Transforming Culture

Michael Angela

Transforming Culture

A Challenge for Christian Mission

Sherwood G. Lingenfelter

BAKER BOOK HOUSE
Grand Rapids, Michigan 49516

Copyright 1992 by
Baker Book House Company

Printed in the United States of America

Library of Congress Cataloging-in-Publication Data

Lingenfelter, Sherwood G.
    Transforming culture : a challenge for Christian mission /
  Sherwood G. Lingenfelter.
        p.   cm.
    Includes bibliographical references and indexes.
    ISBN 0-8010-5674-8
    1. Missions—Anthropological aspects. 2. Intercultural communication.
    Christianity and culture. I. Title.
    BV2063.L436 1992
    266—dc20   92-4276
                                                                   CIP

To
Dr. Judith E. Lingenfelter,
who for twenty-nine years has been my partner in ministry,
my confidante and friend,
my colleague and professional adviser,
the mother of my children,
and my courageous, patient, enduring, and beloved wife.

For because of our faith, he has brought us into this place of highest privilege where we now stand, and we confidently and joyfully look forward to actually becoming all that God has had in mind for us to be. —Rom. 5:2 LB

Contents

Preface

For nearly two decades I have had the privilege and opportunity of working with missionaries in different organizations in Africa, Latin America, and Asia. A social anthropologist by profession, I have served as a consultant and teacher with the objective of helping missionaries and nationals work more effectively with one another. I have had the opportunity to listen to missionaries and nationals vent their frustrations with one another, and express their desire in the Lord to work together more effectively.

The issues that so often divide Christian workers are not major theological conflicts or questions of spiritual commitment, but rather the daily routines of life. Disputes about the use of mission vehicles, access to mission property, and the use of mission funds seem to be a universal problem. In many places missionaries and nationals have disagreed about how work should be organized, who should be in charge, and whether their partners were doing their fair share. Missionary families are often mystified by the expectations of nationals, and many find themselves feeling either stingy or abused in their exchange relationships with national Christians. In situations where national churches have come of age and missionaries have become partners or subordinate workers to national leaders, disagreements about leadership roles, appropriate authority, and the exercising of authority in the church abound. These kinds of questions have provided the focus of much of my consulting ministry overseas and are the subject of this book.

After completing *Ministering Cross-Culturally* in 1986, I went to Surinam that summer to conduct an anthropology workshop focusing on cross-cultural strategies for the development of indigenous leadership. In Surinam missionaries work with Hindustani, Javanese, Native Americans, and Creole descendents of Africans brought as slaves nearly three

hundred years ago. In the course of this workshop, I saw the participants become frustrated with the basic values model presented in
Ministering Cross-Culturally as they worked with several cultures. While
the model was helpful for identifying tensions in interpersonal values,
when we attempted to apply it to Hindustani, Javanese, Native
Americans, and Afro-Americans, it was not powerful enough to help us
compare the distinctive differences in these four cultures. The values
pairs, such as time and event, allowed us to plot data on a continuum,
but did not provide conceptual distinctions that were useful for cross-
cultural comparison.

After returning to Biola University in the fall of 1986, I began to read
widely in the anthropological literature, seeking tools that would help
me to establish a comparative frame of reference that could be readily
used in cross-cultural consulting. Early in 1987 I discovered Mary
Douglas' model of grid and group, which furnishes the theoretical framework for this book. This model differs from the basic values model in
that its primary focus is the structuring of society rather than interpersonal relationships. Its focus on society is crucial for understanding
value differences that relate to the issues of property, labor, giving, and
authority that produce conflict for missionaries. The model also supplies four distinctive sets for comparison in contrast to the value pairs
employed in the basic values model, creating a more powerful tool for
examining and explaining differences in diverse populations.

The case studies presented in this volume are the result of field
research that I have done in various settings around the world. I am
deeply indebted to Louis and Lisa Shanks, Bob Mantel, and Jay and Beth
Grant for their assistance and hospitality during the summer of 1986 as I
visited and studied with them in Afro-American villages in the interior of
Surinam. I am indebted to Gordon and Lois Koop who were my hosts
and co-workers for more than three months in 1977 in Brazil and without whose assistance I could not have written the material in this volume on the Deni Indians. The people of the Yap islands in the Federated
States of Micronesia have allowed me to study their culture and to live
among them for a period of nearly three years since 1967. I am especially indebted to Fran Defngin, Gabriel Ayin, Cyprian Mugunbey, and an
elderly couple, Fithingrow and Marungweg, for their help on Yap culture.
Many other Yapese men and women, from whom I have learned much,
are too numerous to name here. I am also grateful to many pastor
friends in southern California and my colleagues at Biola University, who
have helped me to understand the people and culture of middle-class
Americans as they relate to other minority groups in the southern
California region.

The ideas for this volume began to take shape in early 1988. The first
version of the chapters on authority was given at a church-planting con-

ference on leadership for Youth with a Mission (YWAM) in Thailand. I am particularly indebted to Kalafi Moala for the invitation to speak at that conference and for many stimulating conversations on this subject during the conference and later during a summer course at Biola University. In 1989 Marilyn Henne arranged an anthropology workshop in Guatemala during which I presented an outline draft of the manuscript for Wycliffe translation and literacy workers in Guatemala. I am particularly indebted to these colleagues for their critical and helpful dialogue on the anthropological ideas presented in this book. In the summer of 1990 Richard Lewis invited me to present the material to a group of missionaries and missionary candidates at the headquarters of United World Mission in North Carolina. The feedback from these missionary colleagues was most helpful and their affirmation of this work spurred me on to develop the manuscript and submit it to Baker Book House. Finally, in 1991 I presented the biblical sections of the manuscript to my adult Sunday school class, the Son Seekers, at Bellflower Brethren Church in Bellflower, California. My church friends asked many questions and helped me to focus on biblical truths that are of practical relevance for daily living in our complex urban society. Without the enthusiastic support of all of these friends, I could not have completed this work.

I am especially indebted to people at Biola University for their support in preparing the manuscript. Wendy Walker typed the first draft of the manuscript and contributed to all of the major revisions, including the preparation of the final manuscript for the publisher. Kimberly Nelson helped with editing a second draft after we received feedback from outside readers. I am especially grateful to Clyde Book, the president of Biola University, who views scholarship as an important part of my work and has freed me to spend time in the summers on the mission field and to continue my scholarship as part of my administrative work as provost.

As in the production of any book, I am deeply indebted to readers who have given me critical feedback. My friend, Marvin Mayers, read the first draft of the volume and contributed extensive, constructive feedback. I am also indebted to the anonymous reviewers for Baker Book House for their contribution to the final volume. Louis Shanks corrected my errors of data and interpretation on material from Surinam. Glenn Flewelling, Steve Barber, and Norie Roeder read a revised manuscript and contributed to the completion of the final version for publication. Dale Kratt led me to Margaret Archer's *Culture and Agency,* which was so helpful in writing the final chapter. My colleagues, Mike Wilkins and Harold Dollar, professors in the Talbot School of Theology, and the School of International Studies at Biola University provided excellent exegetical criticism and helped me to focus more sharply on kingdom principles central to the process of transforming culture.

As I reflect on the process that has led to the completion of this book, I am awed by the many opportunities that God has provided to me for learning, and I am thankful for the many people who have taught me so much from their lives and experience. In sharing these experiences, my desire is that the reader will discover from our struggles, errors, and insights how to become free from the bondage of culture and enjoy the transformation that is ours when the kingdom principles of the gospel of Jesus Christ become our priorities for life.

I
Transferring or Transforming Culture?

Therefore, I urge you, brothers, in view of God's mercy, to offer your bodies as living sacrifices, holy and pleasing to God — this is your spiritual act of worship. Do not conform any longer to the pattern of this world, but be transformed by the renewing of your mind. Then you will be able to test and approve what God's will is — his good, pleasing and perfect will. (Rom. 12:1–2 NIV)

A few years ago some missionary colleagues and I attended a Sunday morning worship service in a large evangelical church in Cameroon's capital city of Yaounde. The African pastors led us in a familiar service, selecting songs from a standard evangelical hymnbook and preaching an inspiring, doctrinally sound message, given in English and translated into French. We missionaries, a few white faces in a sea of black believers, enjoyed the service thoroughly. As I walked away praising God, it suddenly occurred to me that this service was almost identical to those I had experienced in North America. Momentarily stunned, I wondered why I should feel as comfortable in Africa as if I were home.

A week passed. I traveled to the interior in the northwest province of Cameroon, where I attended another worship service. There, the congregation sang unfamiliar music, the musicians played instruments dissonant and grating to my ears, and, while the pastor read from the King James Bible, he preached in a language totally foreign to me. Remembering my experience in Yaounde, I thanked God for the unique expression of worship in this African church. As I observed more care-

13

fully, however, I discovered many familiar things. These people had constructed a church building with gabled roof and steeple, arranged their benches in rows, and copied the platform and pulpit of a New England church. The men sat on one side and the women on the other, as was common in the home churches of early missionary pioneers. In the order of service only the language and the music were unfamiliar. As I reflected further on this African congregation, I discovered a structure nearly identical to that of the Baptist conferences with which I am familiar in the United States.

Why is it that in the process of establishing churches in non-Western nations we transfer our culture of the church? Can we find a biblical basis for this practice? Are missionaries planting biblically founded indigenous churches, or are they transferring their culture of Christianity to every nation of the world?

In Europe, Latin America, and Asia, I have found in every area a similar pattern of church planting. Church distinctives reflect more the home culture of missionaries than those of indigenous cultures. In North Borneo, the Anglican, Evangelical, and Catholic churches are all modeled on patterns brought by missionaries from various denominational and cultural backgrounds. It is difficult to find in the two-thirds world a truly indigenous church. Most churches reflect more the culture of the missionaries who planted them than they do the culture of the new believers.

Missionaries have succeeded in bringing a new worldview, but one that could only marginally be called biblical. Is it possible to have the gospel be truly a transforming presence, or are we always to be limited to reproducing our own cultural reflection of Christianity wherever we carry the message?

Contextualization and Indigenization

After World War II, hundreds of missionaries took up the challenge of reaching a world opened to the gospel by the ravages of war. Everywhere colonial powers began the process of divesting themselves of their possessions and the awesome debt these territories entailed in a world that had suddenly found a conscience about subjugating other peoples. During this same period missionaries also began to reject the colonial history of their missions and the pattern of "transferring" culture that had characterized mission efforts through the prewar period. Missionaries such as Donald A. McGavran, Alan Tippett, and Eugene A. Nida began to reformulate mission strategy to reflect their desire for indigenous as opposed to colonial churches.

Following McGavran, Tippett, and Nida, a second generation of missionary anthropologists, including Paul Hiebert, Charles H. Kraft, and

Marvin K. Mayers, began to define new presuppositions and directions for both missions and theology. They rejected the transplanting of Western culture and the transferring of evangelical church form and practice, and argued for a new vision and method. Their watchwords were drawn from secular anthropology. They preached about functional equivalents, functional substitutes, cultural cues, worldview, contextualization, and the growth of two-thirds world ethnotheology (Conn 1984:89–124).

We owe an enormous debt to these missionary scholars, who have challenged the contemporary mission movement to contextualize the evangelistic message and to plant contextualized indigenous churches. The idea of contextualization is to frame the gospel message in language and communication forms appropriate and meaningful to the local culture, and to focus the message upon crucial issues in the lives of the people. The contextualized indigenous church is built upon culturally appropriate methods of evangelism; the process of discipling draws upon methods of instruction that are familiar and part of local traditions of learning. The structural and political aspects of leadership are adapted from patterns inherent in national cultures rather than imported from denominational organizations in the home countries of missionaries.

On an assignment with a mission in Surinam in 1986, I had the opportunity to observe such a contextualized indigenous church among Surinam Javanese. The pastor of this church was a Javanese man who had concentrated his ministry effort for more than ten years on evangelizing the youth among his people. Deeply discouraged to see these young men and women leave the fellowship of believers at the time of their marriages, he abandoned the youth ministry and began to concentrate on evangelizing adult men.

Through his contact with a Bible translation organization he had gained a great appreciation for the Javanese language. He organized a band and wrote Christian songs using the familiar melodic pattern and appeal of Javanese music. Saturday evening became the prime time for evangelistic outreach; believers and unbelievers enjoyed a time of celebration in Christ. These evangelistic meetings offered food, fellowship, singing, and a brief fifteen-minute sharing of the gospel.

Seeing the response of people to these meetings, the pastor was inspired to launch a Sunday afternoon radio program. Drawing listeners through Javanese Christian music, interviewing men and women who were especially knowledgeable about Javanese culture, and focusing on a message of joy and hope, the pastor brought many to respond to the gospel. He gave his home phone number and address to his radio listeners, and received inquirers any time of the day or night. Within the first year of the radio program more than eighty men, women, and children had received Christ through his ministry.

The organization of local churches growing out of this ministry reflected Javanese values and priorities. The pastor delayed baptizing new believers until the whole family was ready, and concentrated on discipling men. In turn, each family head discipled his wife and children. Worship services were held on Saturday evening, emphasizing celebration and introducing unbelievers to the body of Christ. Small group Bible studies were held in various locations on Sundays to disciple new believers.

The particular patterns developed in this Surinam Javanese church are a combination of Javanese and missionary strategies. The national pastor adapted the Christian faith to the unique needs of his own people. The outcome of his effort was a dynamic, growing church, as many Muslim men and women received the gospel and committed themselves to the Lord Jesus Christ.

In spite of the appeal of contextualization and indigenization for generating more effective church-planting ministries, these strategies are not without risk and potential abuse. Indigenization may lead to dead churches in the third and fourth generation of believers. Even in the New Testament we find Christians very quickly defining the parameters of Christianity in terms of their own cultural limitations. The Book of Acts records an anti-Gentile mentality among Jewish converts. When Peter returned from his evangelistic trip to Joppa, he was immediately challenged by fellow believers who were critical of his eating with uncircumcised Gentiles (Acts 11:1–3). Some were not content with Peter's explanation, and later a faction of Jewish Christians proclaimed that "unless you do what we do in Jerusalem, you cannot be saved" (Acts 15:1). When Paul arrived in Jerusalem late in his ministry, he discovered thousands of Jewish converts, all of them zealous for the law (Acts 21:20). The gospel had become completely conformed to Jewish culture, and the church had drifted to a particular, rather than a universal vision of evangelism.

Gentile churches were no less susceptible to this indigenization problem. Before the death of John the apostle, five of the seven churches in Asia lost their vision, and two, Pergamum and Thyatira, had completely compromised the message of the gospel (Rev. 2–3). Both the indigenous Jewish churches and the indigenous Gentile churches succumbed to the pressures of culture and lost their vision and vitality.

How can we escape the dilemma of the "dead" indigenous church? Andrew Walls (1982:97–99) contrasts the "indigenizing principle"—pressuring people into independence and isolation so that they conform to their own cultural surroundings at the price of detachment from the universal church—with the "pilgrim principle," which draws the church in the direction of the universals of the faith, rooted in obedience to Christ and the Scriptures. Jesus is the author of kingdom teaching and of the pilgrim principle, as recorded in his final hours with his disciples; Jesus prayed and asked the Father to protect his disciples and to keep them pilgrims, not "of" but "in" an evil world. In John 17:13–19, Jesus declares that they were not of the world, yet concludes, "as you have sent me, I have sent them into the world." Walls suggests that "pilgrim" churches arise only when believers receive faithful instruction in the Word of God, and respond with obedience as followers of Jesus Christ in a hostile world.

Contradiction: The Pilgrim and Indigenous Principles

The contradiction between the pilgrim principle, with its emphasis on the universal church and "other-worldliness," and the indigenous principle, with its emphasis on self-support, self-government, and self-propagation in independent "this-worldliness," is implicit in all church ministries. Indigenous churches are very common in the history of the church, and seem to be an inevitable product of the institutionalization of the church. Yet the contextualized indigenous church, while a powerful force for spreading the gospel, may become a vehicle of compromise and death. The pilgrim principle, connecting local believers to the universal church with a vision for outreach to the world, provides a necessary counter-balance. Christians retain a commitment to "bear witness" to the world, without becoming "of the world." The indigenous church without a connection to the universal church and the Word is dead. It becomes so entrenched in its own private vision of righteousness that it cannot contextualize its message to needy people, and has no vision and no outreach.

What in the life of the local church leads to the "privatization" of the vision of Christ for the world? Members of every society hold something of a collective worldview and participate in a structured social environment. They are socialized by parents and peers to accept these values, beliefs, and procedures for action, and to live within them, creating their collective conceptualization of "this-worldliness." Yet these social systems and worldviews become prisons of disobedience, entangling those who hold them in a life of conformity to social images that at their roots are in conflict with God's purpose for humanity as expressed in Jesus Christ. Paul suggests that human beings are in a prison, a cell of disobedience: "God has imprisoned all human beings in their own disobedience only to show mercy to them all" (Rom. 11:30–32 NJB). He repeats the same theme in Galatians 3:22, paraphrasing Psalm 14:1–3. He observes that "the whole world is a prisoner of sin." God has penned up all people in their self-created cells of culture, including Jew and Gentile, pagan and missionary.

This view of culture is at odds with the perspective of earlier missiologists. Charles H. Kraft and Marvin K. Mayers, working from the viewpoint that cultures are integrated, functioning systems, argue that culture is basically a neutral vehicle through which God communicates to human beings. Kraft (1981:113) states that "culture consists of forms, functions, meanings, and usage . . . a kind of road map made up of various forms designed to get people where they need to go. These forms and the functions they are intended to serve are seen, with few exceptions, as neutral with respect to the interaction between God and man. Cultural patterning, organizing, and structuring of life . . . are not seen as inherently evil or good in themselves." Mayers (1987:251) suggests that "it is entirely possible that the gospel can enter a life and a society without change being called for."

In this volume I reject the notion that culture or worldview is neutral. Analogies such as Kraft's "map" or "a tool for communication and interaction" (Lingenfelter and Mayers 1986:122) are inadequate to capture the pervasive presence of sin in the lives and thought of human beings. Using the tool analogy, culture is more like a "slot machine" found in Las Vegas' gambling casinos than a wrench or screw driver. Culture, like a slot machine, is programmed to be sure that those who hold power "win" and the common players "lose"; when or if the organized agenda is violated, people frequently resort to violence to reestablish their "programmed" advantage. Every cultural system brokers power to its members, although the "power" advantage may be held by either individuals or groups. The structures and organizations of cultures are not neutral; people define and structure their relationships with others to protect their personal or group interests, and to sustain or gain advantage over others with whom they compete. Video games provide better analogies to culture than Kraft's "map," because they reflect the various power advantages, access to survival resources, and hostile opposition that typify cultural systems.

Culture then is created and contaminated by human beings; culture is the pen of disobedience from which freedom is possible only through the gospel. H. Richard Niebuhr (1951:165) elucidates how the writings of Paul address this issue, portraying Christ in the role of "the judge of culture and the redeemer to Christian culture." Culture seeks to maintain social control through its rules, norms, and sanctions for behavior, and thus limits certain kinds of "sinful" or deviant behavior. Yet the rules of culture reflect a natural knowledge of God (Rom. 2:14–15) that serves to expose sin rather than bring people to righteousness.

The gospel, in contrast, liberates men and women from the cell of disobedience. The gospel brings a contradictory message to the peoples of the world, challenging their social order and beliefs. The Scriptures show clearly that the gospel contradicts society and worldview. Jesus became incarnate in the Jewish world, but then he began to shatter it with his preaching and teaching. His "good news" brought conflict and change. People in Judea and Samaria hated him and plotted to kill him because he challenged their "system." They did everything they could to destroy Jesus and his followers.

Likewise, when the gospel came into the Greco-Roman world, it brought shattering distress and conflict. The Greeks in Ephesus, furious at Paul's message because it was bad for business, rioted against him. When the gospel challenges with power any "worldview," unbelievers react to defend their view and may inflict upon Christians great distress.

Paul Hiebert (1985) argues that Christianity provides a new hermeneutic for cultural living. Every culture and every person must change in light of a new perspective—Jesus Christ, crucified, risen, and exalted. Jesus did not come to save cultures, but people, and he came to transform them into his likeness. But, whole cultures *will not* be transformed! In fact, the opposite is true. Church and mission history suggests that the neutralization of the church of Christ by the larger culture is a chronic problem, often evident in the third or fourth generation of its new or "renewed" existence.

Perhaps one of the traps into which Christians have fallen is the common belief that God has a "system" that includes particular kinds of behaviors, institutions, and personality traits. Luther, Calvin, Wesley, and other leaders of Reformation theologies and institutions proclaimed that their version of the church most closely represented the "system" called for in Scripture. They all sought to articulate how the kingdom teaching of Christ was to be expressed in the social and cultural world of the local and national church. While church leaders have not always seen eye to eye on the relationship of the gospel and culture (Niebuhr 1951), they have all struggled with corruption in culture, and sought ways to purify the church from that corruption. In every case, however, in just a few generations the resulting churches reflect more the social worlds of Germany, Switzerland, and England than of a dynamic, universally oriented, culture-transforming church.

Transformation is neither bridging from one system to another, nor transferring a "Christian" system to another place and people. Rather, transformation means a new hermeneutic—a redefinition, a reintegration of the lives of God's people (the church) within the system in which they find themselves living and working. Jesus said, "My kingdom is not of this world." He thus denied the existence of a Christian sociopolitical system, but called for the transformation of his disciples' thinking and social relationships with others.

Kraft (1981:348–49) suggests that conversion brings about a "conceptual transformation" in new believers that results in change in values and new habits of behavior. He proposes that they must in Christ learn to live up to the ideals of their own culture and must raise those ideals to those of Scripture (p. 245). While I support Kraft's conclusion, I would add that the Scriptures will inevitably *contradict the ideals of a culture*, and that the life and practice of people within a society and worldview may well conflict with the life example of the Lord Jesus Christ.

The argument of this book is that the social and cultural environment in which a local church is planted exerts powerful pressure on that church and its people to conform to existing standards, values, and practices. The local "worldview" is shaped in large part by the nature of the social environment and the historical cultural traditions articulated within that environment. Christians cannot live apart from social environments, and therefore are subject to these unrelenting forces. Further, the standards, values, and practices of Christian leaders are inextricably intertwined with those of their social environment.

Nevertheless, the gospel may become a significant powerful force in the *continuous restructuring of any social environment and worldview*. As believers become mature in their faith, their interests reflect more and more those of the Lord Jesus Christ. As such, Christians will experience tension and contradiction with old patterns of self-interest and greed, provoking them to contradict old social rules and judge many inadequate as they attempt to imitate the person of Christ in their lives and work. As believers increasingly obey the truth of the gospel, they will discover new ways of managing resources and relationships.

Synthesis: Pluralism, Biblical Contradiction, and Transformation

Conflicts between missiologists and theologians are rooted in presuppositions that, when developed to their extremes, have resulted in rigid absolutism in theology and an uneasy marriage of the gospel and relativism in missiology (cf. Henry 1980). The question, then, is what alternative approach we are to take to avoid the colonial dilemma of the past and a growing theological relativism in the present. The solution presented in the chapters that follow is similar to that presented by Mayers (1987:247–60) in his combination of biblical absolutism and cultural relativism. We agree on the truth and authority of Scripture, and on the pluralism that characterizes cultures and affects the missionary enterprise. We differ in our view of culture and worldview: Mayers has a "high" and neutral view of culture, while the view of culture presented here is a "low" view, that of culture inextricably infected by sin.

First, we need to adopt a pluralist perspective on the world and its many distinctive social environments and worldviews. Beginning with respect for host cultures, we seek to know and understand how other peoples see and interpret their world. We must recognize that our own worldview and social environment are not biblical; that we have in fact interpreted and conformed the Scriptures to our own cultural images. Therefore, when we enter another culture we must examine the life and beliefs of those people; we must discover their significant questions; we must search the Scriptures to find biblical answers, recognizing the limitations of our own views. While a pluralist perspective is a valuable corrective to ethnocentrism in our work and ministry, however, it is to be moderated by a commitment to the truth and authority of Scripture. Throughout this book we will move from pluralist case studies to the Scriptures, asking how biblical truth contradicts the values and behavior of the missionary and/or the national.

Second, we must clearly grasp the relationship between the forces of social environment and worldview, and understand how the issues of economy and social relationships play a crucial role in the formation of belief communities. To help us in this process, we turn to the comparative study of social environment and culture. Using a model of social environment presented in chapter 2, this book will enable the reader to understand how values and practices relating to property, labor, and sharing of wealth are inextricably linked to the order of social relations, personal identity, and worldview. Social identity is formed in the structured relationships of the household into which an individual is born and nurtured, and is played out in the community where the daily economic routines that supply the subsistence of life are conducted.

Working from an in-depth analysis of four specific societies reflecting four distinctive social environments, the reader will begin to grasp the idea of social context and see how people and context together become the forces of power seeking to squeeze us into a mold, and hold us in a "pen of disobedience" (Rom. 11–12). Through the exploration of contrasting values regarding such issues as preservation of property, working by rules, granting authority to others, and procedures for settling differences, the reader will gain a clearer vision of imprisonment in a social milieu and how to break free from this bondage through the redemptive work of Christ.

In a most practical way, the cross-cultural worker—evangelist, church planter, teacher, nurse, community developer, linguist, literacy worker, translator—will discover the social roots of interpersonal conflicts endemic to living and working with people of different cultural and social heritages. Chapter 3 explores the social values that lie behind conflicting values between missionary and national regarding maintenance of property and equipment. In chapter 4 we shall focus on tensions over labor and productivity, and what constitutes appropriate work goals, schedules, and rewards. Chapter 5 examines the perceptions and accusations of theft, selfishness, greed, and stinginess between expatriates and nationals, and how each have failed to appropriate biblical priorities in their relationships. In each of these chapters we shall seek to discover why attempts to resolve conflict fail and broken relationships seem impossible to mend, and why nationals resist missionary efforts to "move the ministry ahead."

Chapters 6, 7, and 8 grapple with the issues of authority in family, community, and the church. Working through case studies from Scripture and from the four contemporary societies introduced in chapter 2, these chapters suggest that our perceptions about authority, family, and community are shaped more by our social environments than by our understanding of Scripture. Chapter 6 identifies the distinctive "sins of the fathers" in each of the four social environments, and how they might be transformed by the teachings of Scripture. Chapter 7 illustrates how missionary and national leaders arrive at an impasse because of misunderstandings about authority, and that both fail to understand the call of Christ to "servant" leadership. Chapter 8 returns to the subject of conflict and conflict resolution, illustrating how Christians who have the best intentions fail to understand one another, and thus engage in actions that frustrate rather than facilitate the resolution of differences.

Eating provides the central theme of chapter 9. The chapter opens with a discussion of how the study of eating provides important insights into the social order of a particular social environment. The chapter examines eating in the Gospels, with the purpose of better understanding their social content. The study of eating practices illuminates key features of social structure, and provides insight into first-century Jewish society.

Chapter 10 grapples with the question of how to "make a church" out of a heterogeneous collection of new believers. Reviewing the history of the early church in the Book of Acts, the chapter suggests that making disciples is more than personal "mentoring." It is a social process in which people share food and commit themselves to periods of intimate fellowship, study, and prayer. The chapter also explores the changing social environment of the early church, and proposes that successful, growing churches embrace pluralism and diversity rather than uniformity.

The final chapter returns to the theme of "transforming culture." Reflecting on the roots of tension and sin that enter so readily into the life and ministry of Christian workers, and linking these to bondage to a particular social environment and worldview, the reader may begin the process of thinking theologically apart from that worldview. When we carefully examine ourselves, we shall be forced to admit that, more often than not, we conform theology to practice; we perceive the kingdom of God on earth in our own cultural terms. This is why conforming to the cultural standards of the day has been such a pervasive characteristic of Christianity, as evidenced throughout the history of the church.

Only by recognizing that cultural blindness is the rule, not the exception, and that our philosophies are our windows onto the world, can we free our fellowship and our theology from the bondage of our cultural philosophies and worldview. We must look through multiple windows if we are to genuinely apprehend the transforming power of the gospel and apply kingdom principles interculturally. Each believer sees through a glass, narrow and constraining, but together as disciples with differing perspectives, we can begin to comprehend the wider impact of the Scripture in a pluralistic world.

Of course, escape from the cell of disobedience is never total until we are with Christ. Because we are born into a social world, socialized into its language and thought, we will always be blinded by its sin. While this book may enable the reader to see more clearly a particular social "pen," escape from the prison of disobedience is a work of grace, empowered through the Spirit in the body of Christ. That is why we need other believers, redeemed and being transformed in their "prisons," to help us understand how God's Word contradicts our thinking and our way of life. Together we may teach one another about the sources of our mutual blindnesses.

Although the pages that follow are filled with pluralist descriptions of societies, values, and worldviews, the author is committed to Scripture as the constant, unchanging revelation of God in Christ, reconciling the world unto himself. Paul captures the argument in Romans 12:1–2: "Don't let the world squeeze you into its mold" (Phillips). I ask the reader to join me in asking this question: How does the gospel contradict what I think, what I believe, and how I live? If we ask this question daily, we will certainly change the way we live. If we take the gospel into every culture, and help others ask the same question, they too will change. Yet, we will not all end up wearing "Western grey suits." Rather we will become transformed people, wearing the multicolored coats of the world's diverse cultures, but living transformed lives within them.

2
A Model for Analysis of Social Order

S ocial anthropologist Mary Douglas (1982:190) has identified two social factors (grid and group) that enable field workers to decipher the unique features of a social environment and to begin the process of analyzing social order. Grid and group represent distinctive dynamic social forces that generate diverse types of social environment. Grid refers to a "dimension of individuation" in which a social environment pressures individuals to conforming behavior through elaborated status and role distinctions (hierarchy) and social rules (high grid), or to nonconforming behavior where individuals must exhibit unique value and autonomy (low grid). Group refers to a "dimension of social incorporation" in which a social environment emphasizes insider/outsider relationships, placing high value on collective support for the survival of the group (high group), or rejects communal commitments in favor of individualistic activities (low group).

Recognizing that each of these factors is present in every social situation, Douglas suggests that we may measure the relative strength of these forces and identify four different types of social environment resulting from their combination. The "individualist" social environment promotes personal autonomy (low grid) and resists concerted collective action among individuals (low group). The "collectivist" environment demands concerted corporate action (high group), but insists that persons are unique and minimizes status differences among them (low grid). The "bureaucratic" social environment emphasizes role specialization and carefully defined rules of authority and action (high grid), but rampant individualism keeps people from forming community larger than private interest cliques (low group). The "corporate" environment combines a very strong emphasis on group cohesion, identity, and cooperation (high group), with strong hierarchy, specialization, and customary rules for action (high grid).

The Concept of Grid

Douglas (1982) introduces the concept of grid as a means to examine and compare the degree of autonomy given to individuals in diverse social settings. The simplest way to illustrate this concept is to picture a rolltop desk containing many little boxes for letters and papers. In a desk with four boxes, papers and letters must be grouped into large categories; sorting is limited to these four groups. If we multiply the number of boxes, then it is possible to sort letters into an increasingly diverse number of categories. If we had a desk with a box for every letter in the alphabet, for example, it would take twenty-six to do a systematic sort.

The idea of grid, then, focuses on how a social system sorts and constrains individuals by distinctive role categories. The larger the number of role categories, the greater the number of social distinctions and the more constrained the autonomy of individuals in social relations. More social distinctions usually imply more sharply defined expectations and social rules. The larger the number of rules the greater the constraints upon individuals in the structuring of social relationships. Douglas would characterize such a social environment as strong grid, in which individual relationships tend to be regulated and persons experience social isolation and restricted options (p. 192).

At the lowest end of grid a society has few social distinctions among its members. Some of the simplest and most fundamental distinctions in human societies are those between male and female or between parent and child. These distinctions anthropologists have called ascribed statuses. They are universal in human groups. In a low grid social environment the emphasis on social distinctions is submerged, and may include only a few distinctions other than these fundamental roles. Perhaps members will identify individuals who have particular skills that are respected or they may identify individuals as leaders. The skills and positions of leadership are generally open to the ambitious and the individuals who occupy them are considered best among equals.

Figure 2.1
The Concept of Grid

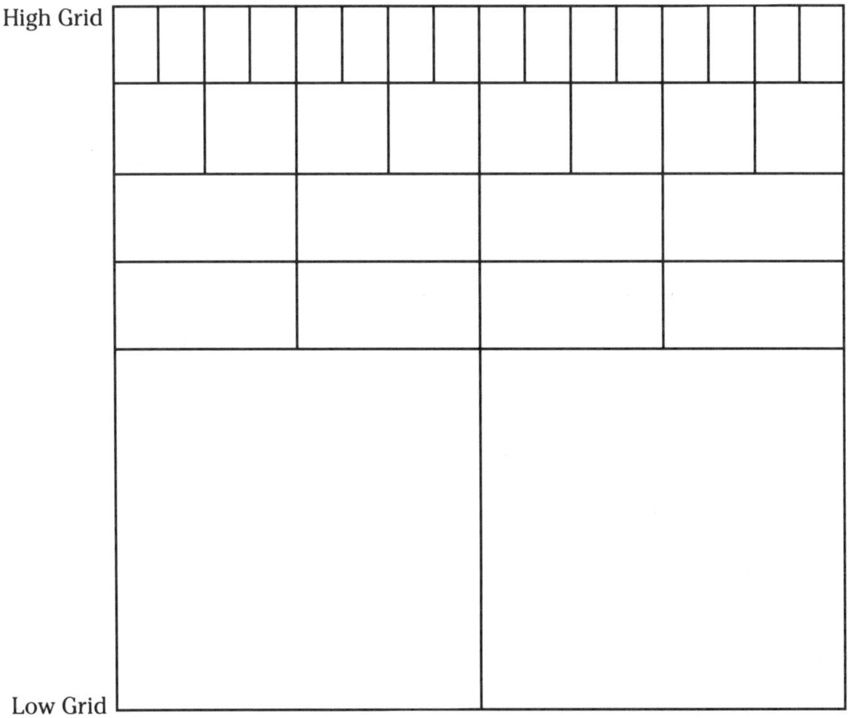

Social environments characterized by low grid emphasize the unique value of individuals within an open, competitive environment. People are known by their life history and for their character rather than by particular role distinctions. People have the options "to deal or not to deal, to choose their own partners" (p. 193). Since most individuals have potential access to all of the roles available, no particular role is given distinctive value over other ones. People emphasize "fair" competition and each individual is valued for personal history and character strengths.

Higher grid social environments entail multiple social distinctions (Figure 2.1). Such environments generally are hierarchical with a few role distinctions at the top and many role distinctions at the middle and bottom rungs. The roles at the top of the hierarchy have uniquely defined value and power. Generally these roles are limited to a small number of individuals within the total social environment. For example, in a private university the president is the chief executive officer of the

Figure 2.2
A High Grid Social Environment

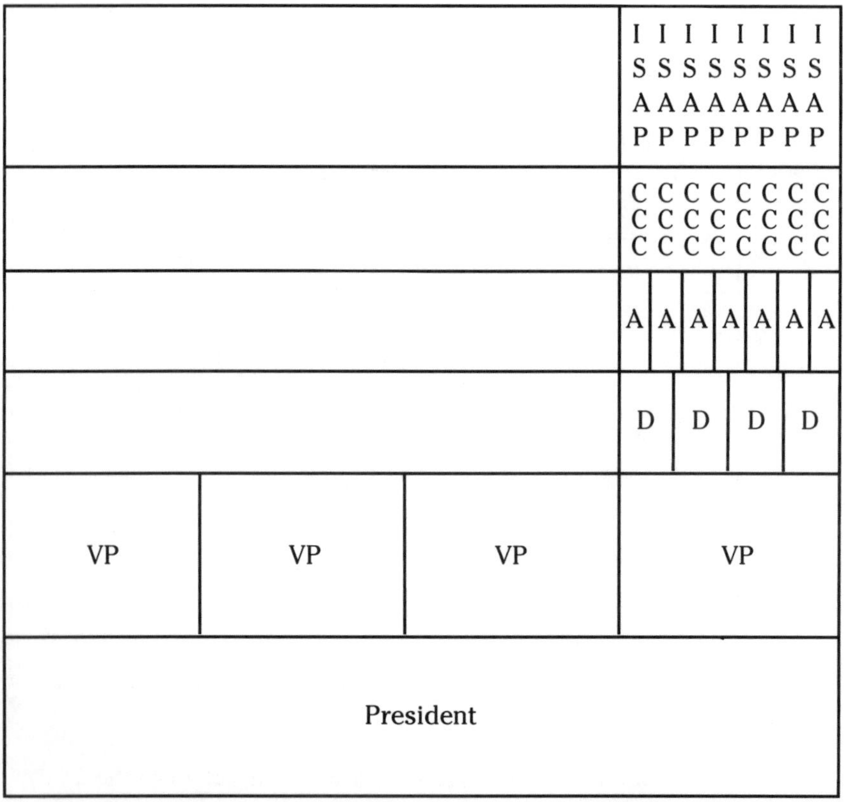

	I I I I I I I S S S S S S S S A A A A A A A A P P P P P P P P
	C C C C C C C C C C C C C C C C C C C C C C C C
	A A A A A A A
	D D D D
VP VP VP	VP
President	

institution. Underneath the president, there are usually several vice-presidents who have diverse responsibilities. The individuals who occupy the roles of president and vice-president have distinctive recognition and authority within the community. They are given honor and respect because of the roles that they occupy.

In contrast, those individuals who occupy mid- or lower-role positions of a high grid environment are embedded in the hierarchy (Figure 2.2). These individuals have much less autonomy and are constrained by the hierarchy and the rules regulating their position. For example, within a university setting, department chairs and faculty members occupy middle or lower positions in the hierarchy. While these positions are valued within the university, individuals who occupy them often feel powerless and constrained by the power structure above them. Each individual occupies a particular niche and performs a specific role, having interests and activities that are isolated and unconnected with others in the hierarchy. The specialist in Victorian literature may have no one other than students with whom to discuss that speciality. As a consequence, that faculty member feels isolated and alone, enjoying the support of peers only at professional meetings of other Victorian specialists on one or two occasions a year. Such specialization and isolation result in a sense of loneliness and powerlessness within the social environment.

In high grid social situations the importance of role is given higher value than any other factor. Individuals are judged on the basis of their role performance and are rewarded for achieving role expectations. The high grid social environment punishes those who refuse to meet role expectations.

Grid should not be confused with the traditional anthropological and sociological concepts of achieved and ascribed status. High grid social environments may be characterized by both achieved and ascribed status positions. For example, in a university, most faculty and administrative positions are achieved status positions. Individuals must earn doctoral degrees and promotions to obtain specific positions within the hierarchy. At the same time, the high degree of role specialization that separates the English faculty into Victorian, seventeenth-century, and contemporary American specialists creates distinctive positions within the hierarchy and isolates individual faculty members from one another. The degree of distinction and personal isolation may be greater than that within the classical ascribed status systems such as caste in India. While the Indian leatherworker and barber are born into their ascribed occupations, their role performance is no more constraining than that of the English Victorian specialist in the academic department in the university. Both the Victorian specialist and the leatherworker must fulfill a prescribed set of occupational duties that are attributed to a specific status. Whether achieved or ascribed, both of these situations define a high grid social environment.

The Concept of Group

The second variable in Douglas' model is the concept of group. While this is a familiar concept in social science literature, it is helpful to define clearly what is meant by "group." First, let us distinguish social group from social identity. Social identity—such as American versus Canadian, or Christian versus Muslim—defines a position from which the content of a relationship may be negotiated. Social group, on the other hand, defines a collective to which individuals belong, having specific criteria of membership, such as local Presbyterian, Conservative Baptist, Calvary Chapel, or Free Methodist churches.

Social identity may be defined as an aspect of self, while social group may be defined as an aspect of others. Personal identity is dependent upon the context in which a person is living and working and the content of that identity may be negotiated by people who participate together. Group on the other hand is characterized by boundaries and distinguishes those who are inside the group from those who are outside. Groups, such as the Evangelical Free Church of America, have corporate organizations and resources. The organization is comprised of the leadership structure, rules, and procedures of membership by which people act together to accomplish collective goals and activities. Corporate resources are those material and social assets that members use to accomplish corporate goals. Within a group, there are leaders who work to accomplish corporate goals and mobilize the membership to support these objectives and activities.

The dynamics of relationships within groups include support and opposition in relationship to goals, authority, legitimacy, and group process. The members of a group actively engage one another in group processes to identify goals and to make decisions regarding means to achieve those goals. The leaders of the group have been allocated authority by the members through which they coordinate and mobilize the group for these common objectives. Groups have standards of behavior and values that define the legitimate means for group action.

Douglas argues that social environments differ to the extent that they vary in their emphasis on the survival of the group as opposed to the survival of the individual. Those societies that place high value on the survival of the group are collectivist in orientation, whereas those societies that place low value on the group are individualist in orientation.

In the low group social environment pressure for group-focused activity is weak, and individuals cooperate with one another primarily for instrumental ends. For example, people stop at a gas station, give money to the cashier, and then pump gas into their cars. The name of the cashier is unimportant; the names of customers are unimportant; exchanges are strictly cash for gasoline. Social courtesy is kept to a minimum and interactions are conducted at the most efficient speed possible for the parties. The order of relationships is technical rather than moral in meaning.

In a high group social environment pressure to consider group relationships and interests is high, and individuals must continually evaluate collective as well as personal interests. Economic transactions are never merely instrumental, but always require consideration of the persons involved, their group affiliations, and what those affiliations mean for relationships. Stopping at a gas station becomes a social as well as an economic encounter. The customer and attendant will respond to one another on the basis of their personal identities and respective group affiliations. If they do not know one another by name, they will ask others to identify the unknown person by both name and group. Once they know these crucial social facts, they will then adjust their behavior appropriately; pumping gas involves appropriate patterns of address, of respect and deference or of joking, of paying or expecting credit, and of time committed to social interaction while buying gas. The order of relationships has high social and moral meaning as well as economic content.

In a low group social environment people create social groups, but they are often temporary and exert weak pressure on the members. Members of these groups tend to focus on activities rather than long-term corporate objectives, and their allegiance to the group fluctuates and changes. Usually these activity groups form for a particular period of time and to meet a certain objective. Once the objective is met and the time has passed, the members scatter, never to reunite as a group again.

The high group social environment involves relationships imbued with social meaning. Cooperation is based upon the quality and duration of relationships rather than upon instrumental objectives. Membership involves personal intimacy and social meaning. One cannot conduct business without first giving attention to the social constraints of respect and mutual interest. A high group social environment is characterized by corporate enduring institutions. The group has a life that lasts beyond that of its individual members and perpetuates its resources and meanings over a much longer period of time. The goal of group interaction is to perpetuate the life of the group rather than the life of its individual members.

Social Environments

Combining the concepts of grid and group to form a social matrix, Douglas identifies four distinctive types of social environment. These social environments are merely the recombination of these two variables into four distinctive sets. The low grid/low group set comprises the "A-Individualist" social environment. The high grid/low group set comprises a "B-Bureaucratic systemic" social environment. The high grid/high group set constitutes a "C-Corporate systemic" environment. The low grid/high group set yields a "D-Collectivist" social environment (Figure 2.3).

This typology provides an analytical framework within which I will compare and contrast diverse human social behavior and values. Four

Figure 2.3
Types of Social Environment

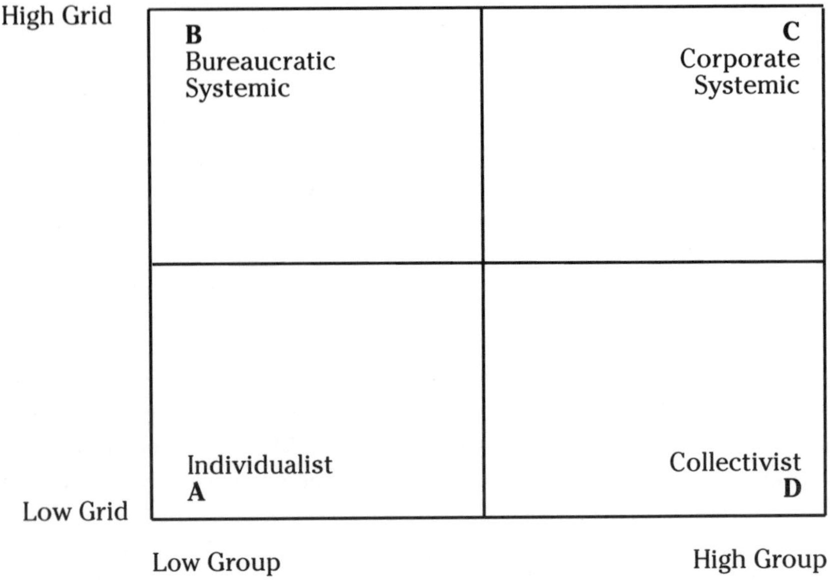

High Grid

B Bureaucratic Systemic	C Corporate Systemic
Individualist A	Collectivist D

Low Grid

Low Group   High Group

ethnographic cases presented throughout the book will furnish concrete illustrations of each of the four social environments. The variables of grid and group provide the constants through which to explore economic and social behavior, foundational to each of the societies described. Issues of property, labor, and economic exchange often create tension and even open conflict between the expatriate and the national. Working from the grid/group typology and using case studies of conflict between nationals and cross-cultural workers, this book will allow the reader to reflect upon personal and cultural values and behaviors, and then to compare and contrast these with the values and behaviors of others. The assumption of this analysis is that grid and group are powerful social forces, generated out of basic social relationships in the family and community, that strongly influence and constrain the values and behavior of people in a given social environment.

As with any analytical tool, the grid/group model has inherent strengths and weaknesses. As a four-part diagnostic matrix, it is complex enough to show variation and distinctions that are blurred in simpler tools such as the basic values model (Lingenfelter and Mayers 1986). Sometimes it may prove too complex for a reader new to the sociological and anthropological study of society and culture. Yet for the professional, the constants of grid and group will prove too restrictive, and the explanatory power of social environment will be too weak to capture even a glimpse of the vast historical and sociocultural diversity of the human species.

The application of this model is not intended to reduce social and cultural differences to a simple, four-variant social matrix, but rather to release participant-observers from the conceptual bondage of their own social environments by providing a means for contrast and comparison. The grid/group model provides conceptual glasses through which we may discover new perspectives on the people, the social activities, and the expressed meanings and values that are part of living and working cross-culturally. The societies used to illustrate the four variations are expressive of these differences, but by no means comprehensive or "typical" of the vast range of societies and cultures found around the world.

The Deni Indians of Western Brazil: A-Individualist (Low Grid/Low Group)

The Deni, located on Marrecao Creek in the Cunhua/Purus river region in western Brazil, were studied by Gordon Koop in the mid-1970s. The Deni speak a language from the Arawakan family of South American Indian languages. Koop was residing among them to translate the New Testament into their language. I joined him as an anthropology consultant in 1977 and spent several months conducting research with him in the village (Koop and Lingenfelter 1980). The Deni are farmers, hunters, and fishermen. Their staple food is bitter manioc, a root crop that must be processed to remove potassium cyanide. Villages are set in the midst of cleared fields, where the people plant and harvest their crops. Villages are not permanent; people often shift location every two or three years, usually in response to illness or disaster that signifies bad luck or evil spirits in that place.

This particular Deni village had only sixteen households of eighty-six people. Their village and surrounding fields consisted of several adjacent clearings in a vast tropical jungle. Typically, each married couple had their own house, built on poles about five feet above the ground. The houses surrounded a sandy plaza in the village. Brothers built adjacent houses, forming residential clusters in the village. Two widows lived adjacent to their brothers, who provided meat and other assistance. The adaptation of these people to the hardships and hostilities of life in the Amazon rain forest, with only peripheral contact with Brazilians, provides an example of an A-Individualist, low grid/low group social environment.

The village is a very unstable social unit. At no time in the last fifty years have these people lived in the same location for more than five or six years. They move often, and suddenly, provoked by conflict with one another or outsiders, by the fear and threat of spirits, or by accidents, sickness, or death. When they move, individual families scatter to other locations, often in clusters of two or three households. If a particular location proves satisfactory over time, the village expands as other families move in. After several people died due to accidents and illness in 1980, the Marrecao village split into three smaller clusters that settled within a mile and a half radius of the mission airstrip. These clusters do not constitute permanent groups, but shifting cooperative arrangements of mutual convenience to member households.

Social roles among the Deni are limited primarily to male/female, kinship, and skill recognition. People look for leadership from more aggressive individuals in the society, people who are willing to take the risk of leading in communal activities. Headmen and shamen, like cheerleaders at a football game, encourage people to engage in group activities but have no power or authority to coerce their obedience. They lead in public activities, but people deny them status or privilege. There is no limit to the number of headmen or shamen. This village of eighty-six people had four men who were recognized as such.

People assess the behavior of these self-declared headmen to see if they merit the rank. The man who calls frequent feasts and motivates villagers to participate receives approval and praise. The people readily support a man who offers economic or social advantage. If, on the other hand, he fails to satisfy their expectations, the people will shift their loyalties quickly to another leader or even move to another settlement.

About two miles by foot or an hour by canoe from the village is a small settlement of Brazilian peasants with whom the Deni visit and trade. Most Deni men have allied themselves with this local family and several other Brazilian patrons in the region. Acquisition of trade goods is their primary motivation and value. Individuals request trade goods from each patron, to the extent that the patron extends credit. When called upon to work to pay off their debt, individuals play one patron against the other, avoiding debt service and risking retribution for as long a time as they may safely do so. As with their village chiefs, Deni shift loyalties to the patron who offers a perceived advantage.

U.S. Christian College Faculty: B-Bureaucratic (High Grid/Low Group)

Christian College is a nondenominational liberal arts institution located in a major metropolitan area in the western United States. I have chosen the faculty of this institution as a case study because I have been both participant and observer in this social environment for more than seven years. At the same time, I have found similar social behavior and values at other institutions in the region. I believe the behavior and values described in this case study are broadly typical of the social class of Americans to which the faculty of Christian College belong. (Individuals and subgroups within that social class may take exception, and rightly so, to my analysis. Individuals express their own unique life histories and personal worldviews, and thus often depart from what I or another observer might describe as the "norm" for their social environment.)

The members of the faculty of Christian College do not live in a common community, nor do they constitute a formally organized group. Yet because they work daily in the same institution, share commitments to a common mission, invest their lives in the students who choose their department and discipline, and cooperate and compete with one another in the institutional social structure and culture, they constitute a legitimate population for comparative research. The social relationships of these faculty within the context of Christian College illustrate the B-Bureaucratic, high grid/low group social environment.

When faculty members are hired to work at Christian College, they enter into a scaled hierarchy of relationships that establishes their relative position in relation to their professional colleagues. The scale is graded on the basis of educational level, years of teaching in a college or university, and success in the publishing of professional monographs or in professional journals. Instructor rank is the lowest on the scale, requiring a masters degree in a given subject area and little or no experience in college teaching. To achieve promotion to assistant professor, one must have at least three years of college teaching and have made considerable progress toward earning a doctorate or the degree that is "terminal" in that subject area. To gain promotion or appointment as associate professor, one must have at least six years of college teaching experience, in most cases have earned the doctoral degree, and show evidence of success in professional publication. The rank of professor is the final step in the scale, and is awarded only to those who demonstrate long-term effectiveness in teaching, and who have earned national recognition for their professional publications or other achievements.

The faculty see themselves as the social heart of the institution. While staff and administration are essential to enable them to accomplish their tasks, the mission of education is carried out in their classrooms. Administrative and staff roles are of lesser consequence in the order of things, and faculty sometimes, in their frustration with both, wish they could get along without them. The pay scale of the institution reflects these hierarchical differences: faculty are nine- or ten-month contract employees, and are paid on a graded scale beginning at $22,000 and capped at about $47,000 (1990). Staff are hourly employees, and their annual wages range from $10,000 to about $24,000 (1990). Administration are twelve-month employees and, depending upon their background and qualifications, their salaries range from $24,000 to $50,000 (1990). Only the senior level administrators—deans, vice-presidents, and the president—receive salaries in excess of $50,000.

The institution is bureaucratic in its organization, yet lacking in corporate solidarity. The faculty are highly individualistic. Each individual is trained in a very particular field of research, and teaches specific courses. Most faculty prefer to teach only in their field of specialization; some are very protective of their courses and their place in the curriculum. Faculty prefer their own private office, desire to set their own schedule for classes and office hours, and have particular students who identify closely with their interests rather than with the interests of colleagues. While they are organized into departments and schools administered by department chairpersons and deans, their personal routines, agendas, and careers take priority over collective interests. When collective concerns do emerge, such as in budget matters, curriculum decisions, or program changes, faculty usually support the private interests of their department or school, and see themselves in competition with other interest groups in the institution.

The faculty are also pitted against one another in the promotion system. Each rank has at least two grades within it, and the individual must apply for advancement in rank. A committee of peers and the academic dean review and evaluate each application, and judge the teaching and professional performance of the individual. Some who are gifted move rapidly up the rank system, while others who lack the required degree or publications become stuck at a particular rank or grade.

Faculty carry these values of individualism and autonomy over into their private lives. Their choices of residence are highly personal, and they live scattered across the metropolitan area. Many commute nearly an hour to the campus, and a few live even farther away. While there is ample housing in the city in which the college is located, commuters choose to do so because of personal interests and agendas—cost of housing, quality of local schools, type of neighborhood, employment of a spouse, or proximity of the beach or mountains. While they sign the doctrinal statement of faith of Christian College, in their personal lives and worship they attend churches that range from charismatic Calvary chapels to fundamentalist Baptists, and from elder-ruled Plymouth Brethren to liturgical Episcopalian.

Participation in the activities of the college community is also a matter of individual choice. A few faculty regularly attend college chapels; most come only on special occasions; a few do not attend at all. The faculty who are responsible for basketball games, concerts, and recitals press their department colleagues and friends to support these events, but the remaining faculty forgo these activities for personal agendas. Only those events that are mandatory, such as graduation, bring out the majority of faculty. "Community" is a word used around the college campus, but the social lives of the faculty demonstrate higher priority for individual autonomy than for collective or corporate commitments.

The Yapese: C-Corporate (High Grid/High Group)

The people of the islands of Yap in the western Caroline Islands are brown-skinned, black-haired Micronesians, numbering approximately ten thousand in the 1990 census. The ancestors of the Yapese are a mixture of island peoples from the western islands in Indonesia and the Philippines, from Melanesia in the south, and from the eastern islands in Micronesia. I first lived in Yap from 1967 to 1969, doing research on traditional culture and political change, when Yap was an administrative district of the U.S. Trust Territory of the Pacific Islands. I returned to Yap in 1979/80 to conduct research on the impact of twenty-five years of American administration and education on marriage and family relationships. Today these islands are part of Yap State in the Federated States of Micronesia, independent politically but under a "free association" agreement with the United States.

While the economy and material culture of the islands have changed much over the last twenty-five years, the fundamental features of the Yap social environment remain the same. Yapese people today continue to place very high value on membership and obligation to traditional kin and village groups. They also have a highly developed traditional and contemporary hierarchy, with a strong, high grid social environment. Throughout this book the Yapese illustrate the C-Corporate, high grid/high group social environment.

People live in nearly one hundred villages, which occupy all of the viable agricultural land and fishing reef on Yap. A port town is located along the harbor on the eastern side of the islands, where about two thousand people live. Many others commute to work daily. About half of the adult male population works for wages in the small government town, and they buy canned fish, rice, and other imported goods to contribute to the household economy. The villagers are farmers and fishermen; women work on the land to produce vegetable foods, and men work on the reef to provide fish for their daily diet. The major source of vegetable food is taro, cultivated in large, communally constructed swamps located along streams or behind land reclaimed from tidal flats along the seashore. The prime village locations are along the seashore or on small rivers, where taro can be readily cultivated; the less desirable locations are inland, where the land is suitable only for sweet potatoes and yams, or small, family-constructed taro plots.

Over the last two hundred years the people of Yap have responded to population pressure on very limited land and sea resources by creating a high grid/high group social environment. Yapese rank their villages in a hierarchy with five distinctive levels: the top three include the highest or chiefly villages, villages of noble rank, and commoner villages. Most of these villages are located on the prime lands and along the seashore of the islands. Village leaders own land and fishing resources crucial to the survival of the people. Each of these villages encompasses resources that make people somewhat self-sufficient; however, a few control fishing rights on the reef nearby and others control specialized resources, such as mangrove swamps, timber in the uplands, clay formations for making pottery, and garden territory for the production of yams. On the interior mountains of the islands most villages are classified as either chief's servants villages or serf villages. The people who live in these villages have received less desirable land from the higher ranking villages in return for perpetual servitude to their high caste benefactors.

Even the Yapese who live and work in town identify themselves by their village of birth. Every Yapese name belongs to a particular parcel of land on which ancestors built a stone house foundation. Each foundation has a "pool" of ancestral spirits and names from which every child born to that family is named. House foundations and names are passed from fathers to children; people who share names from an ancestral foundation belong to an "estate group." Male children are entitled to inherit, by virtue of their name, parcels of land and rights to use resources that belong to the estate group. Female children may not inherit, unless there are no male heirs, but they have rights to subsistence from the estate until their death. A woman usually resides on the land of her husband, and her children become heirs in her husband's estate group.

In each Yapese village, the family house foundations have political and social significance. Yapese say that "the land is chief." Each village is divided into higher and lower ranking sections; within each section, certain house foundations and estate groups hold political titles. Titles are ranked in order of their significance in the village; the highest are the chief of the village, the chief of young men, and the chief of ritual. Village sections also have section chiefs, section leaders of young men, and other lesser titles, all assigned to particular parcels of land and estate groups. The family that holds a particular parcel of land "speaks" for the land and thereby exercises the authority and power vested in the title.

Succession to titles and leadership roles in Yap villages are governed by inheritance and competence. A man cannot succeed to the head position in his estate group until his father and elder brothers die or voluntarily relinquish their right of succession. If a man proves to be incompetent in a position, people will either work around him, or in the most serious case, remove him by force from the leadership role. Today, as increasing numbers of men are educated in American colleges and find careers in the government and business of town, competence has become a larger factor. In the villages, however, land is still chief, and the village fisherman may still be the highest ranking authority for village affairs, provided he speaks for the estate group that owns the land which is village chief.

Yap today blends together traditional and modern life. In the same village two neighbors—lifelong friends or members of the same estate group—will arise in the morning. One will put on a long pants and a shirt, the other will wear a traditional loin cloth. They will chew betel nut together in the predawn darkness. One will get into his jeep to drive ten miles to work in town, and the other will walk down to the beach and begin to mend his fishing nets. In town, the villager will work with men and women from other parts of the island; his status will be based upon his village, his title within his village, his title in his government position, his age, and his competence. In the village, the fisherman will work with his neighbors and with men from adjacent villages; his status will be based upon his age, his village, and his title within his village. When they come together in the evening, the fisherman may share his catch of the day, and the government employee may share tobacco or beer that he has purchased on his way home from town. Wherever they are, their family, village, personal status, and group affliation go with them.

Afro-Americans in Surinam: D-Collectivist (Low Grid/High Group)

The Aukan and Saramaccan Afro-Americans are descendents of slaves brought from Africa to Surinam on the northern coast of South America. Each of these language groups is scattered throughout the interior of Surinam, living on islands and along the banks of the two major rivers. These villagers, whose ancestors escaped from the slave plantations and reestablished a matrilineally focused culture, practice ancestor veneration and exhibit many other cultural features carried with them from West Africa generations ago. Their languages are distinctive English- and Portuguese-based Creoles, yet their cultures have remarkable similarities. The Aukan people are described in most of the following chapters, yet much of what is said about them is true of the Saramaccans. While I have visited both groups and worked with mission teams who have long-term and intimate knowledge of each, I am indebted to the works of Richard Price (1975, 1976), Louis Shanks (1987), and Thoden van Velzen (1978) for detailed ethnographic information. Aukan and Saramaccan villages are described to illustrate a D-Collectivist, low grid/high group social environment.

The Saramaccans and Aukan are organized in groups based upon matrilineal descent and residence in compact villages on the islands and banks of the major rivers that extend into the hinterland of Surinam. The farmlands are located in the hills along the river banks, and the people subsist on rice, plaintains, sweet potatoes, and manioc. Men hunt and fish to supply protein for their daily diet. Each matrilineal clan occupies its own territory, and as the population has increased, the lineages have spread to form several villages. I have visited the village of Manlobi, which is the government center of the Beei clan, encompassing three adjacent villages—Manlobi, Fandaake, and Saye—and have, with Shanks interpreting, interviewed the captain and elders.

The history of the Aukan and Saramaccan people, celebrating the bravery of the leaders who led them in resisting slave masters and leading the bands of runaways to new settlements in the interior, plays a very important role in their present identity. Many of their matrilineal clan names can be traced to plantation owners from whom their ancestors fled, and people trace their ancestry to the "sister" of the founding leader of the band of runaways. The leaders of the runaways became culture heroes, and the office of *gaanman* ("chieftain") served as the political symbol of the group's unity and exclusiveness.

To insiders, the most visible symbol of lineage unity is their *avo*, or ancestress, from whom the members are descended and thus receive rights to lineage territory. Men or women may own houses and land in their ancestral village. However, men often live in the village of their wife until they are old enough to begin working toward an "elder" role in their own village. Typically, the women of Aukan and Saramaccan villages are the major labor force for the production of food. Sisters and daughters work together in groups to produce the vegetable foods necessary for survival. The men aid their sisters and wives in the clearing of land and preparing the fields for planting, and spend time in hunting and fishing activities. Many Saramaccan and Aukan men today are involved in cash-producing activities to supplement their family income and diet.

The general community is characterized by limited distinctions of matrilineal clan and lineages, and of sex and seniority for individuals within them. People recognize the elders in the community because of their age, their nearness to becoming ancestors. They are regarded as the leaders. Everyone—all adult age groups, male and female—participates in decision making in the community. They discuss issues openly; anyone can speak in these meetings. Distinctions are not based upon principles of hierarchy, but upon personal character, age, and influence in the community.

The government of a clan is collective, shared among the elders, the village *kabiten* ("captains"), the *kunu* ("avenging ancestors"), and the ritual specialists such as the shamen, herbalists, and funeral foremen. None have exclusive power over the others, but rather they work together to assure the safety and well-being of the clan and communities. Succession to the offices of *gaanman* and captain is strictly matrilineal; most villages have at least two captains, with larger villages having more. These men are the most respected senior men in their lineages, and they are the most visible symbol of a lineage's unity. Shanks (1987:12) notes that "When one is first introduced to a village, it is the height of rudeness in the eyes of the Aukaners, if he does not announce his presence to the lineage headman."

Aukan carefully watch young men and women in their community and evaluate their loyalty and commitment to public goals. If they see an individual who is hard-working and trustworthy, they increase that person's responsibility and recognition. Clan elders recruit men and women for the positions of ritual leaders and assistants (*basia*) to the captain and the elders on the basis of their personal character and the quality of their commitment to and work for the community. Aukan men and women achieve these positions of leadership and service to the clan by fulfilling the expectations and public goals of the community. Any individual who desires such honor must work hard for recognition for faithful service to the community.

Social Environments as Units of Comparison

The concepts of social environment and society are separate and distinct throughout this work. The term "societies" refers to a widely diverse range of economic and political arrangements. Anthropologists have recognized distinctive levels of sociocultural integration, ranging from band and tribal societies to chiefdom, state, and complex industrial societies in the modern world. The concept of social environment applies to a smaller unit of comparison that may be found in any one of these levels of sociocultural integration. Any given society may have one or all four of the social environments described above. Christian College faculty may participate in more than one social environment: some work daily in the B-Bureaucratic environment of the college, but belong to a C-Corporate church. Others may belong to D-Collectivist or B-Bureaucratic churches. The metropolitan area surrounding the college is so complex that it offers individuals options to participate in any of the four social environments we have described.

Participation in two or more social environments will create tension and conflicts for individuals, yet people are generally flexible and capable of adapting to such demands. In the case of the two Yapese men described above, the commuter to town has adapted to the B-Bureaucratic system introduced by the American administration, yet continues to live effectively in his C-Corporate village environment in the evenings and on weekends. Having grown up in the village, he brings to the B-Bureaucratic system many of his village values and expectations, yet he has learned to set them aside or to compensate when bureaucratic values have priority.

The concept of social environment, then, applies specifically to the presence of factors in a specific social setting of grid (the relative elaboration of status differences that constrain [high grid] or confer [low grid] personal autonomy) and group (the relative value placed upon belonging and acting in concert [high group] or detachment and acting independently of others [low group]). These factors are measurable in a specific environment in terms of how social roles constrain or confer autonomy upon individuals, and in terms of how membership and collective participation in groups are deemed essential or marginal to the social relationships and transactions.

The grid/group model classifies social environments in an attempt to draw specific observations about the value and belief dimensions that are characteristic of those environments. In the following chapters we will explore conflicting values about property, labor, and exchange from the grid and group perspectives. Using material from the four societies above, the book will identify key value differences in economic and social relationships and specific values characteristic of each social environment. By exploring Scripture on the same subjects, I will point to similar social environments in biblical societies, and seek to discern "transformation" principles from Scripture that apply for motivating and modeling Christ-like behavior in all social environments. From this diagnosis of environment and value differences, the Christian worker will be able to determine how best to develop a ministry to obtain maximum effectiveness within that social environment, and even more important, to live more like Christ in relationships with nationals.

3
Property

The Silent Enemy of Church Growth

A pastor in an inner city church in Los Angeles regularly challenges people in his denomination to reach out to Hispanics and other ethnic groups in southern California, yet he finds people less than eager to follow his lead. A man in one of the suburban churches was clearly upset about the possibility of people from another ethnic background coming to the church. As the pastor pointed out the responsibility of Christians to minister to the poor and foreigners, the parishioner interrupted with evident irritation. Pointing to the steeple on top of the church, he said, "See that steeple up there? I built it with my own hands. No Mexican is ever going to be on the board of this church as long as I have anything to do with it!"

Investment in property and values about property stir very deep emotions among American Christians. Pastor, church elder, church member, and missionary alike share this concern about property. One of the most pervasive issues infecting both local church and mission outreach is conflict over questions of property. The parishioner described above is hardly unique. Many evangelicals, from the mission field to the local church, share his frustrations and concerns.

Case Studies

A Fruit Tree in California

In southern California the anxiety among Anglo Christians about personal or church property is one of the key obstacles to reaching immigrant populations. After a Sunday service in which I spoke on this particular subject, a member of the congregation related an incident that illustrates this problem. He told how Vietnamese children came to his house a few years before and asked if they could pick the fruit from a tree in his yard. He allowed them to pick the fruit. In their enthusiasm they broke numerous small branches. Distressed at the appearance of the tree after they had finished, he decided that he would not let them pick fruit again. Over the next couple of years when the fruit was ripe, children came, pestering him to pick the fruit, but each time he turned them away. Even though the fruit fell to the ground and rotted, he did not want to deal with the trouble or damage these children might cause. Finally, in frustration over their continual asking, he cut the tree down. As he told me the story, he was aware of the lost opportunity to share the love of Christ with many children who had come to his house for fruit.

The tree had become the focus of his interest. Compelled to protect his interest, he cut the tree down rather than share its fruit with those who had need. Not only did he fail to share the fruit, but he failed to share the good news of Christ with those who came. Unfortunately, his situation is not unique. Many have chosen to protect property rather than to share the good news of Christ. He said, "I have been so blind. The Lord has been bringing people to my door, but instead of reaching out, I have turned them away and cut down the tree that brought them. What I saw as a bother and a threat was in reality a great opportunity which I have lost." Missionaries often come from a similar social environment as this committed Christian layman, and they experience similar frustrations on the mission field.

Property Maintenance in Central Africa

A pastor friend in southern California related the story of a visit to his denominational mission in Africa. At one mission station, a missionary complained bitterly to him about the time he had to spend on maintenance at the station. He said, "I spend 90 percent of my time on maintenance and only 10 percent on ministry. I am deeply frustrated! Please carry the message back to our churches of how desperately we need maintenance help."

To complicate matters further, the missionary described how disputes about property had alienated him from his African neighbors. Complaining that they had no respect for private property, he described how hostile neighbors frequently cut the plastic water pipe that brought water from their storage tank. Sometimes a woman was "too lazy" to walk to the river for water, and used the convenient method of cutting his pipe to supply her need. Needless to say, he responded angrily to these acts of vandalism, which also created a hardship for the missionaries, draining their water supply.

Neither the pastor nor the missionary considered the possibility of forgetting the maintenance and getting on with the ministry. The maintenance of the property was clearly of higher priority than the ministry of the gospel in that missionary's life. He would not say this with his words but he clearly showed it by his actions.

The missionary maintained the property because he was compelled to do so by his social values and resultant expectations. Having learned from the time he was a boy that property has great value and must be preserved and sustained, he believed that to fail to do so was sin. He felt a moral responsibility to keep up the property, even though that responsibility kept him from ministering to the people for whom he had gone to the mission field.

Property and Ministry

Stories like the ones related above can be retold again and again on every continent of the world. Missionaries open up new fields and plant churches. Inevitably, after the harvesting of souls they find it necessary to build a church building. Oftentimes they deem local materials inadequate, because if one is to build a building one should do it "right" ("right" usually means the way it was done at "home"). The missionary may solicit money from home churches to build an impressive building, evidence of God's power and wondrous work in this place. The dedication of the new church is frequently followed by other building projects. Sometimes it is a school, sometimes a youth center, sometimes a bookstore, sometimes housing for other missionaries. Often these building projects take years of work and energy, with negative impacts on evangelism and church planting. The growth of the church becomes internal, through the children of converts. Evangelism dies out and the ministry now becomes one of nurturing the flock.

Missionaries have many responsibilities in maintaining physical facilities. Buildings must be painted. It is not good to have a building without grass, but grass must be mowed. Of course it's important to have motor vehicles to save travel time with so many responsibilities, but cars require maintenance and upkeep. And so as the missionary compound grows so does the work to keep it running, and field workers find themselves in the situation of the missionary in Africa, spending 90 percent of their time on maintenance and only 10 percent on ministry.

Many mission organizations try to rectify this situation by sending more missionaries to the field. Of course, only a few of these new missionaries are involved in evangelism and church planting. Most come in supporting roles, to maintain the property, to teach in the schools, to work in the print shop, to supervise the youth center, and generally to keep the system set up by the first wave of church planters running. All of this new staff serve at great expense to the home church, and in the long run, contribute more of their energy and work to the property than to the ministry of the mission. Church growth slows when the building program begins, and it rarely regains its momentum.

Only by increasing the missionary staff threefold can a mission effect a sustained program of evangelism and discipleship. In many of the missions conferences I attend, I find mission leaders appealing for support workers to do the jobs that will free the evangelists and teachers for evangelism and teaching. Unfortunately, I hear very few people asking if some or many of these jobs could be eliminated, or how to mobilize evangelists and teachers with minimal property and equipment.

What values compel us to commit ourselves so inextricably to property? Why is it so important for us to have it? Why do we fight so strongly to protect it? How is it that we allow concern for material possessions to come between us and our call to ministry? What can we do to focus clearly on these conflicts, and to identify alternative strategies to cope with them? How can we begin to make choices that enable us to be more effective in our relationships and ministry?

Property: A Model for Analysis

In keeping with the general assumption of this book, the theoretical perspective of social environment, with its grid and group dimensions, provides an explanatory framework for discussion and analysis of cultural values with regard to property. More specifically, we want to look at the relationships between property and grid, and between property and group strength in social relationships. The objective of this chapter is to provide the Christian worker with an understanding of how values about property vary with the social environment, and to facilitate comparison and analysis for strategic trouble shooting and planning.

How do high and low grid generate different values regarding property, and what variations do we see in cultures? To what extent does the group exert control over property that is owned by individual members or at least used by individual members within the group? What is the ongoing tension between the individual and the group in relationship to property?

Grid: Holding versus Competition for Property

Let us first consider the issue of grid. How is the individual's personal estate significant in terms of conception of self, personal significance, and uniqueness? Clearly, if people have no personal estate—in other words, no property of significance—then property will contribute little to conception of self in society. When property is held by individuals it confers significant social and economic value to those who hold it. It becomes important in a person's conception of self and social esteem.

In a high grid social environment control over property is usually connected to those who hold the higher positions in the social hierarchy, and people place high priority on holding property. Since property often confers personal prestige and symbolizes social class, preservation of holdings becomes a high value. People learn to conserve their resources and thereby enhance their social standing. Achievement in this setting is highly structured by factors of status and role to which property values have been attached. Saving becomes a high value and individuals are motivated to protect their personal property interests (Table 3.1).

In a low grid social environment competition rather than control is the primary value. The increased individual autonomy of low grid dic-

Table 3.1
Society and Value Profiles: Property

B-Bureaucratic (Christian College)	C-Corporate (Yap)
(high grid, low group)	**(high grid, high group)**
Priority of individual property	Priority of persons and group property
Preservation of individual holdings	Tension—interests for persons/property
Conserving, protecting self-interest	Selective preservation/consumption
Saving is highly valued	Sharing is highly valued, save for group
A-Individualist (Deni)	**D-Collectivist (Aukan)**
(low grid, low group)	**(low grid, high group)**
Priority of competition	Priority of persons
Expansion of holdings	Preservation of group interests
Risk taking, individual interests	Consuming in the interest of the group
Acquiring/investing is highly valued	Sharing is highly valued

tates freedom to manage property according to individual designs. Where property confers economic advantage or power, individuals may engage in significant risk taking to expand their property holdings and thereby improve their personal position and reputation. Achievement in this environment is associated with risk and investment of individual energy and skill. The autonomy of low grid promotes a free-for-all attitude toward acquiring and risking property.

Group: Individual Interests versus Corporate Interests

Group control over property is an ancient practice in human societies. When Joshua divided the land of Canaan among the tribes of Israel, he distributed the territories according to groups—the tribes, clans, and families of Israel. Careful examination of the historical books in the Old Testament shows that rights to land in Israel were held by both the individual and the group. The law stated clearly that land could not be alienated from the group. If for some reason people were forced to sell their land, during the sabbatical (seventh) year, or in the year of Jubilee, all alienated lands were to be returned to those families from which they had been separated.

This corporate principle is illustrated further in the Book of Ruth. Naomi was not free to sell her lands to anyone she pleased, but had to follow the required rules of succession that granted rights to those lands to other members of her husband's clan and lineage. Boaz, according to the text, was not the first in line to inherit the property and so he had to negotiate settlement with the kinsman who had first priority. It became clear as they negotiated for the property (Ruth 4) that it was not merely property at stake, but also a person. Naomi's kinsman not only had to redeem the property, but also had to marry Ruth and provide for her descendents. It was for this reason that the kinsman redeemer gave up his rights to Boaz.

This tension between individual and group rights is a very important issue in understanding property cross-culturally. Societies vary distinctly in their values and rules with regard to the control of property. Some place a strong emphasis on individual control, whereas others focus on corporate control. To help us to develop an understanding of this diversity we will examine the degrees to which societies differ in terms of their individual freedom or corporate control over property.

In a high group social environment the priority of persons and group interests becomes the dominant value factor. Members of the group place strong value upon sharing with one another, and to a lesser degree with outsiders. Leaders may demand that members contribute family or personal property for the interest of the group, and they will sanction those individuals who fail to contribute. The group will mobilize to protect its collective property against the threat of outsiders and to redistribute its resources fairly among its members.

In a low group social environment collective considerations are spurned by individuals, who have only an instrumental or material interest in cooperation. Acquiring, rather than sharing, motivates individual behavior, and the use and consumption of property are governed by individual considerations. Self-interest has priority over other persons, shaping economic and social decisions.

Case Studies

The Deni: A-Individualist Environment (Low Grid/Low Group)

Around the Deni village three men each cleared a separate field with the cooperative help of other villagers, and from these fields they and some of their partners in labor acquired their staple food. Each field owner had a section of the field that he planted and harvested; and each owner had allocated part of his field to men and women who contributed in a substantive way to clearing it. However, Deni do not hold permanent rights to these plots, nor do they pass them on to their children. In fact, most of the time they abandon these fields in two or three years, or sooner if a disaster has afflicted the village. Historically, at sudden death or misfortune, people abandon their village and form a new village in a distant place.

Deni hold other items of personal property lightly in their system of values. Houses, constructed from jungle materials, serve only three or four years. Deni do not hesitate to abandon a house at a moment's notice if they feel danger threatens them and the village. The only significant material possessions to which they attach importance are steel tools and shotguns. These rare items, purchased at some cost from Brazilians or other outsiders, are highly valued and carefully kept. These items are rare, however, and knives and other steel tools wear out long before they can be passed on to children.

The group has no special value for Deni property interests. Individual leaders select the place of a village settlement in a vast virgin forest, and those who wish join in clearing the land and planting the fields. People shift residence from one area to another and from one leader to another. They share jointly cleared fields, but in privately planted and harvested parcels. They distribute surplus meat from successful hunts, but participation is voluntary and a hunter's wife makes the final decision about sharing.

Having little durable property of value yet seeking greater access to consumable manufactured goods, Deni embrace outside contacts and seek to expand their personal prosperity and consumption through these relationships. They openly compete with one another, and manipulate their external contacts in a competitive manner in order to gain more material goods. They do not practice conservation of resources, and have nothing that is worth "saving" for a "rainy day"; yet they risk alienating patron and neighbor in order to acquire what is in their personal interest.

Christian College: B-Bureaucratic Environment (High Grid/Low Group)

The most common concern of prospective recruits to Christian College faculty, and of those who are already employed at Christian College, is the acquisition of an appropriate house. The house must be located in a neighborhood that is consistent with class expectations, must be near schools that are appropriate for children, and must be within a price range that is economically feasible. Since Christian College is located in an area of high real estate inflation, potential recruits have turned down job offers, stating explicitly that the salary offered will not allow them to purchase an appropriate house. The privately owned house, with its implied social class affiliation, is a major element in Christian College faculty's conception of themselves.

While owning a personal home is essential to these people, they have done nothing as a group to support one another in this enterprise. With regard to personal economy, the Christian College faculty share only their mutual identity and individual contracts with a corporate organization. The faculty themselves do not constitute a corporate group, and they share no mutual resources or economic support. Their relationship is contractual rather than organic, and they make independent decisions about property and personal finances. They compete for the resources of the corporate school and know little or nothing about the personal finances of one another. They do not constitute a group in any formal sense of the term; rather, they are individuals working under contract in a legally defined bureaucracy.

The Christian College faculty operate in a B-Bureaucratic social environment in which there is a moderately strong emphasis on hierarchy and a negative emphasis on group control over personal economic life. As such these people place a very high priority on property, and emphasize its intrinsic value for personal identity and ascribed status. Individual faculty work to preserve their holdings and maintain them carefully, since they represent a significant dimension of their personal status. People share concerns for saving, conserving, and protecting their individual interests against those who would undermine or destroy them.

New faculty to Christian College reject the changing neighborhoods of older faculty, perceiving them as less secure and supportive of their private interests and the welfare of their children. Because people in a B environment lack any strong group organization, they are helpless against powerful individuals who threaten their property and livelihood. The classic illustration of this is "white flight" in ethnically changing neighborhoods; in Christian College the pattern is "each to the best neighborhood he can afford." Rather than work as a group to defend and sustain their economic interests, they act as individuals, attempting to buy, sell, and relocate in what they perceive to be a more secure community.

This analysis of Christian College faculty does not deny that they have group affiliations of church and school. Rather, as a faculty they have no corporate property interest or action. Without shared personal resources, they act as individuals rather than in concert. At the same time, each of those faculty members may belong to a group that does have corporate interest and shares corporate identity. Most, if not all of the Christian College faculty belong to a church organization in which their membership is voluntary, and to which they contribute a significant amount of personal income that is redistributed for the good of the local church. However, their commitment of time and resources to the church is only a limited part of their total economic experience. As a consequence, their economic values are shaped more fundamentally by their isolation as individual faculty than it is by their membership in an occasional corporate group.

The Yapese: C-Corporate Environment (High Grid/High Group)

The people of the Yap Islands define the structure of society in terms of land. Since the economy is agricultural and only a small portion of the thirty-eight square miles of the island is arable, land is both scarce and valuable. The Yapese say that the land is chief in the village. They allocate positions of public authority, ritual authority, and economic obligation to particular "landed estates." They define wealth and poverty, strength and weakness in terms of control over the land.

In addition, people's access to land is defined in terms of corporate groups. Yapese assign every parcel of land to particular family estate groups, which are owned by a corporate group of men and women who have inherited joint rights from their fathers. The Yapese estate group controls the land and resources of the estate; the leaders have the right to tax members of the estate group for produce from their fields, and to demand labor from members for estate group projects.

Yapese experience a strong tension between the priorities of persons and property. Because of the significant emphasis on group, they place person-group goals first and foremost in their thinking. Yet, because hierarchy is so inextricably tied to personal estate, individuals engage in intense competition for authority over estates, producing significant tension among close and distant kin. People must not voice openly their dissent or conflict with others in the society. At the same time, they have strong individual competitive interests. As a consequence, the social environment is one fraught with tension, yet subverted to public consensus because of the inherent controlling power of the group over property.

Property defines a Yapese person's place in both grid and group. Yapese individuals must maintain a significant degree of self-control in this social setting, so that their personal interests do not appear to be in conflict with the group's interests. Living under these pressures, Yapese engage in both selective preservation and consumption of resources, depending upon the contradictory interests of the individual and the group. They respond to pressure from the group to be generous, sharing that which they control for the benefit of the corporate estate. Yet they plot and execute strategies for acquisition of land and valuables for which they have even a marginal claim, since a man gains power and prestige by controlling the land estate to which authority and title are ascribed. Inevitably, people criticize the powerful for being grasping and stingy, and denigrate the poor, who cannot produce wealth to give to others.

The Aukan: D-Collectivist Environment (Low Grid/High Group)

The Aukan have corporate matrilineal clans that claim rights to land and territory. The clan provides individuals, born into the clan, with a distinctive identity in relationship to all other members of Aukan society. Each lineage segment of a clan occupies specific territory, including sections of the villages where people reside and agricultural fields on the hillsides surrounding the villages. The Aukan clan acts corporately, controlling access to land and other resources of significance to the Aukan people.

Aukan women control the village and farm lands inherited from their matrilineal ancestors. Men work on the land of their clan sisters in their village of birth, or for their wives on their land in the village in which they have married. Aukan are excellent wood workers and build wooden houses made of rough hewn planks in their villages. Men build for their sisters or wives, who own much of the village property. A woman provides a home and land for each daughter, and sisters collectively control their village and garden territory. An Aukan man circulates between his village of birth and the village(s) of his wife or wives.

Aukan give priority to persons over property and their primary concern is the preservation of group interests. They spend little effort on preservation and maintenance of houses, which are primarily utilitarian in value. However, men and women spend considerable effort on the preparation of fields and the cultivation of food resources that support members of the extended family. When people act in conflict with the interest of the group they may be publicly criticized or even publicly sanctioned with supernatural or magical coercion. Aukan fear the punitive action of ancestors, who are the protectors of group interests, and the retribution of living members of the clan who perform magic or sorcery against other individuals in the group to punish them. The force of the group is a consuming pressure in Aukan society, and individuals gain prestige and rank only in relationship to their commitment to the group.

Biblical Perspectives on Property and Mission Conflicts

Returning to the case studies that we considered at the opening of the chapter, it may now become apparent that the two laymen and the missionary in these cases shared similar values. Each was preoccupied with the preservation of property; each placed great value on maintaining the existing value of the property; and each was defensive about outsiders who threatened their property interest. These values are typical of the B-Bureaucratic social environment.

In each case, conflict arose because of interaction with others who did not appreciate the values of the individuals affected. The suburban church member viewed Mexican neighbors as a threat to a building that he had helped construct with his hands. The Anglo neighbor was distressed at how the Vietnamese children damaged his tree in picking its fruit. The American missionary in Central Africa felt harassed by his African neighbors who insisted on obtaining unauthorized access to his water by cutting the plastic pipe to save a trip to the river.

In each of these cases, the ethnic group with whom the persons were in conflict came from social environments that placed a much higher emphasis on group. While we do not have adequate data to determine in what precise social environment these ethnic participants came from, it is evident from their behavior that sharing was highly valued among them. The Central African woman cut the water line because she believed that the missionary was stingy and unwilling to share a valued water source. The Vietnamese children asked to pick fruit because they saw it falling to the ground and rotting. The inner city pastor was encouraging the suburban church member to share his facilities with Hispanic immigrants living in the neighborhood.

In each case, those involved responded with deep emotion. They were not able to think objectively about the situation or make a decision based upon the real needs of the people involved. They responded from deep feelings and emotional values growing out of a long commitment to a particular worldview.

The effect of any social environment is to squeeze its members into a particular social and value mold. The Central African who cuts the

water line is acting just as much out of social pressure as is the missionary who is angered by the act. Both of them are products of their social
contexts and worldviews, albeit different ones. Neither is able to actual-
ize the admonition of Romans 12:2: "Do not allow the world to squeeze
you into its mold."

In all three situations, the values expressed by these Christians are in
conflict with their Christian faith. The synoptic Gospels are replete with
references to how priority for property should be peripheral in the life of
the Christian disciple. Matthew 6:19–24 calls the believer to lay up treasures in heaven rather than on earth. In the same chapter (vv. 28–34)
Jesus challenges his disciples not to worry about clothing or food, "but
seek first his kingdom and his righteousness and all these things will be
given to you as well." Matthew 19:16–22 recounts the story of the rich
young man who came to Jesus and asked what good thing he needed to
do to gain eternal life. Jesus told him to sell his possessions and give to
the poor. He went away in despair, because he had great wealth.

In spite of these texts, missionaries struggle more with nationals over
property than perhaps in any other area of their relationships. Some
missionary candidates have asked us if it is okay to take a microwave
oven and an ample supply of shoes and clothing for their children. Their
rationale is that things are cheaper in the United States, than in the
country to which they are going. When they arrive in their field of ministry and find people asking them for the things they have brought, they
find they must defend and protect their property interests. All of this
results in spiritual as well as social struggle. Pacific Island missionaries
have engaged in endless disputes with national leaders over the use of
mission vehicles. Missionaries living in compounds in Brazil and Africa
struggle with pressure to dissolve their compounds and enter the
national society and culture. In all of these situations nationals view missionaries as both wealthy and stingy, denying the benefits of their
wealth to national co-workers.

These missionaries know the text in Mark 6:8–11 in which Jesus
instructs his disciples to go with no bread, no bag, no money, and no
extra clothing. They find such instructions incomprehensible and
archaic, clearly not applicable to their life and ministry. They have read
many times Luke 9:58: "foxes have holes, and birds of the air have nests,
but the Son of Man has no place to lay his head." They know of the cost
of discipleship described in Matthew 16:24–28 and Luke 14:33: "any of
you who does not give up everything he has cannot be my disciple."
Some may even recall Hebrews 10:32–34, which talks about how early
believers joyfully accepted the confiscation of their property. Yet, the
pull of their own social environment is so powerful that they can only
with extreme difficulty incorporate such principles into their own lives
and relationships.

Students and missionary candidates are no different from their prede-
cessors in the field. Some of the most common questions I am asked in
my classes have to do with anticipated requests for money and personal
property. Usually these students are concerned about someone taking
advantage of them, about not having enough for themselves, and about
"stewardship" and using "wisely" the resources they have been given.

I should make it clear that neither I nor the Scriptures are antiwealth
or antireward. Luke 19:11–27 relates the parable of the ten minas, in
which the faithful servants are given great reward for their faithful service. It is clear in Luke 8:2–3 that women of means supported Jesus and
his disciples in their itinerant ministry. Jesus loved and accepted those
who had wealth and owed his personal support in large part to these
women of means. Jesus' disciples were also property owners. Peter,
James, and John came from families that owned houses and fishing
boats. They were independent businessmen who supported their families through the property resources that they held. Barnabas perhaps
paid the bills on his trips with Paul; Paul had a room in Philemon's
house and requested the service of one of his servants.

The issue is not having wealth or property, but rather the values that
lie behind our attitudes toward property and ministry. Acts 4:37 notes
how one of the disciples, Barnabas, sold a field that he owned and
brought the money to the apostles. The text does not say that he sold
all of his property, but only a field. It also records how he did this to
encourage and support those who had need.

Reflecting on the four distinctive social environments and the respective values of those environments, it should be clear by now that each
of them holds specific values in relationship to property. A careful examination of each of the social environments should produce critical
insight into ways in which these values are used in respect to other
people. The biblical message is that we are to be freed from the bondage
of property regardless of the social environment in which we find ourselves. The rich young ruler described in the three Gospels was not
from a B-Bureaucratic social environment. If we had adequate data, we
probably would have described the social environment of his world as a
C-Corporate environment. In spite of that fact, property was a stumbling
block, interfering with his relationship with Jesus Christ. He was unable
to accept a call to ministry because he valued his property more highly
than eternal life.

Resolving Property Conflicts

To work toward the resolution of conflicts about property, we must
first ask what it is we fear. Once we identify our fears, we may then deal
with them through application of the truth of Scripture.

The man who owned the fruit tree in California was upset by its appearance, perhaps fearing that it was a negative reflection on him. Each subsequent year when the tree was ripe he was further frustrated by the loss of peace and quiet and the inconvenience created by children coming to his door. The fear of disruption of his personal life finally led him to cut the tree down. As this man reflected on his actions, he identified two key principles that are crucial for cross-cultural Christian workers. The tree actually created an opportunity for building relationships with people he did not know. Each child asking for fruit from his tree presented another opportunity to share the love of Christ. If we can interpret requests for access to our property as an opportunity to demonstrate our love in Christ, our attitude about the person making the request and the potential depletion of our resources will change drastically. Fear of inconvenience and fear of loss of image pale in contrast to the opportunity to build relationships and to proclaim Christ.

If we could ask the missionary in Central Africa what fears pushed him to spend 90 percent of his time on maintenance, he might include fear of an inadequate water supply; fear of breakdown of necessary equipment; fear of the loss of time because of the failure to do preventive maintenance; discouragement over the disorder in his living circumstances; and fear of being dependent upon others who might be helpful, but only with strings attached. Property begins to own the missionary, instead of the missionary owning the property. Preservation becomes a matter of preserving self-identity and well-being, as well as fending off disorder.

Jesus admonishes us not to fear for these things. Yet our faith is often weak, and we cry out for a few practical strategies. The most important is to adopt a simplified lifestyle. The less property we own, the less energy we will have to expend to prevent disorder. By simplifying their lifestyle missionaries remove the temptation to hang on to the social values of their home culture.

Missionaries must also relinquish independence and become more dependent on nationals. In Central Africa, for example, many women would be happy to carry water for missionaries. While the men would need to learn to do maintenance work, they would be delighted to have jobs. If missionaries learn to accept less precision and be open to alternative ways of accomplishing things, they will probably find that national workers can take care of most of the maintenance that must be done. Further, the mutual relationship between missionary and national worker can become a means of discipling new believers.

To help us change our attitudes we may challenge one another with a question: Whom do we worship? God? Or the creation of our hands? Reviewing Scripture passages, such as Isaiah 44, can help us come to terms with the issue of false worship. Only when we are willing to surrender to Christ all that we have, are we free to enjoy all that he gives to us. Jesus reminds us in the Gospels that if we struggle to save our lives we are certain to lose them.

The solution for the missionary, then, is to not be enslaved to the values of the social environment. Norman Dietsch, a missionary to people on the island of Manus in New Guinea, told me the story of how he was instructed by his colleagues to buy pots and pans, plates, utensils, towels, and other items to set up his household as a single man in Manus. When he arrived on the beach, the Manus people (D-Collectivist) began to request from him each of the items that he had obediently purchased. As Dietsch tells his story, he said he naively accepted the text in Matthew 5 that says "give to the one who asks you, and do not turn away from the one who wants to borrow from you." Soon, all of the items that he had purchased were gone; the people had taken every one. But then Dietsch discovered a marvelous thing. When he needed to cook, all he had to do was ask, and there was always a pan available. When he needed utensils, they were provided. When he needed a towel someone always produced a towel. During that first year of ministry the people were faithful to their own value for sharing, providing every one of his material needs, returning in kind everything that he had given to them.

The point of this illustration is that practicing kingdom principles does not place missionaries at risk, in spite of the fact that our background values cry out against the action path demanded. God is faithful to his people, and rewards those who obey his commandments. The challenge for cross-cultural workers is to learn to discern when the values of the home social environment become obstacles to obedience.

4
Labor
and Productivity

Divisive Values in Mission

Case Studies

The Deni and Mission Conflict

My colleague, Gordon Koop, occasionally sent radio messages to Deni villagers asking them to clear the airstrip of grass and jungle weeds in preparation for his return to the village. Understanding the importance of the task and the urgency to have it completed before the day of the scheduled flight, the people responded promptly; they generally cleared and maintained the airstrip to the satisfaction of the pilot.

Koop's problem came in paying the people for their work. Most of the villagers had worked on the strip and they all expected some pay for their work. Because he was not in the village, Koop found it impossible to distinguish between those who worked hard and long and those who had merely come to collect a reward. He wanted to pay people according to the quality and time of their work, and he wanted each person to be treated fairly. He also had limited funds and could not give indiscriminately.

Asking the village chief to pay people according to the amount of work that they had done, he provided a quantity of shotgun powder and enough bolts of cloth to pay men and women what he deemed an appropriate fee for the work. The village chief took the shotgun powder and the cloth to his house, and invited the men and women who had worked to come. The aggressive men quickly took as much powder as they could get and the aggressive women took more than their share of cloth, leaving those who were less aggressive with little or nothing.

The disgruntled workers complained to Koop, who was deeply frustrated by the whole process. He confronted the chief, telling him of those who were angry and reprimanding him for not paying people according to their work. The chief, in turn, did not understand the time-pay equivalency, and told Koop that there was not enough material to satisfy all the people who had worked. Koop tried to explain the work-pay equivalency rule, whereas the Deni demanded a specific personal objective without reference to quantity of work needed to fulfill it. The outcome was a stand-off: Koop said the chief was weak and let things get out of control; the chief and people said Koop had the goods, but he wouldn't give enough to pay everybody. All grumbled openly about the others who had grabbed for themselves.

Nehemiah and the Wall

The Book of Nehemiah in the Old Testament provides a very different case study of the organization of labor. Nehemiah came from the citadel of Susa to his ancestral home in Jerusalem with letters from King Artaxerxes authorizing him to cut timber and to rebuild the city gates and city walls of Jerusalem. After surveying the ruins (Neh. 2:13–16), Nehemiah informed the priests, nobles, and officials that he had received authorization from the king and organized them to begin the work of rebuilding the walls.

Nehemiah used two key principles for the organization of the workforce: residence and kinship. The text (Neh. 3) details how each gate was assigned to a particular leader and the residents of a particular district. In most of these situations the residents of districts were also kinsmen or extended families. Nehemiah assigned repairs on the walls to leaders of particular districts in the region or to families who lived immediately adjacent to a particular section of the wall. It is clear from reading through the text that each gate and each section was repaired by an assigned group of people. The work was organized along the lines of existing leadership, territorial, and kinship divisions within the society.

The local governor, Sanballat, opposed the work of Nehemiah, seeing him as a threat to his own leadership and promoting the welfare of the subject Israeli population. He attempted to arouse other ethnic groups in the region to mobilize against the Israelites and stop them, even by force, from completing this task. Nehemiah reports that there was intense opposition and fear of attack among the people working on the project.

Nehemiah responded to this threat by organizing half of his work-force for defense and the other half for labor. "I stationed some of the people behind the lowest points of the wall at the exposed places, post-ing them by families, with their swords, spears, and bows. After I looked things over, I stood up and said to the nobles, the officials, and the rest of the people, 'Don't be afraid of them. Remember the Lord, who is great and awesome, and fight for your brothers, your sons and your daugh-ters, your wives, and your homes'" (Neh. 4:13–14). From that time on, half of the people worked while the other half stood guard against the threat of hostile outside forces. Nehemiah kept a man with a trumpet near him, and told the workers and warriors to come to the sound of the trumpet to quell any attack from their enemies.

Apparently during this same time period, the people had experienced a famine. The poorer members of the community were forced to mort-gage their fields, vineyards, and homes to get adequate grain to eat. Nehemiah confronted the nobles and officials, accusing them of exacting interest from their countrymen and forcing them into slavery. He insisted that these wealthy leaders lend money and grain to the people without interest and without confiscating their fields, vineyards, olive groves, and houses (Neh. 5:9–11). Nehemiah reports that he had ample food to feed the 150 Jews and officials who ate at his table, but did not demand the food allotted to the governor because he felt the tax load was already too heavy on the people.

Working at what seemed an impossible pace, the people labored day and night, completing the rebuilding of the wall in fifty-two days. Nehemiah reports, "Neither I nor my brothers nor the men nor the guards with me took off our clothes; each had his weapon even when he went for water." Through his leadership, he inspired the people to finish this great task, and thereby remove their disgrace, shame, and vulnera-bility.

Labor and Social Values

Nehemiah and Koop faced very different social environments for the organization of work. Nehemiah found an already existing political orga-nization, with a hierarchy of leadership and an organization of residen-tial and kinship groups. These groups had a past history of cooperative labor and were mobilized quickly for a task that seemed impossible to their enemies. They worked intensively and collectively, and supported one another for the corporate objective of rebuilding the walls of Jerusalem. Koop, in contrast, faced a group of unorganized, self-motivated, and independent workers. Each of them expected payment from him according to their own estimation of their work. They had no effective centralized leadership, and were unaccustomed to any kind of corporate work activity or corporate reward.

Labor and productivity may be measured by two key characteristics: the extent to which labor and productivity are organized by rule or goal, and the extent to which labor is left to the decision of the individual or is governed by group relationships. The unique emphasis upon one or more of these factors in a social environment leads to particular values and practices for social labor. By defining more explicitly the nature of these differences and identifying specific values and behaviors that typify particular social environments, we can understand better the dynamics that leaders face when they attempt to mobilize a workforce.

High Grid: Labor by Rule

The simplest rule found universally in human society is a sexual division of labor. In some societies the division of labor for men and women is prescribed and violations of these rules arouse great social reaction. In others, the sexual division of labor is negotiated, allowing individuals to decide, at least among certain tasks or on specific occasions, which tasks they will do.

The most elementary rule of hierarchy in the organization of labor is that of relative age among kin. For example, within the Yapese family estate group the senior male has the authority to organize work. This elderly man calls the younger men and women who have been given access to estate group property to work for the good of the group. If they fail to fulfill their obligations this man has power to confiscate their resources or to withhold other estate group benefits from them. The key distinguishing factors are age and sex and kin relationships. Younger individuals are under the authority of elders within their kin group in such a setting.

A more complex rule of authority is that rule of tradition that extends beyond the kinship group. In the same village setting in Yap, leaders have traditionally delegated to particular family estate groups specific tasks in major community labor projects. If, for example, a village chief organizes a large fishing expedition, some estate groups have customary labor obligations to manage the canoes, other estate groups have assigned tasks to put out the nets, and other estate groups have authority to distribute fish caught in this group fishing activity. Rules of tradition define authority and specialization in work activities that engage the members of the community at large.

In complex societies, the division of labor becomes increasingly specialized, as illustrated in traditional societies, such as the caste system of India, and in the broad range of industrial societies. In the Indian caste system, specialization is the function of ritual purity and caste specialization of labor. For example, the leatherworker caste occupies the lower scale of ritual purity. Its members produce leather goods, such as buckets used to irrigate the fields of higher caste farmers. Each of the other castes in the system has some specialized role in the organization of work in the total society; there is reciprocity among the various caste groups.

In industrial societies the same kind of specialization occurs, but is more highly differentiated. The rule of law or bureaucracy becomes the key differentiating factor for job specialization. Members of a university staff formally differentiate each job in terms of the degree of prestige, job status, and hierarchy necessary for job completion. The people who clean and maintain the facilities are absolutely essential to the ongoing process of the university, but their specialized jobs are low status and low hierarchy. They receive pay equivalent to their position in the hierarchy. Professors occupy assistant, associate, or professorial ranks, and are paid on a salary scale graded by rank and time in service. Administrators hold the ranked offices of chair, dean, vice-president, or president, and also are paid according to the differences in hierarchy and degree of responsibility defined in their legal job descriptions. The system has a clear outline of positions, rules, and procedures, and the law of bureaucracy governs the relationships among the parts.

In a traditional society such as India the law is one of purity rather than process. The position that each person has in the specialized division of labor is not only one of occupation but also one of religious purity. The highest, the Brahmins, are also the priests. Those who are in the bottom specialized classes are unclean and untouchable. The rule of purity becomes the law of differentiation in this type of society. In the university setting described above those who occupy the highest positions have no greater religious purity than those of low position. In fact, in a Christian university, those who are in low positions are counted to have the same Christian purity as those in high positions because of their relationship to Jesus Christ. All are covered by the blood of Christ and are one in terms of their ritual purity.

Low Grid: Labor by Goal

Rather than differentiate according to the type and the strength of rules operating in a society or organization, the division of labor in a goal-oriented system is an achieved or negotiated assignment. Individuals work together not because of prescribed structure, but because they perceive cooperation to be to their advantage and the specific arrangements to be to the mutual advantage of participants. By focusing on the goals in work activities, people free themselves to arrange their labor relationships according to the most expedient, reasonably negotiable process.

The simplest type of goals found in societies are the goals of subsistence. All human beings must provide for food and other needs on a daily basis to survive. The Deni Indians are motivated primarily by goals of subsistence. In most societies of the world people struggle for more than subsistence in their daily lives. Many people seek to obtain surplus that they can utilize to enhance their own personal lives and gain advantage in their relationships with others. In many societies in the world this surplus must be used for public as well as personal good. In others the surplus may be used exclusively for personal ends.

When a society allows individuals to compete, the differences that emerge when people gain surplus often lead to patron-client relationships. A classic case of this is found in New Guinea, where "big men" embark on political careers that are based primarily on patronage. Individual men gain renown through hard work and the production of significant surplus in their fields and herds of pigs; they achieve "big man" status when they utilize that surplus to gain clients in the society around them. The process of gaining clients is one of giving out wealth to incur the debt of those who become clients. The larger the number of clients a man can mobilize, the greater are his standing and prestige in the society around him. Every position is negotiated; individual "big men" compete for clients, each trying to outgive his competitors. Clients may have more than one patron in such a system.

In other social settings individuals may accumulate significant wealth and thereby gain prestige in their relationships with others. Where accumulation is the name of the game, patronage may be an important part of the individual's power, but the wealthy must accumulate wealth more rapidly than they distribute it to sustain prestige. One gains power and wealth in the same process. It is out of such systems that the growth of modern capitalism emerged. Within modern capitalism it is possible for an individual to gain not only wealth but also capital. Capital wealth is defined as wealth that is used to produce more wealth rather than to confer prestige. Men such as Karl Ichan, T. Boone Pickens, and Donald Trump use their personal wealth to buy other major companies, primarily to demonstrate their personal power and business acumen and to expand their sphere of economic control.

Low Group: Individual Autonomy to Labor

All human societies have activity groups through which work is done. To what extent do these activity groups create obligation and coerce individuals to accept group authority in work relationships? To what extent are individuals able to work independently of these groups and to establish or sustain an individual freedom of group authority? The issue is one of individual freedom or social interdependence in labor arrangements; we must explore the full range of possible expressions of these variables in social environments.

It is useful to distinguish between degrees and levels of interdependence in social settings. Some societies, such as the Deni, rely upon activity groups for seasonal economic interest. Deni individuals organize activity groups to clear fields or to engage in the frequent feasting activities that are part of their cultural interests. Even more frequently, Deni work together in pairs for farming activities. These work pairs allow significant individual freedom but provide some interdependence and support that enhance each person's ability to achieve personal goals.

In other social settings interdependence may be defined primarily in terms of role. Individuals may have very little opportunity to work in activity groups and may have little or no experience with the dynamics of group relationships. The individual may be only required to fulfill a role (gas station attendant) that prescribes an isolated task, interdependent with other roles (manager, attendants) yet involving little or no activity that can be characterized as group activity.

As individuals become masters of their own economic careers, they may achieve a greater degree of autonomy in their relations with others. In an industrial or commercial society where an individual may establish an independent business, role and business career may allow people to labor independently of others in the society. To the extent that people must rely upon supporting businesses or customers to achieve personal economic interests, they are interdependent. Yet it is possible for individuals to become so wealthy that they are able to manipulate resources independently of the constraints of others in the system. The individual who has great capital resources has the greatest individual freedom and independence, and may not need to labor at all.

High Group: Group Coercion to Labor

On the other side of the scale group integration and group control may transform the interdependence of activity groups into the obligation of group membership. Once an individual becomes a member of a group, that formal membership carries with it certain inherent obligations varying in degree and character, constraining factors on the freedom of the individual.

The most common form of coercion inherent in group membership arises from the dynamics of social interaction and economic interdependence. As individuals commit to membership and joint access to resources, daily social interaction produces pressure for conformity and consensus. The more extensive the economic and social interaction of the group, the greater the pressure that emerges from that group to control the interests of the individual.

Table 4.1
Society and Value Profiles: Labor

B-Bureaucratic (Christian College)	C-Corporate (Yap)
(high grid, low group)	**(high grid, high group)**
Schedule by rule	Schedule by consensus, rule
Work by role assignment, work rules	Work by role, group, and situation specs
Work/interaction separate by rule	Work/interaction mingled by consensus
Productivity = time rule/product	Productivity = role, group value
Motivation = norm of behavior, pay-off	Motivation = group incentives, group pay-off

A-Individualist (Deni)	D-Collectivist (Aukan)
(low grid, low group)	**(low grid, high group)**
Schedule by goal considerations	Schedule by goal, group interest
Work by objective requirements	Work by personal/group concerns
Work/interaction defined by goal	Work/interaction optional by interest
Productivity = effort/product	Productivity = individual effort within a group context
Motivation = goal at any acceptable cost	Motivation = balance of group/person pay-off

The degree of group integration and group power over labor seems to be directly proportional to the extent to which the group shares economic resources and rituals. Conversation and social interaction provide the basic glue of group cohesion; sharing resources and food, participating in integrating rituals generate the strongest bonds of mutual interest. These in turn lead to coercion of individuals and submitting of personal interests to those of the group.

This is illustrated by the Yapese. Members of each eating class and each social rank in society share betel nut, signifying their identity as members of a given social strata. The eating of betel nut is both a food activity and a ritual activity. When the leaders of a particular kinship group or village gather together for a work party, the first step in the activity is to sit together to chew betel nut. After the time of conversation and betel nut chewing is completed, the work activity may begin.

Yapese reject individuals who do not participate in chewing betel nut as deviant and in conflict with the interests of the group.

Table 4.1 illustrates how the organization and motivation of labor by rule or goal and by individual or group incentives combine to produce four distinctive value profiles. In the A-Individualist social environment, people schedule and organize work according to specifications of goal, and measure productivity and incentive according to relative personal costs and pay-off. In the B-Bureaucratic social environment, role and rule dominate schedule and organization. Reward for labor is regulated by considerations of time and social hierarchy, producing wage scales in modern societies and scales of material and ritual standing in traditional societies.

In the C-Corporate social environment, group values, incentives, and decisions periodically supersede the interests and activities of individuals, and the high grid factor of role and rule serves to organize group labor. In contrast, people who reject role and rule, and give goal and group interests priority to organize labor, create a D-Collectivist social environment.

Case Studies

The Deni: A-Individualist Social Environment (Low Grid/Low Group)

The Deni work as individuals and schedule their daily activities according to their personal goals. Deni men decide early in the morning whether they intend to hunt or fish, and whether they intend to do it alone or with others. Both men and women determine their daily activities in accord with their individual and domestic interests.

Deni order their lives around objective goals, and their daily routine is negotiated on a day-to-day basis. Deni schedule their work according to the particular requirements of the goal that they have defined for that day. If they determine to go on an extended hunt, they organize themselves and schedule their activities according to that objective. If, on the other hand, they intend to sit or to work with a Brazilian patron, they determine their work routine accordingly.

Social interaction is a very important part of Deni life, but they do not hesitate to sacrifice social interaction for their particular goals. Men will spend long hours alone in the forest hunting wild game. On some occasions they will go in pairs, or even in larger groups, but much of a man's life is spent in the forest alone. Women, on the other hand, tend to work in social groups. Mother and daughter will harvest or process manioc together. These are not permanent arrangements; they vary day by day and by the particular activity involved.

Deni measure productivity on the basis of their success. If they have gotten meat, they call it a successful hunt. When men spend long hours in the forest and come back with nothing, they are discouraged. People express frustration with individuals who do not give their best effort to produce. One individual in the village was crippled and unable to go hunting. People in the village criticized him openly because he did not fish, nor did he attempt to plant a garden. Because he was mobile, able to go from place to place, they expected more from him. Citing his unwillingness to work, people called him lazy and his relatives sometimes refused to feed him.

Motivation among Deni is goal-oriented. Critical of those who do not have goals and do not work, Deni measure success in terms of what people produce and the effort they expend to be productive. One man whose left arm was amputated above the elbow was highly esteemed by the people because of his commitment to achieve personal and village goals and his evident hard work. People admired his aggressive, hard-working behavior, and commended him for his achievements.

Deni compete with one another in terms of their individual work activities and measure the achievements of individuals in the community on the basis of their productivity. Some individuals are recognized as good hunters, others for special skills such as shamanistic ritual, clearing fields, or cutting trees.

Christian College: B-Bureaucratic (High Grid/Low Group)

Christian College is a fairly typical example of a B-Bureaucratic social environment in a modern complex society. At Christian College each position has its job description and specific assignments. Work is always by role assignment and follows very specific rules. A person who checks meal tickets when students enter the dining hall is not able to sell tickets; tickets are purchased in a different office where other people have the assigned task of selling meal tickets.

Another distinctive characteristic of B-Bureaucratic societies is that work and interaction are separated by work rules. People are given a specified number of hours or minutes in which they are to work; they are granted short periods of time in which they may stop work and interact with one another. While Christian College faculty members are expected to spend time interacting with students, if staff are found spending excessive time in interaction they will be criticized and even disciplined by their supervisors. Too much social interaction is considered loafing or stealing from the employer, and such behavior is discouraged.

Productivity in this work environment is defined in relationship to time and product. Individuals are expected to expend a certain amount of labor in a given period of time. In the college, faculty have a regular class workload (e.g., four three-unit classes), while staff are expected to be at their desks from 8:00 A.M. to 5:00 P.M.

In business or industry with a similar social environment the amount of work produced may be more carefully regulated. At Eastman Kodak in Rochester, New York, the quantity of products is timed and counted. Laborers must maintain a certain production rate if they wish to maintain good standing with the employer. Employees are given special benefits for producing a surplus above the work rate and may receive bonus pay for that activity. If they are highly motivated and produce more than the specified surplus, however, the job may be recalculated so that all workers must produce at that higher level. Veteran Kodak workers are careful not to upset this balance.

Motivation in B-Bureaucratic societies is carefully tied to the rules. People in B-Bureaucratic social environments expect that individuals in assigned roles will perform their role obligations without additional compensation. Christian College faculty and students experience deep frustration when they go overseas because third world bureaucrats often expect tips or special compensation for doing their normal work. Many Americans find this unacceptable because, in their own cultural setting, the role carries with it the obligation of completing the work assigned to the role. The pay received for a role is contractual and acceptance of the contract means that a person agrees to do the job on those terms. No additional pay is to be expected.

The Yapese: C-Corporate Social Environment (High Grid/High Group)

In Yap, scheduling of work activities is done by consensus in the community. All who anticipate being part of the work project agree to an appointed time and task. Their expectations are that work will not be scheduled for them without their approval. Yapese assign work by role; the elderly and the skilled lead in every public or family work context. These experts, skilled in a special craft, give knowledge and direction to the work.

The benefits of labor are both social and economic. People organize cooperative projects because it is socially good to do so. Outside observers are astonished at the leisurely pace at which Yapese build houses (it may take several years) or work on other major projects. The initiators of such projects invariably include a cooperative phase, which will involve significant costs in terms of food and drink needed to pay the laborers, who are kin, fellow villagers, and friends. The cooperative phase seems to move very rapidly, yet the preparation for this social event often costs builders more than if they had done the work themselves, or contracted with others to do it for them. The cost of collective labor is rarely a consideration; the social benefit has higher priority.

When I asked a man why he used six men on a job that he had contracted for four, he replied, "With six it is more fun."

Scheduling of work is a matter of social importance; economic agendas may be set aside for social reasons. Co-workers may come and go according to their specific individual needs, as long as they work within the consensus expectations of the group. People engaged in cooperative work expect to spend at least half the time in conversation and social interaction. If the fellowship is good, more of the day will be given to talk than to labor. If the work is out of doors and the weather becomes intolerable, the workers, by consensus, delay their activities until a time when the weather is suitable.

Yapese make social interaction as high a priority as labor. People expect to enjoy being together while they work, and make little or no distinction between work time and social time. To socialize on the job is considered part of the job and generally the group acts in consensus with regard to this expectation. The men building my house back in 1967 alternated each hour between work and conversation, in spite of the fact that they were not being paid by the hour but by the job. Conversation was more important to them than the time/pay ratio.

Productivity is also evaluated according to group priorities and in accord with the assigned roles of individuals. Yapese evaluate how well a job is done on the basis of comparison. They also assess the achievement of one group in opposition to the achievements of another group. Productivity is defined more in terms of comparison of group achievements than in terms of a particular rule of time and product. Group competition is a chief factor in a Yapese definition of productivity.

Motivation in C-Corporate environments is a combination of group-focused incentives and pay-offs that benefit the group and the individuals who participate in them. Oftentimes a primary motivation in Yap is the dynamic of group interaction and satisfaction. If people enjoy being together and working together, they have a positive experience in their work relationship. At the same time, it is important that the group achieve its objective. If the group fails to achieve its objectives, individuals participating within the group will also have a sense of failure.

The Aukan: D-Collectivist Social Environment
(Low Grid/High Group)

The Aukan Afro-Americans reflect a D-Collectivist social environment in terms of their labor relationships and practices. Men and women work according to their individual and group interests. Women usually plant and harvest open fields on the plateau and hills inland from the river in small groups of three or four households. They go as a group and work together in their individual fields over a period of several weeks. After they have completed their field work they return to the village, again in a group, where they process and consume the food that they have gathered. Men likewise work as individuals and in groups. Men help their sisters or their wives in their fields and they also hunt and fish for meat. Hunting and fishing activities tend to be individual.

When the village mobilizes men to work together for a community project, the leaders especially watch the participation of individual men. Those men who show a strong and consistent effort to serve the group will be selected as the future leaders of the group. Leadership is identified on the basis of group service and submission to the group leadership. Leaders watch and evaluate individuals over a long period of time (up to ten years) before they grant to them public recognition and incorporate them into the leadership corps. Aukaners place strong emphasis on the effort of individuals in support of group values. Self-interested individuals are rejected as potential leaders and may even be sanctioned by economic, social, or supernatural means.

The Aukan group exercises very strong coercive power over individuals within it. This coercive power resides predominantly in the spirits of the ancestors, who are a continuing threat to the welfare and well-being of Aukan people. Aukan believe that the spirits of the dead punish the living for social misdeeds. Therefore when someone is sick, or some other significant disaster befalls people in a village, the village leaders divine which ancestor is angry and for what reasons. Through this divining process, they identify the guilty individuals, and punish them by demanding sacrifice and purifying ritual. The only way an individual can escape this sanction is to flee from the village and join some other group. Even at another village, however, the ancestral spirits may punish through illness or other kinds of disaster. As long as people maintain residence within the network of Aukan communities they cannot escape this supernatural force that sustains the power of the group. Even when they go to the city they are still subject to the punitive powers of the spirits of the dead, although the "posse" is less effective, especially should an individual seek refuge in a new community of Christian believers.

D-Collectivist societies focus on objective goals, but these goals are defined by group interests rather than individual interests, and the activities of individuals are subject to the requirements of the group. Aukan work is organized in terms of personal and group concerns. People may work on individual projects as long as the demands of the group do not interfere. However, because of the high group interest and integration, when Aukan village or clan leaders call for concerted group activity all individual interests are subject to group demands.

The relationship between work and social interaction is dependent upon the interest of the group. Because clan and village solidarity is so crucial to sustaining group interests, much social interaction is included in work activities. Decision making is governed by group consensus and work activities involve collective labor and reward. Aukaners define productivity in terms of the value of individual effort for group interest. Public expression of group acceptance and threats of group sanction motivate people to participate. The success of the group is its own reward and individuals receive special group recognition for exemplary service.

Labor, Productivity, and Value Conflicts

The patterns of social labor in world cultures are significantly diverse. In B-Bureaucratic and C-Corporate societies the ascribed hierarchy plays a very crucial role in the organization of work; rule and procedure are fundamental to work relationships. In contrast, in A-Individualist and D-Collectivist societies, objective goals are the primary consideration by which individuals organize their labor activities. Achieving the goals and fulfilling the interests of the individual or the group are essential. As we consider ministry in any of these social environments, we must recognize that the organization of and reward for labor are important considerations.

Conflict in Christian College

There may be several social environments in the same society. People interacting across two social environments will inevitably have conflict. I have used Christian College to illustrate the B-Bureaucratic social environment, but in fact Christian College has variants of both B (high grid/low group) and C (high grid/high group) social environments in the community. This is not only a fact of college life, but also the source of one of the perpetual tensions in that life. The social environments are "upper campus" and "lower campus," in which the upper is the domain of the administration, faculty, and classrooms, and the lower is residence halls, dining hall, and athletic facilities.

The "upper campus" is a B-Bureaucratic environment. The "lower campus" constitutes a C-Corporate community. Students and staff live together in a common residential setting; they eat together in a common dining facility, and they form cohesive small groups in the various floors and sections of the residence hall. Within this setting, the staff emphasize group unity and collegiality among the students who are residents and the resident directors and assistants.

Conflict among people in these environments is usually the result of different values, rules, and procedures. When students in the lower campus have significant needs, the resident advisers, who are participants in the community, respond according to their relationship to the students. When there is destruction of property, resident advisers respond with compassion and personal interest.

In contrast, the office of housing operates in a B-Bureaucratic environment. Individuals who work within the office have work assignments by role and work rules. The rules specify that students who have damaged property in the dormitories must pay specific fines. The officer who is in charge of administering the rules usually assesses the fines, sometimes in spite of objections by the resident adviser. The official in the housing office has no relationship with the students and is working in a setting in which reward is based on work done according to the rules. As a consequence, conflict arises between the resident director, who is part of the C-Corporate environment, and the housing official, who is part of the B-Bureaucratic environment. They argue with one another; they feel frustrated by the demands that each is making because they are participants in different social environments.

These same conflicts may be carried outside of the college to other social settings. This is clearly one of the problems that affects missionaries working in third world countries. Most Western missionaries have spent significant parts of their lives in B-Bureaucratic environments like Christian College, where they have learned to work according to rule and role. When they begin church-planting activities or establish institutions in which they are in positions of supervision over nationals, they define the work situation in terms of B-Bureaucratic social expectations.

Oftentimes, individuals who are nationals in these settings come from C-Corporate social settings. As a consequence, missionaries and nationals find themselves in conflict over work rules, schedules, and definitions of productivity. Missionaries judge nationals as loafing and inconsiderate of authority. Missionaries also evaluate the spiritual life of the nationals and conclude that they are slothful and unwise in the use of resources. As a consequence, the relationship between missionaries and nationals is threatened. Nationals, on the other hand, judge missionaries accordingly. They see missionaries as insensitive and unconcerned about the needs of those who work with them. Nationals find missionaries harsh and rigid. The importance of rule is excessive and misunderstood. Further, nationals see the missionaries as unresponsive to the group and to spiritual issues. Missionaries seem unloving and interested only in how much money they spend for the labor that they supervise. Such conflicts are pervasive in cross-cultural ministries.

Mission Employment of Aukan Co-Workers

The penchant of Aukan people to sacrifice the interests of the individual for the good of the group carries over from traditional society into evangelical churches. My mission colleagues in Surinam confronted those values in their attempts to enlist the support of local churches for the Aukan translation project. Mission staff desired that the local Aukan churches support two individuals they had chosen to be translation workers. These two men were multilingual; they could read and write in Dutch and in English, and had been trained to write in their own language and to translate. However, they were relatively young men who were not recognized in the church as spiritual leaders. Mission leaders felt that the churches ought to provide partial support for these men to do translation work, and sought to motivate church leaders to support them.

The elders in the churches not only refused to provide economic support for these men, but they also questioned whether they should be entrusted with the responsibility of translation. When the mission team explored the situation further, they discovered that the pastors did not receive pay. Rather, they were "working for the Lord"; they were chosen by the senior pastors because of their long-term commitment to and work for the group. They had demonstrated faithfulness over many years in supporting group interests and working toward group goals; as a consequence they were entrusted with spiritual leadership of the group.

In contrast, the Bible translators were primarily concerned about the technical requirements of the work. They defined Bible translation in B-Bureaucratic terms. They had a job they wanted done. This job required certain technical skills and individuals who could fill that goal assignment. The mother tongue translator was a role, and the task was an assignment to be done by rule and paid according to time-work equivalents. The church, in contrast, had no rule of time-work equivalents, but rather of work-group equivalents (D-Collectivist labor terms). Individuals should be working for the group because as members it was in their interest to do so. Their legitimacy was established by the quality and duration of their work. These young men not only should not be paid; they should be working to demonstrate their spiritual maturity by giving of their time and energy to projects of interest to the group. The conflict between the Bible translators' work strategies and Aukan work strategies clearly reflect distinct social environments.

The Bible translators held to their own work strategies but recognized that they had to provide the pay for these mother-tongue translators. Since the job was defined according to the Bible translators' hierarchy and work rules, it was impractical to expect the Aukan church to support it. The two systems were in distinctive conflict with one another and a resolution would require a change in the social structure of either of the two groups. Neither, of course, was willing or able to change.

This kind of social conflict is inevitable as we attempt to move from one social setting to another. The Aukan churches were extremely effective in mobilizing members for group interest. On several occasions we observed many Aukan men working together around the church building to maintain it, to clean it, and to make improvements on the general property. They also organized themselves to care for the membership. Different individuals had responsibilities for visiting the sick, for holding Bible studies, or for organizing youth activities. All of these individuals worked for the Lord and for the good of the group. None of them received pay, including the senior pastor. Individuals received leadership responsibility because of their regular, consistent performance in support of the work of the group. The success of the group was its own reward, and individuals received only prestige rewards and recognition for their commitment to group goals.

Outside of the church many of these individuals were employed in jobs in the national economy. The pastor that we interviewed worked for the national government and was paid there for his role performance. It is not that these urban Aukan did not understand the other arrangements. In fact, many of them worked in B-Bureaucratic social environments. However, they could not redefine their church environment. They saw the Bible translators as an institution like the Surinam government, capable of paying out of its own resources for technical work. As a consequence, the Aukan did not see and could not appreciate why the Bible translators wanted them to support the Bible translation efforts of these two men. As members of the church these men should work in secular jobs as the other people in the church and support the group and its interests. Bible translation was in the group interest, but it was really not a group project; it was the Bible translators' project. Therefore, it was only right that they should pay these men to do Bible translation if they wanted them to do it. The concept of church support for translation was inconsistent with church work procedures and in conflict with their understanding of how the church should work.

It should be evident from this case study that it is possible to have two different types of social organization and two different patterns of work relationships in the same setting. Conflicts will arise when we attempt to mix these kinds of social expectations and rules about work and overturn the social structure within which they are contextualized. The context of the Bible translators requires work by rule and procedures characteristic of B-Bureaucratic societies. The work in the Aukan church requires work by goal, the primacy of group interest, and procedures characteristic of D-Collectivist societies. When the mission leaders demanded that a D-Collectivist society work and support a project according to B-Bureaucratic society rules, it was not possible nor was it considered legitimate by Aukan people.

The Bible and Labor

Some people come to the Scriptures seeking normative instructions with which they may solve conflicts like those described above. Some Bible teachers might choose the case study of Nehemiah to teach "effective leadership" and to show Aukan pastors why and how they should "get with the program" that the mission leader has chosen. Such a Bible study has limited relevance unless the teacher understands Jerusalem in the fifth century in terms of a C-Corporate social environment. When Nehemiah proposed reconstruction of the wall, the people, in their Oriental worldview, understood and shared the shame that Nehemiah felt. They agreed that the task was both worthy and urgent, and committed themselves to carry out this work in spite of opposition and danger. This case is a classic illustration of how tasks may be assigned to corporate groups and how work might be organized and directed by corporate leaders, whose authority comes from their status within their respective groups. To apply the principles in Nehemiah to other social environments without careful recontextualization can lead to false applications and even destructive leadership training.

It is essential to understand that the case studies in Scripture reflect a distinctive social environment and worldview, and that both the cases and the contexts vary. For example, the case study of Jacob (Gen. 30:25–43) reflects an A-Individualist organization of labor. Jacob and Laban negotiate the matters of labor and wages. Jacob pleads with Laban to release him to return to his own homeland. Laban in return pleads with Jacob to stay and says, "Name your wages, and I will pay them." Divining that Jacob is bringing him good fortune, Laban seeks to capitalize on that advantage as long as possible. After they have agreed that Jacob will get the speckled, spotted, and dark-colored sheep and goats, Jacob uses magic and planned breeding to increase the size of his own herds (Gen. 30:37–39). Laban and Jacob compete with one another, each seeking to enhance his own wealth and to use the labor and resources of the other to assist in that effort.

In contrast, Jacob's son, Joseph, who becomes ruler over all of Egypt, provides an excellent illustration of the B-Bureaucratic organization of labor (Gen. 47). Joseph uses the huge quantities of grain, stored up during the seven years of plenty, to extend the control of Pharaoh over all of Egypt. After the people of Egypt had exhausted their money and livestock to buy grain, the text reports that Joseph bought all the land in Egypt for Pharaoh. "The Egyptians, one in all, sold their fields, because the famine was too severe for them . . . and Joseph reduced the people to servitude, from one end of Egypt to the other." In the organization that followed, one-fifth of the crops of Egypt belonged to Pharaoh and four-fifths were allocated to the laborers as food for themselves, their households, and their children. Joseph's success affects both the descendents of Egyptians and Israelis; in Exodus we find the Israelites serving as slave laborers for a descendent of Pharaoh, who authorizes foremen to force them to produce the bricks to meet a daily quota (Exod. 5). When Moses seeks to free the people, Pharaoh instructs the foremen to withhold the straw, forcing them to gather stubble in the fields, yet produce bricks at the same rate that they had done in previous days. The nomadic individualist herders from Canaan had been transformed into slave laborers, working by production quotas and work rules imposed upon them by authoritarian foremen in Pharaoh's bureaucracy.

The scriptural case that illustrates the D-Collectivist social environment is found in the New Testament. Following the resurrection of Jesus, the disciples form a D-Collectivist social environment. The data for this appear in two places: the fishing incident reported in the last chapter of John's Gospel, and the description of the birth of the church in the opening chapters of Acts. In the final incident recorded in the Gospel of John, seven of Jesus' disciples had gathered by the Sea of Tiberias. Peter decided to go fishing and the other disciples joined him. At least two of those, Nathaniel from Cana and Thomas, were not fishermen, but by this time they were intimate members of the group. While the focus of this text is not labor, it is a collective labor activity that provides the opportunity for the miracle of the draught of fish and Jesus' instruction of Peter.

Following the resurrection of Christ, the believing disciples, numbering about 120, gathered frequently for prayer. In a short period of time, the group enjoyed a remarkable degree of unity and collective interest. Peter initiated the decision to select a replacement for Judas, but the decision was accomplished by group prayer and the casting of lots. The outpouring of the Holy Spirit occurred when they were all gathered together in one place. The work of the early church emphasized collective action (Acts 2:42–47), with the apostles providing leadership for the new believers.

The Holy Spirit has anointed leaders to serve in all four of the social environments illuminated by the grid/group model. Further exploration of the details of these cases shows that these leaders acted consistently and appropriately within the context of that historic social environment and worldview. Peter followed the "first among equals" leadership expectations of the D-Collectivist gathering of disciples, while Nehemiah acted with the compelling authority appropriate to the C-Corporate structure of fifth-century Jerusalem. Each case provides an illustration of spiritually empowered leadership appropriate to the context in which it occurs.

"Working for the Lord"—Labor in Christian Context

Scripture does not prescribe a particular social environment or worldview. The Spirit of God works in the lives of people in whatever social environment they find themselves. This is an essential fact if we are to understand how to apply the teaching of Scripture to the practical questions of life in various social environments of ministry. The theme of Scripture is not the restructuring of social environments into some ideal kingdom type, but rather the application of "words of life" or kingdom principles to ordinary working relationships.

Paul's message to high grid/high group Greeks at Ephesus and Colossae compel new believers to rethink their relationships in the world. While Paul accepts the master-slave relationship as a given, he challenges both master and slave to redeemed relationships with one another. The slave is to work "with sincerity of heart and reverence for the Lord" (Col. 3:22); the master is to "provide your slaves with what is right and fair, because you know you also have a Master in heaven" (Col. 4:1). Paul reminds his readers that "anyone who does wrong will be repaid for his wrong, and there is no favoritism" (Col. 3:25). The central pervasive theme of Paul's message to masters and slaves is summed up in his command, "Whatever you do, work at it with all your heart, as working for the Lord, not for men, since you know you will receive an inheritance from the Lord as a reward. It is the Lord Christ you are serving" (Col. 3:23–24).

The text in Colossians and the parallel text in Ephesians (6:5–9) are not a rationale for particular structural relationships, but rather an argument that those relationships in their natural social contexts must be redeemed. Paul challenges new believers to discharge the duties of their roles in family, community, and ministry as if they were working for the Lord and not for men. This attitude of submission to Christ and service to others pervades New Testament teaching on transformed labor relationships.

These texts take as given the existing structures and worldview of Greek or Jewish society, both of which are high grid/high group social environments. The objective of these texts is not to justify the abuses and sins of the social environment, but rather to call Christians to be followers of Christ even in those abusive contexts. Peter (1 Pet. 2:18) advises Jewish believers to submit even to harsh masters, recognizing the unjustness of their behavior. Peter calls them to a consciousness of God and to an endurance for the sake of the gospel. Peter uses Jesus as the illustrative example, noting how he did not retaliate when he suffered, but rather entrusted himself to God. Peter sums up the purpose of suffering for the believer: "But rejoice that you participate in the sufferings of Christ, so that you may be overjoyed when his glory is revealed" (1 Pet. 4:13).

The social norms of each type of social environment serve to regulate the behavior of the members within that environment. As we have seen in the discussion above, labor may be organized either by rule or by goal considerations and by priority given to individual or group demands. In each of the respective social environments, people seek to control their own labor and the labor of others for personal and group advantage. The message of these texts is that personal and group advantage are not to be our priority. The priority of the believer should be the glory of God and working in His service. This may be accomplished in various ways, depending on the social environment we encounter. As my New Testament colleague, Mike Wilkins, has suggested (personal communication), people labor in response to the incentives of reward and/or gratitude; yet the particular rewards that motivate people or the acts for which they might express gratitude vary with each social environment.

The Aukan church in Surinam (low grid/high group) emphasizes that its members should work without pay. They hold up Colossians 3:23 as their motto and claim that they are "working for the Lord." Serving the church is the primary group value. Individuals are measured in terms of their commitment to serving the Lord and his people. Senior men and women are rewarded with leadership roles in recognition of their years of faithful service.

In my local church in southern California (high grid/low group), we operate from a more bureaucratic type of social organization. We have elected officers, paid staff, and many lay leadership positions. The board, the trustees, the deacons, and the Sunday school staff all have their respective roles and responsibilities. In our meetings we talk about job descriptions and tasks to be done. We typically recruit workers to fill particular tasks that we have identified as necessary for priority ministries. Members push as much work as possible on the paid staff, and volunteers often quietly complain about the burden of responsibilities that they have for the church. The reward typically given to the volunteer is that "you have done your duty" as a member and as a servant in the body of Christ. Only on rare occasions do people rally in collective excitement to support an all-church work day or to move a pastor into his new home. Their motivations are based upon definitions of duty and anticipated personal rewards for service.

The Javanese church in Surinam (high grid/high group) emphasizes corporate activity, perhaps stimulated by the pressure of their Muslim neighbors and friends, and the fact that they have few other opportunities for fellowship with Javanese believers. The Javanese church focuses on corporate authority relationships among pastors, lay leaders, and lay workers, with a strong emphasis on following the leader and supporting the activities of the leader and the group. Leaders organize and promote group celebration, corporate affirmation of faith in Jesus Christ, and "serving the body" and "doing their duty" as members in the local church. Church ministries frequently bring the group together as a whole, and work and celebration are inevitably mingled together.

The A-Individualist church is less common than the types described above, yet there are examples in the urban metropolitan areas of the United States. The Bear Valley Baptist Church, described by Frank Tillapaugh (1982), illustrates the low grid/low group urban congregation. The key characteristics of such a local church are a loosely structured organization, individually spawned ministries, and temporary activity groups. Such churches emphasize the diverse interests of their members and promote various activities among them. The people have no need to know what others are doing and the leaders coordinate many different activities. People gain their reward by "exercising their gifts"; the church is seen as the universal body of Christ rather than a local congregation.

In summary, each of these different church organizations described above has accepted the same biblical truth of Colossians 3:23, but each has contextualized this truth in terms of their respective social environment. The Scriptures speak to people, people respond in context, and the Word powerfully transforms the church and its relationship to the world. Each local congregation organizes believers to do the work of Christ, yet each conceptualizes the structure and reward of service in ways that reflect a given social environment. At the same time each has responded to the gospel message and to the call of discipleship to Christ. All seek to discharge the duties of ministry (2 Tim. 4:5) as working for the Lord and not for people.

The Deni Case Reconsidered: A Solution

In the case that opened this chapter, a missionary brought from his own culture specific work rules. The Deni comprehended none of this, but defined work in terms of objective tasks and rewards. To the Deni the time spent, the level of individual effort, and the amount of reward were variable and subject to negotiation. The missionary's concern to pay hard workers more than casual workers was not their concern.

A society such as the Deni is not rule-directed but goal-directed. Work and reward must be negotiated in each situation. I have observed Deni complaining about individuals who continue to borrow from them and do not return; however, they do not stop loaning. They merely complain and try to renegotiate their relationships with these individuals.

Is it possible to resolve such conflicts in a positive way, rather than to go our own separate ways? The answer to this question is yes, if missionaries are willing to change their expectations to mesh with the social environment of those with whom they work. This may be illustrated by discussing how to pay Deni for work on the airstrip.

The solution to paying Deni for airstrip maintenance was a procedural compromise that allowed both the missionary from the B-Bureaucratic society and the members of the A-Individualist society to work according to their own requirements and at the same time be satisfied with arrangements for pay. Koop needed to feel that the amount of money expended on his behalf produced the appropriate amount of labor from the people. The Deni, on the other hand, did not understand his rules or his conception of work. They defined the work in terms of their own personal goals.

The job had to be redefined in such a way that Koop's goals and their goals were met in a way that satisfied both. By dividing the airstrip into segments and assigning parcels to individuals, Koop was able to distribute the work and relate the task to each individual's personal goals. He discovered from each individual what they hoped to earn. One selected a pair of blue jeans and a shirt, another selected a couple of aluminum pans, and so on. If they asked for too much, Koop offered what he felt was legitimate pay for the job. Once the individual reward had been negotiated for each worker, Koop explained what needed to be done to achieve their goal. By redefining a job in terms of goals, the people were able to proceed with the work and complete it to the satisfaction of everyone involved. These negotiations led to ongoing satisfied relationships with the people in the community.

What are the ramifications of such a social environment for moral standards? Missionaries will not find a series of "Ten Commandments" that govern life. For example, Deni complain about the bad behavior of people but do not see that behavior in terms of a series of arbitrary rules. Rather, they view that behavior as conflicting with their own personal goals. Such societies have been mislabeled "amoral." Rather than amoral societies, the norms of morality are negotiated on the basis of the requirements for members of the society to achieve their personal interests. The definition of moral behavior is renegotiated, as are the work rules, when individuals engage in conflict with one another.

Perhaps the most practical rule for a society such as the Deni is the Golden Rule: Do unto others as you would have others do unto you. Because so many of their relationships and activities are negotiated, they understand best the process of negotiation and equal treatment in relationship to one another. A set of standardized rules about behavior does not fit with their understanding of how life and work should proceed. However, the negotiation of relationships in terms of fairness is quite readily understood and accepted.

5
Generosity and Exchange

The Stone of Stumbling in Interpersonal Relationships

Case Studies

Borrowing in America

During my teenage years in northern Ohio, I was socialized into a middle-class social world in which every individual owned all the essential items needed to live an ordinary life. Each of my neighbors had an automobile, a lawn mower, garden tools, and a ladder. These items were neither casually loaned nor easily borrowed, except from a special friend. I learned quickly that we should each have our own things and should not ask others for theirs. My neighbors emphasized by practice that we should be independent and manage our own economic affairs. We did not share money, nor did we share the objects of our material prosperity. If people borrowed tools, they were embarrassed to have to ask, and often, they returned those items quickly so as to not to incur further obligation or to earn disapproval. People talked about those who borrowed as having a flaw in their character. Respectable people provided for their own needs and had no need for the help of others.

Attitudes of economic independence and reluctance to share and exchange with one another are quite common among Americans. Borrowing is carefully regulated and individuals do it only to the extent that they can maintain their autonomy in relationships to others. Only the poorest must borrow from others. Borrowing is a measure of inadequacy in terms of achieving success and prosperity.

Individuals who are socialized in such a social environment struggle with the strong expectations of reciprocity often found in other cultures in the world. Missionaries, anthropologists, and government workers who must live for extended periods of time in such cultures find them confusing at least and frustrating and trying at worst.

Borrowing in Yap

My personal experiences living with the people of Yap produced precisely the conflict alluded to above. For Yapese people, borrowing is an ordinary part of life and people turn frequently to their neighbors for material assistance. Soon after my arrival on Yap, my neighbors discovered the few tools and material possessions that I had brought with me. Shortly, one came and asked to borrow my motor bike; another came and asked for money; soon nearly every material possession that I owned had been the subject of a request to borrow. In every case, I either refused or gave reluctantly. I remember very specifically the incident involving my hammer.

One day a young boy came and asked me if a neighbor on the other side of the village could borrow my hammer. Since this was early in my stay there and I did not understand the rules, I said, "Sure, I would be glad to loan it to you." I gave him the hammer and he went on his way.

Several weeks passed. On one or two occasions I thought of using the hammer, but realized that I had loaned it to this neighbor. One day, quite frustrated because I wanted a hammer, I caught sight of the same boy who happened to be passing my house and asked, "Whatever happened to my hammer?" When he answered that he didn't know, I instructed him to go to that man, find my hammer, and bring it back to me. An hour or so later, the boy returned with a hammer. He told me it was not my hammer, that it belonged to Tamag who lived nearby. He said the handle on my hammer had been broken; some children were playing with the head and lost it. However, Tamag said I could use his hammer as long as I wanted it.

By that time, I was not concerned about who owned the hammer, only that I had one to use for the task at hand. I used it for several days and then placed it in my house with my other tools. Taking a cue from the first borrower, I did not return it, but waited to see what would happen. Several weeks later another little boy came to my house and asked if by chance I had "the" hammer. I said, "What do you mean, 'the' hammer?" He said, "Oh, the hammer that belongs to Tamag down the path." I confessed that I did have the hammer and told him that my hammer had been lost. The boy had been sent to borrow Tamag's hammer. Since Tamag had loaned the hammer to me, he sent this boy to my house. Recognizing that I was party to a growing string of exchanges, I gave it to him, and that was the last time I saw that particular hammer.

The people of Yap are generally willing to share what they have with others. One is not under obligation to return a borrowed object until the person who needs it calls for it. As long as I did not need a hammer, people felt no obligation to return it to my house. However, at the time when I did express need, the person who borrowed it helped me find a hammer from someone else that I could use.

This type of reciprocal borrowing exchange is completely alien to middle-class American culture. The idea that something that I purchased might not be returned to me creates frustration, tension, and even animosity toward the borrower. Missionaries who take up residence in a social environment such as that on Yap struggle over the loss of tools and other objects because of values. Sometimes we accuse our neighbors of stealing rather than participate with them in a system of reciprocity according to the rules of their social world.

Given these differences in expectations, missionaries and nationals often not only do not understand one another, but they build up feelings of hostility because of faulty expectations. I remember occasions when Yapese borrowed money from me. I looked for those persons for days afterwards, expecting them to return the money. According to their values, the repayment need not occur for months or even years. Further, the repayment need not be in kind, but rather might come in some other form or service. My middle-class American expectations are that repayment should be immediate and that the person who has received these goods becomes increasingly inferior to me the longer the payment is delayed.

Borrowing among the Deni

Within a few hours of my arrival in the jungle village of the Deni Indians in Brazil, I was unrolling my sleeping gear on the palm floor of a thatched roof hut, when three Indian men walked up the ladder stairway and entered my semiprivate domain. The owner of the house was absent temporarily from the village and I had been granted permission to stay there. My guests sat down in a semicircle around my suitcase and began to talk with one another. Since I did not understand their language and they did not understand mine, we sat and looked at one another while they conversed. A few moments passed. One of the men then unlatched my suitcase and opened it. They crowded more closely and began to lift out the clothing, notebooks, and the bag of candy that I had tucked underneath my clothes. Soon they had taken complete inventory of all the private items in my suitcase and placed them back in the case. Leaving the lid open, one of the men walked over to a little shelf where I had placed my shaving kit, opened it, and began to sort through its contents. He took particular delight in my shampoo. He showed it to his friends, and then slipped it into the pocket of his old missionary barrel blue jeans. With that I let out a yell and ran to him to retrieve my shampoo. No longer silent, I declared in English that these were my material things and they should not be messing in my private belongings. I retrieved the shampoo, placed it in the case, and closed it tightly. Then I went to the suitcase, closed the lid, latched it, and moved it away from them. They sat for a few moments grinning at one another, conversing further; then they dismissed themselves and departed. This introduction to Deni behavior and values taught me quickly that we had different concepts of "private." I had much to learn.

A few days later, sitting on the open living veranda of my friends, the Koops, I observed a brief conversation between my friend's wife and a Deni woman who then left the house. My friend's wife told me the woman had asked if she could eat with us that evening. When I asked what her response had been, she, with tears in her eyes, said "no." She explained how when they had first arrived, people asked, and they had invited them to eat. Soon, half of the village was eating with them and their food supplies were rapidly depleted. Deni came on a daily basis to ask them for various items of food that they had brought with them. Having planned for a period of two or three months, they knew the limits of their food stores, and learned quickly that to give to anyone resulted in many requests for food. Deciding that the welfare of their children was more important than generosity, they decided to not give food to the Deni.

This decision created strain for the Koops as well as frustration in their relationships with the people. They felt a Christian obligation to be generous and caring for their neighbors, yet they saw the consequences of even small acts of generosity. The Deni seemed to have an insatiable appetite for their food and material goods, and would ask and take until everything was gone.

The Koops did not know how the Deni felt about their refusal. After nearly a year of residing in the village, they still did not have a clear picture of Deni exchange relationships. One thing they did understand: Deni were aggressive in their pursuit of the material goods and food that they brought with them. Yet, for the most part, they did not steal from the Koops and when they were told no, accepted that decision and continued to be friendly and open.

The Deni adapted quickly to the system of exchange established by the translator. He offered material goods in return for meat and contributed coffee on their feast days. They made artifacts that they brought to him in exchange for material goods. He took these artifacts to the city and sold them at market prices, to recover his costs. In this way he attempted to serve them, helping them meet their need for clothing and other goods.

Notwithstanding, my friends felt that at times they were un-Christian in their attitudes about food. In their hearts they desired to give to the Deni, yet because the Deni would take all that they had, they knew they could not do so. They did not understand the rules of Deni exchange relationships and struggled to know how best to work with them.

Asking and Social Exchange

Middle-class American, Yap, and Deni societies have very different systems of social exchange values. In each of these societies, people have specific expectations as to how material goods and food should be shared and distributed among people.

Every society has specific values and expectations with regard to managing wealth. In some societies personal wealth is desired and approved by the members. In others, people employ leveling mechanisms to keep one individual from gaining more wealth than others in their group. In still other societies, people have inherited rules of hierarchy that prescribe the flow of goods to specific individuals who occupy positions of power and may use that power to gain personal wealth.

The goal of this chapter is to discover what patterns of exchange and distribution are characteristic in the four types of social environment, and how these patterns vary as they are elaborated in specific societies and cultures around the world. We shall also identify the patterns of exchange and distribution that characterize our own society and see how these patterns produce value orientations that, when carried into another social environment, may produce conflict and confrontation with others. Conflict arising out of misunderstanding of values about exchange often become a stone of stumbling in interpersonal relationships for missionaries.

High Grid—Asking Is Humiliating

While the Yapese and I had different values in regard to giving, we shared the feeling that asking is humiliating. The fact that my neighbors sent a young boy to ask for my hammer reflects this value. In a high grid social environment, the one who asks is always lower than the one who gives. The giver occupies a position of superiority and power over the receiver. The only way that one can restore the balance in the relationship is to repay the debt. Repayment in a high grid social environment restores equality between the persons involved. In my experience on

Yap, persons in my debt avoided contact with me if at all possible. They were ashamed to meet me in public, knowing my expectation for repayment of their obligation. Only after the debt was paid could we engage in normal social relationships again.

The Yapese sometimes engage in competitive giving with one another. On occasion political rivals seek to outgive one another in ceremonial exchanges. While this is not typical of my urban middle-class society, the neighbor who has the newest lawn mower, the best equipment, or the highest priced car is thought to be superior to the neighbor who owns lower quality goods.

Low Grid—Asking Is Negotiating

The case study of the Deni illustrates graphically the low grid social environment. Not only are the Deni not humiliated, but they ask boldly for whatever it is they desire. They take no offense when what they seek is not granted, but consider the low risk of asking worth the effort. The Deni engage in a series of negotiating requests with missionaries and their Brazilian neighbors.

In a low grid social environment, the giver is in competition with the asker. Each is struggling to gain advantage in a social environment where individual autonomy is highly valued. The Deni expect that their Brazilian patrons will have some competitive advantage in their mutual relationships. They see the missionary through the same eyes. All of the individuals in their social environment compete for similar or shared resources. The Deni see the giver as one from whom they should take an opportunity for personal gain. They also recognize that givers will serve their own personal interests; they therefore have little animosity toward others when their request is denied. Asking and giving are part of a negotiating process in which to give or to receive holds prospect for longer term individual gain.

In this same manner, repayment in a low grid social environment often entails profit to the giver. The Brazilian patron relationship to Deni is a graphic example. When a Deni visits his patron's home, he expects to be fed and he will ask for clothing, aluminum utensils, and other items that he wishes to add to his own personal wealth. The patron will give to the extent that he believes he can induce the Deni to repay him. Often the Brazilian must go after the Deni worker and even coerce him to repay his debt. When the Deni does join him to work, the Brazilian will get as much labor from him as is possible under the circumstances. Usually, the patron profits from Deni labor. The Deni and the Brazilians recognize this and continue to work the system to their mutual advantage when at all possible.

High Group—Asking Places the Group at Risk

In a high group social environment, individuals are not easily isolated from the context and demands of their group. When an individual asks for valued goods or services, the debt may not be only personal; it may also accrue to the social group. In such a social environment, the members of the group see the requests of individuals to outsiders as placing their group at risk. As a consequence, the group exerts significant pressure on the membership to avoid seeking assistance from outsiders. Within the group, reciprocity is often general and members may seek all the assistance they need from their fellows. To request assistance of another group, however, is deemed risky and diminishes the public image of the strength of the group. For example, a group of Aukan villagers sought to build an airstrip on village land. They sent a delegation to an up-river village to request the use of a bulldozer controlled by the regional headman. They did so knowing that the request would probably be denied. Yet they were willing to take the risk knowing that without the bulldozer the airstrip would be an impossible task for them. Their request was denied and the leaders refused to consider going to the headman again. The social cost of their first request was already more than they wanted to risk; they did so in part because they could not appeal to the government for help without first asking the regional headman.

In the reverse situation, a group that gives generously acquires significant social capital through the exchange. In the Aukan illustration above, if the regional headman had granted the use of the bulldozer, he would have increased his social standing and power over the requesting village. By refusing them he not only humiliated them, but he also limited his credit for future support. A group that is generous in a high group social environment gains significant social power and influence.

Because asking places a group at risk, repayment is compulsory for the members. There is never a question of whether the group should repay, but only the question of when, how much, and through what means. The group works to remove whatever risk may have been entailed by asking or receiving material wealth from others.

Low Group—Asking Is Advantageous

In a low group social environment, the person who asks is seeking individual gain. Lacking the constraints of group membership and binding social networks with others, the person asking risks only a specific relationship. In Honoré Balzac's *Eugénie Grandet* (1833), Eugénie's miser father operates in a low group social environment. For Monsieur Grandet asking is a game he plays with all of his friends and patrons to outwit them and to obtain from them some economic advantage.

The story of Grandet is classic with regard to the factors of giving and repayment. Grandet refuses to give to anyone, including his wife and daughter. The family lives on an extremely sparse allowance, eating a diet of bread and water and miniscule portions of meat and vegetables—in spite of the fact that Grandet is an extremely wealthy man. Grandet views any giving as an economic loss and seeks to minimize every possible loss of his funds.

Grandet repays only when the funds are absolutely demanded of him. When his brother dies in bankruptcy, Grandet arranges with the creditors to pay off his brother's debts if they allow him to take over the assets. The creditors agree to this strategy in hopes of reducing their losses. However, Grandet pays them as little as is absolutely necessary, drawing profit from the assets while keeping these creditors at bay.

The case of Monsieur Grandet is one in which social values other than his own play a minimal role in his life and relationships. He alienates his fellow townspeople, his fellow winemakers, and all of those with whom he does business or has social relationships. He does so at will, recognizing that their primary interest in him is also to gain advantage over his resources. While this is an extreme case, it clearly illustrates the factors of exchange in a low group social environment.

Value Profiles and Social Exchange

As we have seen in previous chapters, the particular values of any given social environment are a combination of the factors of grid and group. For example, in a high grid/high group social environment, asking is humiliating and places the group at risk. In a high grid/low group social environment, asking is humiliating but can be advantageous to the individual. In a low grid/high group social environment, asking is negotiating but it also places the group at risk. In a low grid/low group social environment, asking is negotiating and advantageous. The unique values that grow out of the matrix of grid and group with regard to social exchange are summed up in Table 5.1.

The Deni: A-Individualist (Low Grid/Low Group)

As we have seen in the case study presented above, the Deni Indians are low grid and low group. Asking is always negotiating, and they seek their own personal advantage. They view exchange with their Brazilian neighbors and missionaries as an instrumental process. While they know that these outsiders have access to resources not available to them, and therefore greater power in their relationships, the Deni still deem them peers in competition in their local environment. They accept these outsiders only to the extent that they can gain advantage from them and feel free to break off the relationship at will.

Table 5.1
Society and Value Profiles: Economic Exchange

	B-Bureaucratic (College Faculty)	**C-Corporate** (Yap)
	(high grid, low group)	**(high grid, high group)**
Ask:	Borrowing is humiliating, bad form	Borrowing is humiliating, okay
	Debt obligates client	Debt obligates/shames
	Conditional receptivity to gifts	Closed, nonreceptive to gifts
Give:	Loaning is a weak duty, a high risk	Loaning is a duty, honorable
	Fear of exploitation, poverty	Fear of humiliation, inferiority
	High/low exchange—patron/client	High/low exchange—strata/rank
Repay:	Scaled payments	Balanced hierarchical exchange
	Wages for labor, interest for loan	Food, money/labor, respect
	Earn respect by wealth, property	Earn respect by public generosity

	A-Individualist (Deni)	**D-Collectivist** (Aukan)
	(low grid, low group)	**(low grid, high group)**
Ask:	Borrowing is a game	Borrowing is a social risk
	Debt is used to advantage	Debt obligates, group at risk
	Open, receptive to gifts	Closed, guarded receptivity
Give:	Loaning is for profit, a risk	Loaning is for calculated gain
	Fear of material loss, disadvantage	Fear of unequal advantage
	Peer competitive exchange	Peer equality for exchange
Repay:	Negotiated payment, interest	Balanced reciprocal exchange
		labor/labor, food/food
	Earn respect by wealth, expenditures	Earn respect by serving group

Giving and repaying among the Deni are generally negotiated. I observed on many occasions my friend in dialogue with a Deni man or woman with regard to his camp store. Every exchange between them was negotiated in terms of their wants and what they were able to produce to satisfy my friend in the exchange. A similar pattern governs their relationship with their Brazilian neighbors.

The Deni are open and receptive to all gifts from outsiders. They understand that these gifts involve a broadly defined reciprocal exchange, but figure that the return can be negotiated to their own advantage. Some Deni become indebted to as many Brazilian patrons as possible in order to maximize their advantage in material goods. They also play off one patron against the others, paying each only when absolutely necessary.

While the Deni have a very unelaborated social rank system and very limited economic resources, they declare frequently the importance of mutual respect and good talk in the community. Their concern for public respect is illustrated most graphically in their sporadic but frequent public feasts. People dress in their best clothing and gather in the village plaza to eat and talk together; after eating, they dance, wrestle, and joke. People are careful to respect the dignity of one another on these occasions because an insult might result in fighting or someone leaving the feast, thus spoiling it for everyone.

Christian College: B-Bureaucratic (High Grid/Low Group)

The social environment of Christian College faculty is characterized by high grid and low group. For these people, asking is humiliating but can indeed be advantageous. Relationships of exchange in the Christian College social environment are typically characterized by high and low relationships. The faculty member works under the authority of a department chair and dean and has authority over students. The structure of administration-faculty-student relationships often creates a strain for the participants. The persons on top have institutional power over those subordinate to them, creating situations of potential mistrust. Structural rules circumscribe the relationship of high and low exchange among administration, faculty, and students. Exchange outside of this structure is often deemed as an attempt to establish patron/client relationships and may, therefore, be suspect. Individuals in the patron/client context are anxious about receiving gifts, wondering if the giver has some ulterior motive. A student or a faculty member who gives gifts to a superior will perhaps be judged as seeking some privileged access to power. While it is not inappropriate for the administrator or the faculty member to give gifts, this is generally not done outside of the canons of appropriate behavior as defined in the structure.

People in this B-Bureaucratic environment repeatedly measure their compensation against how others in the institution are paid or otherwise rewarded. Some vocal faculty and secretaries are particularly prone to complaining about inadequate pay. Others decry the lack of administrative and secretarial support for their work. People at all levels of bureaucratic institutions struggle over what they perceive as inadequate support and benefits for their labor.

While the members of the faculty share common values focused upon their relationship in Christ, most if not all would be extremely reluctant to give up the material symbols of their rank and years of service. People have very strong expectations that they should be rewarded in accordance with the number of years that they have served the institution and the rank they have achieved in the hierarchy. To suggest that professors should receive exactly the same salary as instructors would be completely unacceptable to most members of the faculty. To most it is inconceivable that a secretary should be paid the same salary as a professor. In the same manner, administrators expect higher pay for higher rank and other material privileges in relationship to their responsibility and authority.

Such material differentiation is most graphically illustrated in faculty and administrative offices. The most junior faculty members receive the least desirable offices in the department. The senior faculty members are given the most spacious offices with the best equipment. Faculty frequently complain that administrators have better office equipment and nicer office furnishings. A quick review of the furnishings in various departments shows that the president has the largest office in the institution, the vice-presidents have the second largest offices, and so on down through the hierarchy. The furnishings in these offices also reflect the degree of rank or positions in the structure. The president has the largest conference table with the largest chairs. The provost has the second largest table with smaller, but appropriate chairs. The other vice-presidents have smaller tables and fewer chairs for conferences in their office than the provost, and so it is through the hierarchy.

Most of these material benefits are regulated by the rules of the structure and by the power given to those higher in the hierarchy to control the resources and their allocation for members of the group. However, the values of those in subordinate positions are just as strong in sustaining the hierarchical structure. While most members of the system resent the power delegated to the administrators over them, they are reluctant to relinquish the power that they have received over others. As a consequence, the majority of the members are willing participants in the hierarchical structure and sustain the high grid/low group social environment.

The Yapese: C-Corporate (High Grid/High Group)

In the Yapese system of stratified villages, the high villages control significant economic resources from which they distribute goods to those who are below them. They may give land, food, or produce to lower ranking communities. The low communities, in return, provide labor, give respect to the higher chiefs, and engage in ceremonial activities that recognize the power and authority of these high ranking leaders. Some lower ranking villages produce specialized products from land or other resources available in their region, which they bring to the high chiefs as tribute.

The exchange between high and low is characterized by strata/rank and balanced by differential reciprocity. The high always give from the material resources they control, whereas the low always return labor and respect. This differential exchange of material resources for labor and respect creates an asymmetrical relationship in which the high groups control the major economic resources and the low groups provide loyalty and human service.

When two high chief villages engage in exchange, it is a carefully formalized public ritual. The objective of such exchanges is to test the other's economic strength. On such an occasion the "giving" village will attempt to humiliate the village(s) receiving by a public display of exceptional generosity (implying stinginess on the part of the recipients). I have observed, on many occasions, high ranking village leaders contributing special gifts at the funeral of a deceased chief. A month or two later the family of the deceased chief returned all of the gifts that they had received, announcing that they were too poor to repay their guests for such great generosity. On this same occasion the family of the deceased chief supplied food and drink in large quantities for their guests and presented baskets of shell valuables, which, while of relatively low value, show public respect for their guests.

The leaders of the highest ranking villages are quite reluctant to receive gifts from other high ranking groups. They seek to control exchanges among leaders of these groups so that an equal balance is maintained between them; valuable gifts are returned, so as to avoid significant debt. In this way, the highest ranking villages maintain independence from one another and leaders protect their own power and interest base.

The Yap case illustrates how a society with a C-Corporate village social environment carefully protects group prestige and resources. By maintaining independence from other powerful groups, they are able to compete on an equal basis with them. They engage in a hierarchy of exchange with lower ranking groups: the high group controls significant resources while the low group provides labor in return for the benefits of those resources.

The Saramaccans: D-Collectivist (Low Grid/High Group)

Saramaccan and Aukan people emphasize low grid relations among people and balanced exchange in their transactions with one another. Perhaps the most graphic illustration of the nature of exchange within these communities is the pattern of eating in the Saramaccan men's house. A group of men affiliated with a particular kin group within the community gather each evening after dark at a central house in their particular section of the village. These men may include brothers, brothers-in-law, sons, and nephews, who gather together to share food and conversation. Earlier in the evening each wife has brought to the men's house a large covered kettle in which there are plates, spoons, and food.

At the appointed time, signaled by the ringing of a bell at the door, the men gather, take their respective stools, and open up their kettles. Each man takes his plate, utensils, and food out of his kettle and places them in open view. On the occasions on which I have eaten, each man had a plate filled with an ample mound of rice. Several had a small, cup-size bowl containing some vegetables or a small portion of fish or meat. As the men began to eat they divided the mound of rice in half, taking one portion for themselves, and pushing the remainder in the plate to the center of the circle of men. Each man also took a portion of his vegetable or fish, and again offered the remaining portion to the others. Men around the circle shared the food that remained in the center of the gathering. When they finished eating, they collected the remnants of rice in their kettles and covered them. They then sat and conversed with one another until some fell asleep, at which time they dispersed to their own distinctive households.

The food exchange illustrated above shows a balanced reciprocity, in which each man takes half of his food and shares the balance with others in the group. In this particular setting meat is always quite scarce, and so the small portions of meat are distributed among all the members of the eating group. Vegetables and soup are also offered to all, so that everyone has something besides rice for the meal. On the particular occasions that I ate in the village no more than four or five of the eight men present had brought meat, yet everyone had some.

This pattern of mutual concern and support is carried into other areas of Saramaccan and Aukan life. People within their respective kin groups call upon one another for labor assistance, for transportation on the river, for use of tools (which only one or two may have), for labor in a public project, or for participation in fishing or other activities that may benefit members of the group.

The matrilineal clans and villages are rivals to one another, and significant tensions exist between them. Women avoid extended obligations with people outside of their own village and clan community. They prefer to deal with a task or economic burden within their own group, rather than to engage in obligating relationships with outsiders. Exchange relationships among women emphasize group cohesiveness and exclusiveness.

Exchange relationships among men extend to outsiders because men find it necessary for their own economic benefit. Men must marry outside of their own matrilineal lineage; therefore, men live part of their adult lives in villages other than those in which they grew up. As a consequence, men develop partnership relationships that help them to survive in another matrilineal community. These partnership relationships serve to increase their own economic strength and to build ties that will be beneficial for them outside of the group. With people who are outsiders and not partners, they follow still a different strategy. While one may give a kinsman or a partner a free ride in his boat, expecting some reciprocal favor later, he charges outsiders for the privilege of riding.

Exchange

Perhaps the most common struggle experienced by missionaries is that of exchange. Missionaries feel pressured by nationals to give goods and money to them. Many missionaries ask how much they should give, when they should give, and what should they expect in terms of repayment. It is difficult to lay down a set of guidelines that will work in the diverse cultures and social environments in which missionaries work. As is evident in the two cases studies that opened this chapter, a missionary in Yap would experience extremely different values and expectations than a missionary among the Deni in Brazil.

The grid/group model, while not foolproof, provides a place to begin. By exploring these four distinctive social environments (see Table 5.1), we may begin to compare and contrast exchange behaviors and through this process sort out those values that are significant in the cultural setting where one works. The two case studies of conflict that follow should help illustrate how this model may be used to understand the differing behavior of nationals and to develop more effective strategies for coping with these distinctive values.

Gifts and Pay in Yap

When I returned to Yap in 1970, I purchased a number of gifts to give to people who had assisted me during the first two years of my field work there. Some of these people were part of the household and lineage in which I had lived for that two-year period. They were like my kinsmen and considered me a part of their group. Other gifts were for people who lived in other areas and to whom I was considered an outsider.

Within my local estate group, people who had become part of my family received our gifts and expressed their appreciation without further comment. However, the response of some old men in another district to my gifts caught me by surprise. The oldest man, to whom I had given a watch, asked me pointedly how much it cost. He did not know that I had purchased a cheap watch at K-Mart, nor what the price of the watch might be. While I didn't have much money, I knew that Yapese were particular about the value of things. I was embarrassed to tell him the price, thinking it would communicate that our friendship was of little value. In fact the friendship was of great value to me, but, living on a limited income and having been reared in a frugal family, I felt constrained in the amount of money that I should spend for these gifts.

My elderly friend insisted on knowing the price. As I resisted he became angry with me and could not understand why I should refuse to tell him. One of the other men explained to me that if he did not know the price he would not know what his obligation was and how to repay me. I refused to tell him the price of the watch, which created a considerable strain on our relationship over the next several days.

As I reflect upon this situation twenty years later, I understand now that his anxiety about obligation grew out of the high grid/high group social environment of Yapese culture. Since I was not a member of his group my gift to him, without stated price, placed him and his social group at risk. He felt obligated to pay me, but because of my refusal, had no idea what his obligation was. My response was incomprehensible to him since any self-respecting Yapese would have made it very clear what the price of the object was so the members of the other group would know their obligation and risk.

My relationship with my Yapese family and neighbors was quite different. I had been accepted as a member of that group and we had engaged in a series of generalized exchanges with one another. They had provided land, food, and a car during my stay on Yap, and I had returned full support for two of their children to attend school in the United States. We had developed an open credit/open trust relationship. Our mutual giving solidified our relationship as insiders and the exchanges between us had become generalized reciprocity. We did not keep track of our obligations, but expected that over a long period of time things would balance out. This type of exchange is acceptable between insiders in a group, but not possible between people who are outsiders.

In 1979/80 we returned to Yap a third time to continue our research. On this occasion I had financial support through a research grant and also had a much better paying job in the state university where I taught. The grant provided funds to pay for Yapese laborers to support me in the research project. For this research I recruited a team of ten Yapese men who worked as census takers and interviewers. Having observed Yapese in hourly wage labor, I knew that paying by the hour would be disastrous. I arranged to pay them for the completed forms that they returned to me. Every week or two as a man completed census surveying in his area, he would bring his completed forms to my office in town. After checking these materials, I would pay him for the work completed.

One evening one of the census takers came to my office and asked if he could talk to me privately. It was evident that he had been drinking, and that he was under stress. He began by saying that he was in a predicament and was looking for someone to help him. The sudden death of one of his relatives placed him in need of money for funeral expenses. Explaining that there was no time to do more census forms, he asked me to give him an advance on his pay for the next two weeks. Understanding the situation, I asked how much he needed and gave him the money. He was very appreciative, thanked me, and left immediately to join a friend waiting for him in the car.

I did not see this man again for more than a month. One day I happened to see him with another man passing by at the main crossroads in the government center. Expecting that he might disappear if he saw me, I moved quickly to greet him and to ask how things were going. He apologized for not seeing me, and said that he had been very busy and hoped that I wouldn't be angry. I assured him that I was not angry; I was only worried that he was going to give up his census work and that I would need to find someone else to do it for him. He assured me that this was not the case and said he had several census forms at home that were completed, but he just hadn't had time to bring them in. I encouraged him to bring in his work to be checked. A few days later he brought me more census forms, yet not enough to cover the advance that I had given to him. After I checked these forms he asked me for another advance.

This dilemma is a very typical one for missionaries and research employers in places like Yap. In the high grid social environment, the missionary or the anthropologist occupies a superior role to the workers that they employ. The dynamics of exchange in that social environment involve both grid and group. In a strata-ranked system, the inferior members look to higher ranks for patronage as well as compensation. If I had been Yapese, there would have been no question about his worthiness to receive the extra help. However, Americans communicate negative vibrations much more overtly than do Yapese of similar strata and rank. It was obvious that I had made him uncomfortable in the manner in which I had given the advance, and he felt embarrassed and demotivated to continue his work. He had anticipated that his relationship with me was deep enough that patronage was a reasonable expectation. I had communicated to him that the advance was conditional.

Fortunately by that time in my work with Yapese I had begun to understand this intuitively. For me, it was more important to keep him as a trained census worker than to worry about the amount of money that I had advanced. I told him how much I appreciated the work that he had done and he could consider the advance a gift from me to help support his need at the time of the funeral. I then paid him for the census forms that he had brought that day, which more than met his financial expectations and need at that time.

The confusion between the two of us arose from our different expectations about high and low exchange. From my point of view, he should receive material benefit only as direct compensation for his labor. From his point of view, we had a relationship that was more than employer-employee; I had become part of his social system, which prescribed not only payment for labor but also patron gift transactions. Once I understood and acted upon this knowledge, he and the other census workers served much more effectively in our cooperative work relationship.

Helping in Surinam

The low grid/high group social environment of the Saramaccans and Aukaners in Surinam create quite a different set of expectations. Young Saramaccan men are unabashed in their economic requests. As I bathed in a stream each morning, I was inundated with requests for my watch, my shorts, and my shirt. These young teenagers declared that I was wealthy, that I had many more pants and shorts back in Paramaribo, and surely I should help them by sharing what I had. I argued that I only had two pair of shorts and they replied that they only had one. I said my mother-in-law had given me the watch, and they said she could buy me another one. No amount of explanation could convince them that I was anything other than stingy. I did not give them my shorts, my shirt, or my watch, but they were undaunted in their requests for these objects.

A few weeks later in an Aukan village, the elders of the village asked us if we would help them to obtain financial support to build an airstrip. As my colleague and I discussed these matters with them, we sensed a deep suspicion about our motives. One of our objectives was to learn more about the leadership structure and process of the Aukan village. When we tried to ask these questions, they responded by asking, "Why do you want to know?" Our dialogue again was one of negotiation. They sought reassurances from us that we would indeed help them and they refused to help us until we could produce something of concrete value. Finally, my colleague and I sat with a group of men and drafted a letter that communicated their specific wants on his word processor to a government official in Paramaribo. After that letter was completed and signed by the village captain, the men were much more cooperative, responding to our questions and interests.

What are the variables in these two different situations? Both Aukan and Saramaccan villages are low grid/high group social environments. The young men negotiating for my watch, shorts, and shirt were challenging me as an outsider. They were giving nothing to me and trying to get as much from me as they possibly could. Since I was really seeking nothing from them, the social interaction was one of cheerful banter and a contest to see if anyone could gain anything out of the exchange. With the elderly men in the Aukan village the stakes were much more serious.

My colleague and I were clearly interested in learning something about them and their culture and they were unwilling to teach us unless they could see some significant benefit for themselves in the exchange. They were guarded in their interactions with us, and closed us out until we could demonstrate to them that we would at least support their interest by communicating to the key government official who might help them. I also promised to send them two "come-alongs," a winch-type tool that they could use to pull out tree stumps. They were skeptical that I would actually deliver, but accepted my promise as of potential value to them. I did, in fact, mail those tools to Surinam upon my return to the United States.

In both of these village situations then, the young and the old operated from a low grid/high group social perspective. Both old and young men sought some significant advantage for themselves or their group in their interactions with us. The young men were very clear in telling us that we didn't need the wealth that we had and we should share it with them. The old men expressed the same idea, but in different terms. They denied us the information we wanted until they were certain that they would receive something of an equivalent value.

Some Biblical Principles: Freedom in Giving and Receiving

The case studies above illustrate how cross-cultural workers struggle with the questions of giving and receiving. Most Christian leaders have internalized biblical warnings about stinginess (Prov. 11:24; 28:27) and admonitions to guard against greed (Luke 12:15; Eph. 5:3). At the same time, missionary and national leaders often remain in bondage to the values and fears of their social environment. While these social systems are useful and good, they have not been designed to create disciples of Christ. Rather, they are systems structured to control greed, to regulate economic exchange, and to enable individuals to calculate interest and personal gains and losses within a social context. As systems to regulate and control individual behavior, they protect members of the society from the excesses of others yet they do not lead people to the freedom and joy promised in the Lord Jesus Christ.

Because these social systems are designed to protect public values of good and to control deviant behaviors of individuals within the social environment, the standards within the culture usually address human fears of loss and exploitation. These fears are addressed in specific values and rules with regard to giving and receiving. These standards define a range of appropriate behavior for giving and receiving upon which people should act, and against which behavior is measured.

The greatest source of anxiety for a Yapese person is not in giving, but in receiving. To receive is humiliating. It places the person in a subordinate role to the giver. Yapese society places great value on generosity and gives high esteem to people who are extremely generous. Those who ask too frequently or show eagerness to get their share of goods being distributed are scorned as beggers and sloughful. The persons who refuse to give are stigmatized as stingy. People who are successful openly deny their wealth, and practice public generosity to reduce social criticism. At the same time, they are often besieged by poorer relatives who see them as inexhaustible sources for their unmet wants and needs. Many prosperous Yapese have locked boxes where they hide valuables, fearing those who would surely ask, if they only knew.

The Deni, in contrast, have no fear at all about receiving. Living in a highly competitive environment, their greatest fears are that others will use coercive force against them in the negotiating process. They fear the loss of profit from their efforts; they fear the loss of advantage in their relationship to others; they fear the power that others hold and may use against them; they fear the random forces of society and nature in which they experience feast and famine, good health and misfortune, or good talk and open conflict. They have no qualms about accumulating goods and wealth through exploitation. They eagerly receive from any who will give to them, and they are bold to ask. At the same time, they give only when pressed by others, or when they believe giving will yield a profitable return or protection from some future disaster.

The Aukan fear that someone will get ahead of them in the competition for resources and wealth. They despise anything that promotes inequality and assert their interest to gain a fair share of whatever is available to the group. Their relationships are calculated in terms of social debt and personal gain. Individuals within a group are pressed to give for the group good. Within the Aukan church this is termed "giving to the Lord." In their relationships with outsiders, Aukan give only if they believe a return is assured. They are afraid of being exploited and exposed to economic loss. They punish offenders by public exposure of their behavior and, if they are unrepentant, exclude these people from the group.

Common fears of missionaries and Christian College faculty are that they will be exploited. They have learned in their culture to view their economic resources as something that is scarce and should be conserved. They believe that each person is responsible for careful management of those resources and responsible for personal welfare. As a consequence, when they are asked to give one of their primary concerns is that what they give will be used wisely and that the person asking them is not exploiting them or their resources. Generally missionaries are very careful to conserve their finances and to use them wisely. When nationals ask for more than they have planned to give, many fear they may exhaust their scarce resources, and therefore will not be able to meet their daily needs. Many feel that they are not teaching nationals responsible behavior by giving unconditionally; these same people are also reluctant to receive gifts from nationals. Taught from their youth to be self-sufficient and independent, they believe that receiving substantive gifts from others casts a negative reflection upon their ability to provide for themselves. Many are reluctant to ask for material help from nationals, fearing further reciprocal obligations. Finally, some fear that they are not respected as persons, but only as a source of money or material things. Feeling demeaned by the asking and giving, they see the resulting relationships tainted by low material motivation and interest.

Freedom to Give "at Risk"

One of the profound truths presented in Scripture is that followers of Jesus Christ may be free from the anxieties that surround material life and resources. Most missionaries have learned very early in their faith the command in Matthew 5:42: "Give to the one who asks you, and do not turn away from the one who wants to borrow from you." They have also been reassured by the promises of Matthew 6:31–34: "So do not worry, saying, 'What shall we eat?' or 'What shall we drink?' or 'What shall we wear?' . . . But seek first his kingdom and his righteousness, and all these things will be given to you as well." We have also been taught to give out of our abundance or our poverty to the Lord. We have been challenged to "bring the whole tithe into the storehouse," and we have heard the promise from God, "see if I will not throw open the floodgates of heaven and pour out so much blessing that you will not have enough room for it" (Mal. 3:10). Yet we have been so conditioned by the standards and practice of our social environment that we doubt the truth of Scripture and find it very difficult to live by it.

Many other passages in Scripture present the same challenge. Proverbs declares that the generous will prosper (11:25) and be blessed (22:9). Isaiah (58:10) addresses the issue of fear of losing personal prosperity for the sake of the poor: "If you spend yourselves in behalf of the hungry and satisfy the needs of the oppressed, then your light will rise in the darkness, and your night will become like the noonday." While we desire the blessing and glory of God, the truth is that we are in bondage to the standards and rules of our social environment. We rely more on the standards of the society around us than the promises of God's Word. Our social environment robs us of the freedom given to us in God's Word: liberation from anxiety about material things, and the desire and joy to give at risk, testing God's capacity to give in return. The Christian worker who has grasped the full meaning of these passages is freed from anxiety about eating, drinking, and clothing, and is released to experience the opening of the floodgates of heaven promised in the Book of Malachi.

The national Christian leader faces the same dilemma as the missionary. Fears about loss, exploitation, social debt, and humiliation inhibit national believers from giving according to the rich measure described in God's Word. However, those who have responded to this message have discovered that God is faithful to his promise. A friend related the story of a missionary working among the Dayaks in Borneo. This missionary challenged the Dayaks to bring their chickens and other food resources to God, which were then given to the poor and those who had dedicated themselves to ministry. After many acted in simple obedience to this command, they harvested a rice crop surplus beyond anything they had experienced before, and which they marketed on the coast. They discovered through obedience that God returned to them far more than they had given or anticipated. They discovered the truth of Proverbs 28:27: "he who gives to the poor will lack nothing."

Freedom to Receive "at Risk"

Jesus said, "Give, and it will be given to you. A good measure, pressed down, shaken together and running over, will be poured into your lap. For with the measure you use, it will be measured to you" (Luke 6:38). This admonition is as much about receiving as it is about giving. Receiving is a very important part of the exchange process. The missionary or national who rejects a gift because of the fear of humiliation, manipulation, or being obligated to others loses a significant part of the blessing of God. Jesus says the "good measure . . . will be poured into your lap." To reject the "pouring" from God because of the social expectations that may come with it deprives the believer of material blessing and of joy and freedom in Christ. Not only do we have the freedom to "give at risk," but we also have the freedom to "receive at risk." These are foundational kingdom principles by which our lives and the lives of others may be transformed.

To "receive at risk" is a central tenet of our faith. The Gospels and the Epistles declare that our salvation in Christ is a gift of God, something for which we cannot pay or work; we do not have anything of value that God would want, and we must accept his gift as an unconditional work of grace (Eph. 2:8–10). The first act that we must comprehend and obey as believers is to accept the gift of salvation in Jesus Christ. Yet we receive that gift "at risk." God demands our obedience and service. Our obedience of faith establishes a pattern of relationship in Christ that should follow into our material life.

In three of the four social environments, people are cautious about receiving gifts and are careful to remove obligations of debt because of the social and economic consequences. Only the people in A-Individualist social environments are open to extensive indebtedness, and they use debt to extend their personal acquisitions with an intent to compete and exploit. In all social environments indebtedness is rejected or embraced in the interest of selfish individual or group advantage, rather than for the good of others.

To "receive at risk" in the biblical context implies a willingness to be humiliated, obligated, or even exploited by being in debt to others. The Christian worker is willing to take the "client" rather than the "patron" role, as Jesus illustrated by his receiving the support of prominent Jewish women (Luke 8:1–3). Missionaries are often cast in the role of "benefactors," having resources far beyond what is available to national leaders. The temptation is to retain the authority and power that belongs to a "benefactor," and to avoid reciprocal arrangements that might make nationals "benefactors" to us. In his final meeting with the Twelve, Jesus cautioned them against this very thing, calling them to be as those who serve at the table, rather than benefactors (Luke 22:25–27).

Addressing Our Fears

The difficulty we have applying kingdom principles may be traced directly to fear. People teach their children what to fear and how to respond appropriately. Asking, giving, and receiving are actions that entail social risk, which in turn creates fear and anxiety among those at risk. The challenge for the missionary is to directly address these fears, to practice "giving at risk" and "receiving at risk."

The most common problem is coping with the many people who knock at the missionary's door and ask for money or other material help. We must first change our attitude. Instead of seeing these people as annoyances, we should view every person who comes as an opportunity for relationship and for sharing the gospel. Giving money or material things should never be a brief transaction. If we do not have time to deal with people at that moment, we should ask them to return at another time when we are free. We must ask these people to explain their needs. We need to explain to them why we have come, how God has provided for us, and what our responsibilities are as stewards of God's provision. We must understand their social environment and their expectations. A gift or loan should be given, understanding their fears and encouraging them toward faith in the God we trusted to provide for our own needs. The opportunity to give is an opportunity for relationship and for witness; when we take less than an hour to talk about the transaction, we have wasted an important opportunity for witness.

Another issue for the missionary is the question of "whose money, mine or God's?" All that we have belongs to the Lord, yet some of us have difficulty putting this truth into practice. We become anxious about our level of support, and worry that too many gifts or loans will place us in financial jeopardy. A helpful technique may be to set aside a portion of financial support to be given to nationals who have need. Making the distribution of such funds a matter of personal prayer, the missionary who gives should acknowledge openly that the gift is from a fund that belongs to God. The debt is to God and not to the missionary, who is merely the steward.

Finally, we must recognize that relationships must be reciprocal, in spite of our fear of obligation; if the giver never asks or receives, the relationship becomes one of domination and subordination. Missionaries must learn to ask for things they do not necessarily want or need (having been taught to be self-reliant) to allow their national friends to repay them. One of my friends working in the Philippines learned to ask others for help, and in becoming dependent upon them, formed relationships deeper than those in her own family. Those friends have also become brothers and sisters in Christ.

In summary, the message of the gospel and the good news proclaimed by Christ is that we can be released from the fears and the selfish interests approved in our cultural system and social environment. While our cultures and social environments are good, bringing regulation and reason to economic relationships, by and in themselves they rob the believer of the freedom offered in Christ. This is not a freedom from "work," not an encouragement to depend upon others for our food and shelter; Paul rebukes the Thessalonians sharply for that attitude (2 Thess. 3:6–15). Rather, the promises of God offer freedom from anxiety about material resources, freedom from fear about exploitation, humiliation, and social debt, and freedom to give and receive in the work of Christ. When we commit ourselves to bless the poor, to feed the hungry, to share with those who are in need, and to express our devotion to our Lord Jesus Christ, we are assured of light in our lives, of provision for our needs, and of receiving the measure that we have given to others, "a good measure, pressed down, shaken together and running over, . . . poured into your lap."

6
Authority and Family

The Foundation of Social Order

The Ideal Man, the Ideal Woman, and Marriage in Yap

During a conversation in 1970 with an old Yapese man, Tamag, and his wife, Rungun, she began to complain about her son's wife. She said the girl was frivolous and lazy. All she ever did was comb her hair, make sweet-smelling garlands, and drive around in her husband's car. Rungun began to complain that Yapese girls were not learning the proper way of life. Most of them did not know anything about gardening or preparing food. How could they ever have children and take care of them the way a Yapese woman should?

At this point, Tamag interrupted and said that he had been like his son when he was a young man. He liked beautiful girls. He even married a few of those girls, but he did not stay married very long. Then, as he got older, he began to realize that he needed a hard-working wife to take care of his need for food and to bear heirs for his estate. He began to look around for the right kind of woman who could provide for him in his old age. He explained that this was the reason he married Rungun.

Rungun nodded her head with approval, and then elaborated further on the ideal Yapese woman. A woman should go to her taro garden early every morning to weed, plant, cultivate, and obtain food for that day. She should have fresh food daily for her husband and children, and if there are leftovers, she should eat them herself. Her garden should be well attended and free of weeds, and she should provide yams, sweet potatoes, and other vegetable crops to add variety to her family's diet. She should cook each morning and evening, with one pot of food for her husband and a separate pot for herself and her children. She should be generous and offer food to her husband's visitors or to others who might have occasion to stop at the house.

Rungun concluded that a good wife should be submissive to her husband and to her mother-in-law. She said her son's wife was lazy and unresponsive. When Rungun asked the girl to come along to work, she always had an excuse and ran away. If Rungun had her way, she would send that girl back to her family and arrange a marriage for her son to another girl in a village close by, who already had her own productive taro and yam gardens on land given to her by her mother. Any girl who drove around in a car and never stayed home could not be good. She was probably flirting with other men, when she should be working with her mother-in-law in her gardens.

The attitudes that Tamag and Rungun expressed about the ideal Yapese woman are not unique. Other Yapese emphasized the same attributes. They also expressed certain expectations for an ideal man. A man who is not a good fisherman makes a poor husband. Fishing is a man's primary occupation; any meal without fish means a man is not doing an adequate job. If a man is a good fisherman, he will get enough not only for his wife and children, but he will be able to share with others as well. Productive and successful men are as much admired as hard-working women. Yapese speak highly of men whose homes are kept in good repair, whose boat or canoe is always ready for use, and whose family always has fish to eat.

Yapese also esteem men who are skilled in public speaking and articulate in conversation. Men who are good conversationalists have great success at attracting lovers, because conversation is a basic element of love making on Yap. Men who can speak with facility and eloquence in public have great potential for political success. Because of their oratory, they may lift the prestige and influence of their family in the community, or obtain lesser punishments for members who have broken community rules, and, therefore, are subject to sanction. Yapese also prize knowledge and intelligence; men who master a body of knowledge and apply it for the good of the community earn public renown.

The ideal man should be generous, modest, and kind. A stingy lover will make a stingy husband, and a stingy husband loses much support in the community. A modest man is trusted as a leader or a confidant, and earns the respect of his fellow Yapese. A kind man treats his wife and children with gentleness and respect, earning in return their obedience and service.

Yapese describe marriage as something of a contest of exchanges between a man and a woman. A man brings the land from his father to his marriage; a woman brings her fertility. The woman works on the man's land and produces food. The man works on the woman's fertility and produces children. The woman nurtures the children with food from her labors, while the man names them with names from his estate, and ultimately confers the estate upon them as his heirs.

A man's contribution also entails resources and labor. Land and names are fundamental to life. A Yapese lacking an ancestral name has no right to inherit the lands of his father. In addition to these, a man provides the heavy labor for clearing gardens. A man's primary work, however, is on the sea. When Yapese sit down to a meal, they must have both vegetable foods and fish. If one element is lacking, someone has not kept part of the reciprocal obligation. A woman's task in the marriage is to work for the estate. Yapese say a woman owns the land under her foot, that is, the land where she lives when she marries; she confirms her ownership by developing it to produce food for her husband and her children who will be heirs of the estate. She is also responsible for the total nurture of the children. She cooks for them, she clothes them in loin cloths and grass skirts, she protects them from danger, and she teaches them the Yapese way of life.

Yapese liken a woman to the traditional round stone disc propped against the stone foundations of a house. She is a fixture in the home. She stays close to the children and to the land, cultivating both to be productive resources for the larger family and society. She is also a stranger, brought from another place and another family to her husband's household. Like a piece of stone, she is liable to theft by other unscrupulous men. Her mother-in-law thus keeps a careful eye on her to prevent casual encounters with interested men who might steal her away.

Yapese liken a man to shell valuables that they exchange at political events over time from one estate to another, and one village to another. A man conducts the public affairs of the family away from home. When a son wants to marry, he carries the request with a shell to the prospective bride's father. When a family member suffers injury from an outsider, he demands recompense or retaliation from the family of the offender. He represents his family in meetings of the local community, and goes with other men of that community to participate in extracommunity affairs. In his travels, he often encounters other women and sometimes engages in extramarital affairs.

Marital conflict and divorce are most frequently precipitated by affairs. If a couple has been married for a short time and have no children, an affair will probably end the marriage abruptly. The woman will take her personal belongings and return to her father's household. If the couple has children, the matter becomes more serious. The husband may beat an unfaithful wife severely until she reforms her ways. A wife, however, has less power over an unfaithful husband. She may first harangue him publicly to shame him for his behavior. If this is unsuccessful, she may refuse to cook for him or to perform other domestic services.

Because of the fragile nature of Yapese marriage, families generally do not celebrate the marriage with a public ceremony until some time after the first or even the second child is born. If the couple has been married for several years, if they have a child or children, and if it looks as though they will have an enduring relationship, the families of the couple may plan a "marriage exchange" of goods and food. Both families expend their best efforts to demonstrate their strength and generosity, and the wife's family aims to give lavishly to anchor their daughter and her children firmly to their new land.

The actual exchange between the two families symbolizes the daily contest between the man and woman as they contribute from their diverse productive activities to the welfare and survival of the family. The woman's family gives stone valuables, symbolizing both the woman's role as the foundation of the family and their desire to anchor her and her children to the land of her husband's estate. In addition to the stone, a woman's family contributes large quantities of the products of a woman's labor, including taro, the major staple food, and yams and other vegetable foods, which the wife and her female relatives have produced in their gardens.

The husband's family reciprocates with the products of a man's labor. The men of the husband's family will attempt to bring baskets of fish and coconuts equivalent to the baskets of vegetable food that they receive from the wife's family. In addition to fish and coconuts, they may contribute shell valuables to match the quantity of stone valuables that they will receive. In these exchanges, as in the routine of daily life, the wife's side often wins the contest, because the staple supply of vegetable crops is assured by diligent work, while fishing is a more uncertain enterprise, subject to the vagaries of weather, tides, and luck. The women are indeed the "strength of the family estate." Without their daily efforts producing and preparing vegetable foods and nurturing the children, the survival of the household and the estate group would be in jeopardy.

Many Yapese marriages today suffer from stresses emerging from wage work, education, and a new town-oriented lifestyle. A man who earns wages can purchase canned fish, beef, and other meats to fulfill his traditional obligations for subsistence. With his cash income he is also able to purchase clothing for himself, his wife, and his children. This effectively eliminates one of his wife's traditional contributions to the marriage relationship. Weaving loin cloths and making grass skirts have become peripheral activities. The man's cash income also permits the purchase of large quantities of imported rice, eliminating the necessity for a woman to do any gardening at all. In brief, a cash income shifts the traditional economic advantage and power from a woman to a man. In the traditional marriage, the woman's vegetable products sustained her household. Today her garden can be replaced with a purchased bag of rice.

Wage work by a husband may lead to a significant loss of power and freedom for a Yapese woman. While in the past her husband was dependent on her for fertility, food, child care, and the products of her labor such as food, clothing, and general cleaning and care, he now relies on her primarily to bear his children, care for them, and act as a general domestic maid. Her role as a provider may be preempted by his money capabilities. Her power as a producer of Yapese staple crops has been shortcircuited by her husband's power through money. The symbolic exchange between a man's family and a woman's family in the marriage no longer expresses the structural facts of the marriage relationship. A man now holds the trump cards (cash) in the contest and the balance of transaction has shifted decidedly in his favor.

Some women have responded to this situation by seeking their own wage employment. Others refuse to cook rice, and continue to produce their own vegetable foods. Some of the younger women are happy to drive their husband's car and live the "lazy" lifestyle deplored by Rungun. A few refuse to marry, and avoid romantic entanglements that might result in pregnancy and an unwanted marriage.

Some couples have worked out personal strategies to cope with these changes; others have given up and divorced, hoping to find a more satisfactory relationship in a future marriage. Divorce is a relatively simple matter. The woman returns to her own family and the relationship is finished. Children, however, create serious complications. Since the names and legal status of children come from their fathers, Yapese insist that they remain in their father's household. The women, on the other hand, are loath to leave their children, and the new wife is often reluctant to care for a previous wife's offspring. Some men ask their mothers or sisters to take care of their children, while others permit them to live with their ex-wives. In any case, the presence of children creates much more serious dislocation and conflict in a divorce.

Domestic Authority

The Yapese marriage described briefly above seems strange to most Americans, not merely because of the different economic relationships, but more so because of the priorities for reciprocity between husband and wife, which is also extended to their families. The idea that the wife/mother is the "strength of the family" is transferable, but that the reasons behind this strength come from her role as the primary producer of the staple crops leads most Americans to think Yapese men are "lazy fishermen." The ease and frequency of divorce are disconcerting to American Christians, and the idea that the man's family has the legal right to the children is almost a reversal of American thought. The thought that employment could have such a destructive effect on husband/wife relationships never entered the minds of the American government officials who introduced wage work into Yapese society.

Most Christians assume that there is a biblical model for family relationships. The family structure with which they are most familiar (their own) is the one that they believe is biblically based. When they read the Scriptures they find proof texts that support their analysis and conclude that any other form of family relationships is against biblical doctrine. Few if any scholars have done a careful comparative analysis of family structures in the Scriptures, and some who have researched the topic have ignored the diversity and imposed a systematic uniformity upon Scripture addressing family relations.

Most of the extended case material on family in the Bible is found in the Old Testament. A careful analysis of this case material will show that the structure of family relations changes from one period of time to another and from case to case. The data presented in the New Testament are much more sparse, but again careful analysis suggests a diversity that one would expect with grid and group analysis.

Anthropologists have engaged in extensive comparative study of family relationships over the course of this century. The outcome of this analysis demonstrates both a marvelous diversity and some distinctive but common patterns of relationship that are found in the structuring of families around the world. The classical work on this subject is George Peter Murdock's *Social Structure* (1949). Murdock identifies thirteen major types of kinship and family systems among the world's diverse cultures. While we will not explore the rich diversity of family systems, this chapter will show how significant values in family are linked inextricably to variables of social environment. I will argue that issues of authority in the family are shaped primarily by the social environment. Further, contrary to common theological opinion, the teachings of Scripture do not support one particular kind of authority as prescribed by a specific social environment, but rather call for transformation of authority relationships in any social environment into a pattern shaped more in the image of Christ.

The application of the model of grid and group to family units has some inherent limitations. First, family units tend to be the smallest and most variable units in society. As such they reflect the individuality and diversity of their members; no two families are exactly alike. Second, family structures vary significantly across cultures. Comparative research (Netting, Wilk, and Arnould 1984) has documented significant structural and functional variation that makes generalizations hazardous at best. The grid and group model has not been used by others as a tool for analysis of domestic units, and I proceed here with caution, acknowledging the tendency to oversimplify very complex human behavior.

Let us begin with the subject of family relationships. The faculty of Christian College tend to think of family first in terms of the husband/wife relationship. This is a horizontal relationship of people in the same generation, who establish their own household and live independently of others in the society. Many peoples of the world think of family more in terms of vertical relationships, referencing first the parent/child relationship, and sometimes including grandparent or higher generations. The vertical focus is a necessary element of societies that value kinship groups and place authority in the hands of elder members of the group. The horizontal focus is possible where individuality is highly valued and accountability to others is restricted to role obligations or negotiated personally.

The second factor of importance is the nature of domestic authority. The faculty of Christian College tend to think of authority in family relationships in terms of role definition and obligation. "Father" is "head" of the household, sometimes called the "old man." "Husband" is "provider" even when both husband and wife produce incomes. "Mother" is the all-around utility person, "the cook, cleaning lady, the driver, the nurse, the nag." "Wife" is both "lover" and "maid." Other people in the world have a much looser attitude about roles and domestic authority, focusing more on personal skill, interests, and relationships. The Deni, for example, occasionally switch sex roles; women go fishing, while the men stay in the village, cook manioc, and care for the children. Such behavior would be scandalous in Yap, where it is absolutely forbidden for women to enter men's fishing waters.

To describe variation in the structuring of grid and group relationships, the terms "authoritarian," "egalitarian," "vertical," and "nonvertical" are helpful. Grid is represented in the degree of authority assigned to role relationships in families; high grid is "authoritarian" while low grid is "egalitarian." Group is represented by the degree to which authority is "vertical" or "nonvertical," with high group having "vertical" authority and low group possessing "nonvertical" authority. Family units such as the Yapese, which locate authority in the senior generation and keep junior generations subordinate, are "vertical" in orientation and "authoritarian" in perspective. Family units such as the Deni, which allocate authority variably from father to father-in-law to mature male, are "nonvertical" in orientation and "egalitarian" in focus. The middle-class American family is "nonvertical" and "authoritarian," placing great emphasis on role definition and obligation.

The formation of high group environments over time is facilitated when domestic groups prescribe or encourage specific rules or patterns of residence. When a society such as the Yapese prescribes the place in which families must live (lands owned by the estate group and passed from one generation to the next), the end result is a corporate group that has duration long beyond the lives of the individual members. Individuals in the domestic unit co-reside with others for a lifetime. Their relationships become cohesive and binding. The Deni in contrast emphasize residence by individual choice, thus limiting the possibility of strong group allegiance. Individual family units may change residence every two or three years in the course of their life histories and align themselves with other Deni in relationships that are mutually instrumental and convenient. Only the father-in-law/son-in-law relationship has prescriptive value, based upon the authority of the father-in-law over his daughter and his granting access of the son-in-law to that daughter until a time when the daughter is able to exercise her own independent authority.

Bringing together the factors of authority and residence yields four distinctive patterns of domestic authority (Table 6.1). Comparing the different types of domestic authority allows us to observe significant patterns of variation. The grid factor produces different structures in the parental role in these family units. In the low grid societies (A-Individualist and D-Collectivist), parents take primarily a nurturing role in their relationship to their children. As children mature and grow the parents and children become co-laborers in the common activities of the household. In contrast, in high grid societies (B-Bureaucratic and C-Corporate) parents take authoritarian and disciplinarian roles. While children are clearly nurtured in these social settings, the emphasis is given to authority relationships and that authority is focused in either of the two parents. In both settings, children receive nurture but for that nurture they return obedience and respect.

Sibling relationships in these four social types vary according to both grid and group. High grid tends to produce significant distinctions between elder and younger siblings, in which the elder hold authority and privilege. Low grid emphasizes relative equality, skill distinctions, and personal autonomy. In the low grid, A-Individualist social environ-

Table 6.1
Society and Value Profiles: Domestic Authority

B-Bureaucratic (Faculty-CC)	C-Corporate (Yap)
(high grid, low group)	(high grid, high group)
Father is disciplinarian	Father has total authority
Nurture until of age, then separation	Lifelong nurture-obedience reciprocity
Siblings are equal	Elder siblings have authority over younger siblings
Independent personal estate	Elders oversee corporate family estate
Children select mates, limited by incest rules	Children select mates, according to family/kin relations and rules

A-Individualist (Deni)	D-Collectivist (Aukan)
(low grid, low group)	(low grid, high group)
Parents have nurturing/training role	Parents share authority/nurturing role
Children are co-laborers with parents	Children are co-laborers with mother
Siblings are equals, co-laborers, or competitors	Sisters share family estate, men aid sisters and wives
Households shift residence according to domestic interests	Ancestral residence, elders oversee corporate family estate
Father controls marriage of daughter, labor of son-in-law	Mother controls marriage of daughter, outside of matrilineal clan

ment, siblings have egalitarian relationships with one another and their lives from childhood to death reflect individual autonomy and "what's in it for me" sibling ties. Brothers and sisters may share with one another but their relationships are negotiated rather than prescribed. When high grid is combined with the low group, B-Bureaucratic social environment, the elder/younger distinctions between siblings are important, but may not result in differentiation in inheritance or other family rights. Responsibilities of older for younger may be discarded when siblings reach adulthood and their relationship may emphasize equality and personal independence. In C-Corporate social environments, the relationship of elder and younger is spelled out in customary rules or duties.

Frequently the eldest are assigned authority over the resources of the family unit. Among Yapese the eldest sibling holds first right to complete authority over the estate group and all its resources. In low grid/high group societies (D-Collectivist) sibling differences may be based primarily upon descent rules. In matrilineal descent systems, sisters provide the cohesive organizing relationship and in patrilineal societies that comes through brothers. In cognatic or bilateral descent systems, it may be brothers and/or sisters who relate to one another such as we find among families in North Borneo. In these latter cases, the sibling relationship is shaped by the rules of inheritance but low grid prohibits any emergence of the social distinctions and authority invested in single members of those groups.

The Deni: A-Individualist, Horizontal, Egalitarian Families

Family authority among the Deni is best illustrated by the co-laboring relationships between father and son, and between father-in-law and son-in-law. When a boy is seven or eight years old he begins to accompany his father into the forest on hunting and fishing trips. His father teaches him the basic skills of tracking, survival, and gleaning key food resources from the forest. By the time a boy is ten or twelve years old he is able to forage in the forest alone. At a very early age boys begin practicing the skills of shooting with the bow and arrow and fishing with both bow and line. Boys soon become equals to their fathers in the skills of hunting and fishing. They become competitors as well as friends.

As a boy reaches adulthood, his father seeks to negotiate a marriage for his son with the daughter of another member of the community. Usually such marriages are arranged by the exchange of daughters. Once a marriage is accomplished, the son becomes subordinate to the authority of his father-in-law. For a period of three years the son-in-law works under the direction of his father-in-law. When he goes hunting or fishing he brings the meat to his mother-in-law, who prepares and distributes the food. The father-in-law demands and receives his assistance in clearing fields, making dug-out canoes, and helping with other domestic support activities. Since the father-in-law may nullify the marriage, he has control over the son-in-law. If a young man fails to meet his obligations, his father-in-law may take back his daughter and force the son-in-law to return to his own family.

The authority of the father-in-law over the son-in-law is temporary. After a period of approximately three years, the son-in-law has fulfilled his obligation and is no longer required to fish or hunt for his in-laws. Over a period of several months he gradually diverts his meat from his mother-in-law to his wife. The young couple soon takes up independent residence in the community and people recognize the daughter/wife as a fully independent woman in the community having the right to distribute her husband's catch. As the control of the young man's game shifts from his mother-in-law to his wife, so the control of the father-in-law is lessened.

After five or six years of marriage, the couple may separate totally from the community. Now independent in their domestic relationships, they may establish themselves in any of the available Indian or Brazilian communities nearby. They may continue to support either set of parents, but are not obligated to do so.

Deni men frequently cluster in groups with their brothers and widowed sisters. Individuals negotiate these arrangements according to domestic interests and may change them at any time they find relocation convenient. Men often leave their wives in the company of their brothers so they can work for extended periods for Brazilian patrons. They find these residence arrangements mutually beneficial, but do not feel constrained by authority or group ethic.

Deni values and the structure of parent/child relationships show striking similarities to those found in the Old Testament between Jacob and his father-in-law and Jacob and his sons. In both cases children serve as co-laborers with parents, and married brothers share labor and food with one another's families. The father's authority is restricted and sons exercise much independent power. The value ethos of the families are also similar. Deni brothers negotiate with and deceive one another, as did Jacob and Esau. "Right" is what can be sustained by personal shrewdness, skill, and influence, not a matter of moral or social code. The sense of authority and law found in Yap and in postexilic Hebrew families (Nehemiah) is totally absent in the families of Jacob, Laban, and the Deni.

Christian College: B-Bureaucratic, Horizontal, Authoritarian Families

Families at Christian College have high expectations for their children. When they select their home and church, they usually choose locations that have high quality schools and a strong youth program in the church. Children are expected to make their marks in both school and church. Children must earn good grades; those who fail are a source of deep concern for parents. When a child is having trouble, the parents explore every alternative to help the child achieve at an acceptable level. In addition to good grades, parents expect good, if not perfect attendance and high social marks from school.

At home Christian College parents make certain demands upon their children. Some time between the ages of six and ten children are assigned chores. Usually they are expected to clean their own room and perform other chores, such as mowing the lawn, vacuuming the carpet, loading the dishwasher, or doing other routine maintenance of the family property.

Church, recreation, and skill development are also important. Each child is encouraged to select a sport, musical instrument, or some other artistic skill and work in a disciplined manner to demonstrate growth and to earn recognition for achievements. Parents get great satisfaction from their children's superior performance in a sport or in music or the arts, and children gain a positive self-image from these achievements. The church provides a place for children to participate in Christian community, to meet other Christian youth, and to learn more about the faith of their parents. Parents hope that their children will adopt their faith, and are very sensitive to the success or failure of church leaders and programs in this regard.

Relationships within the family have fairly well defined role expectations. A child may argue with the mother, but not usually with the father. The language of argument must be constrained and show respect. Older siblings have responsibility for younger siblings, but may not act as the parents. Each member of the household has personal space and property. Each member of the family has a separate bedroom or part of a bedroom, a separate seat at the table, and place for personal items (mail, books, etc.). Children learn to respect the individual space and property of their parents and siblings, and parents correct them when they violate these rules. Siblings compete with one another for their "fair share" of space, attention, and recognition from their parents.

Family members pursue individual interests outside the home. Often father and mother have separate careers, especially after children are old enough to be in school. Children pursue their own private interests, striving for separate identities from one another. Younger siblings resent teachers who expect them to be like their older brother or sister, and they often choose courses of study or sports, music, or drama activities that differ from that of their siblings. As children grow older family life becomes disconnected by conflicting schedules, as parents and children go in many different directions.

Christian College families have contradictory goals, valuing on the one hand "close relationships," yet organizing their lives to focus on individual interests, private space, and personal achievement. Christian College family life is so individualistic that members often have unrealistic expectations for holidays and vacations, hoping that they can capture the unity they have lost in their daily lives.

The career choices and marriages of children follow the same pattern of increasing independence that parents teach in their daily domestic relationships. Choice of college, career, and spouse is usually left to the child, depending upon the degree to which the parents provide financial support. The more money the parents give to the child, the greater right they feel to express their opinions and will on these matters. On the choice of a spouse, however, parents feel great restraint; they often want to advise, know they should not, and struggle with either choice. Once children select their mates, they know they must establish their own household, independent financially from their parents. If they need parental help, it is something of a disgrace to them and to their parents. They should be able to make their way on their own.

Aged parents feel the same need to remain independent from their children. Ideally parents and married children live their separate, private domestic lives. Holidays remain times for gathering and symbolic unity, but distance may make these gatherings infrequent. When elderly parents have need, most refuse to ask their children for help, and would feel exceedingly embarrassed to do so. The children likewise do not expect to help their parents, but will do so when and if their parents' health or financial situation require it. Both believe it is best to remain independent, leading their separate lives for as long as is humanly possible.

The Yapese: C-Corporate, Vertical, Authoritarian Families

During my first field work on the island of Yap in the late 1960s, I developed a close friendship with a Yapese man of approximately forty-five years of age. As I began to know him more intimately, he shared with me some of the personal dimensions of his life and family relationships. I was surprised to discover that for over twenty years he had brought his biweekly paycheck home to his father, who kept the bulk of the money and returned only that which his son needed. The son began this practice when he first started working and continued it until his father's death just a year before I arrived.

Coming from America, where I had been taught by my father to develop my own independent resources and very early in my adulthood had been set free to support myself, I was stunned by this disclosure. I asked my friend how he met the needs of his family of eight children. He replied that his father had given him an allowance to cover his expenses and needs, and provided the resources for any major expense. His father exercised authority and control over the family income until the day of his death.

Exploring this issue with other men, I discovered that among Yapese, fathers expect sons to render absolute obedience and respect. In return the father will provide all of a son's material and nurture needs. The son who presents his paycheck recognizes his father's authority over all of the resources of the extended family. In return the father makes sure that all the members of the extended family are cared for adequately. Following the social implications of these expectations, sons show great deference to their fathers. It is unusual to see fathers and sons engage in conversation with one another, and it is extremely rare to see a son argue with his father. If such an argument occurs, it is the talk of the village and a source of deep embarrassment to the members of the family.

The respect distance between fathers and sons is illustrated most graphically in the organization of domestic work. Men and women will take preadolescent sons and daughters with them while they work in fishing, farming, or construction activities. These children do not come along as co-workers, but to learn and "play at" the activities of their parents. In this "play" activity children learn to work alongside their parents. They are gradually given responsibility to care for their younger siblings and to share in the routine maintenance tasks of the household. When children reach puberty they are separated from the "children" in the family and join a sharply defined, generational peer group. As the youngest generation of adults, they are drafted into service for family or community as a group, and are subject to the authority of the senior generation. The generations provide a hierarchy of authority, with the eldest generation exempt from labor and holding the supervisory role. The middle generation of men or women provides the knowledge and skilled labor for the task, and the junior generation contributes unskilled labor. During the activities men and women in each generation work in partnership with their peers, and in subordination to their elders.

Generally, fathers and sons avoid social situations that might result in overfamiliarity. Yapese men address their fathers by their first names and fathers address their sons by their first names. Respect is shown by patterns of conversational avoidance rather than by the use of affection and kinship terminology. The dependency relationship between father and son is sustained by the practice of naming one's sons after one's own father and one's father's brothers. When elderly men engage in conversation with one another, sons, if present, sit quietly at the side as observers rather than participants. Play or recreational activities are restricted to members of one's own peer group.

Many Americans judge Yapese father-son relationships to be dysfunctional. They believe that father and sons should joke with one another, that children should learn to be independent, and that children should have the freedom to make their own decisions and control their own resources. Teachers and missionaries from the United States have brought these values with them to Yap and suppose that their own family relationships are more biblical than those of the Yapese, although text and verse are difficult to produce. Some would argue that the mutual pattern of avoidance in the Yapese father-son relationship has very negative developmental consequences for Yapese individuals. This conclusion is of course based upon certain cultural and social expectations of Americans for personal development, and disregards the evidence that many Yapese have rich and healthy relationships with their fathers.

In fact, contrary to the opinion of some American school teachers and missionaries, many Yapese men have very healthy, deep love and respect for their fathers. Even as there are troubled families in every culture, some Yapese families are dysfunctional, but that dysfunction seems to arise out of broken relationships between husbands and wives and between fathers and sons within the context of the generally accepted family pattern.

The Aukan: D-Collectivist, Vertical, Egalitarian Families

Louis Shanks (1987:14–16) describes the marriage of a man named Da Sonobi in the village of Manlobi. Da Sonobi was reared in his mother's home and his marriage was arranged by his lineage-father (mother's elder brother) rather than his father. Da Sonobi's first wife came from a different clan and lineage, but lived in the same village. After they were married, Da Sonobi moved to his wife's lineage and built a house for her there; at times he returned to his own lineage and stayed in his deceased lineage-father's house.

Some time after his marriage, Da Sonobi had an incestuous relationship with a girl in his own clan, which created an uproar in the village. In punishment for this violation of the incest taboo, he was beaten by village priests at the mortuary in an attempt to appease the ancestress spirits. He was then banished to another village. A girl was born from this taboo union, but she died (as people expected) when she was about three years old.

Da Sonobi's affair created tension with his wife, and they were separated. He then married a woman from the village of Keementi, and lived there until the storm over the incestuous relationship had died. As Da Sonobi grew older he took another wife, this time closer to home in the adjacent village of Fandaaki. Taking up residence with this woman allowed him to resume a role in his lineage of birth where gradually over many years he became a leader. During these years he traveled back and forth between his two wives, spending time with each, and with the men in their villages, until they died. Finally, as an old man of more than seventy years, he married a third woman from the village of Tabiki. While he spent some time in her village, they lived most of their time in Manlobi, residing in Da Sonobi's lineage where he was an elder and village leader.

Da Sonobi's case is a fairly typical one for Aukan men. The Aukan prefer that a marriage partner come from the same village, but from a different matrilineal clan. Aukan men say, "It is better to get a wife from your own shore—you don't have to travel back and forth on the river." A young man may then participate in co-laboring relationships with his father, lineage-fathers, brothers, and boyhood friends. Yet, this practice of marrying and living on your own shore creates extensive opportunities for violating the rules of clan and lineage exogamy and, therefore, angering the ancestors. Such "incestuous" clan liaisons create great conflict and must be punished by beatings and excommunication from the lineage group to deter ancestral acts of vengeance.

A man's father or lineage-father takes the initiative to seek his first wife. Often these marriages are arranged between families from different lineages within the same or adjacent villages. After marriage, the young couple will reside for a time in the girl's village. The new husband has a responsibility to build his wife a house and to clear a section of the forest owned by her lineage and help her plant a garden. In addition to these major economic responsibilities, a young man must give his new wife pots, pans, dishes, hammocks, and water buckets. He is also responsible to keep her supplied with salt, kerosene, and meat. Living away from his home village, he must also form friendships and working partnerships with men in his new residence.

The young woman tends the garden, cooks for her husband, and makes his clothing. Since the residence of the couple is in the woman's village and lineage section, the woman has the support of her mother and sisters and her male matrilineal kinsmen. Sometimes in such a context a woman "overpowers" a man by her attitudes and actions. The Aukan say that in such circumstances a husband should divorce his wife and return to his own village where he may live in a house vacated by a deceased relative.

Because a man can have more than one wife, Aukan residence for men is complicated. Some men take a second and even a third wife and spend time traveling back and forth on the river from one spouse to another. If a man shirks his duty and fails to build a house for his wife, his reputation is ruined, particularly if his failure results in divorce and a later husband builds the woman her first house.

As a man grows older, his status within his mother's family grows and his duties toward his matrilineage increase. Every man has a responsibility to help rear his sister's children and to support the interests and work of his maternal lineage and clan. In Aukan culture the maternal uncle, or lineage-father, is a more influential person than one's biological father. As the man's authority increases with age, he will establish his primary residence in his matrilineage and future wives will come to his village for long periods of time. These senior men settle lineage disputes, supervise village-wide councils, and serve as ruling elders for funeral rites and other village activities.

The Role of the Domestic Family Unit in Social Environments

Family authority relationships reflect the domestic organization of labor. This authority structure serves to organize production in family economic activities and provides the basis for the subsistence of the domestic group. The Yapese, for example, promote their sons only on the occasion of the death of the fathers and all of their younger brothers. The elder generation holds authority over the younger until all its members have died. This is reflected in the organization of domestic and communal labor; the elder generation of men "give the word" and the younger generations "run to do it." Domestic and community work groups are nearly always organized on the basis of peer relationships; each generation forms its peer work groups. When it is convenient to mobilize the extended family, the senior generation (male and female) takes the administrative role, and the junior generations serve as laborers.

These case studies are by no means unique in human societies. The domestic unit in every society provides a foundational, organizational unit for the survival of the individual members. As such, a society lives or dies on the basis of the success of the organization of the domestic unit.

The domestic unit serves not only for subsistence but also as the means of transmitting the material and cultural inheritance of the group. Children learn from their parents the basic means of production and the cultural values and standards by which people organize their activities with one another. The Deni Indian father teaches his son the skills of hunting, the value of self-sufficiency, and the independence of domestic units by frequently realigning his own domestic unit with others and by releasing his son to a father-in-law to establish his own independent household. The Christian College father emphasizes success in school, respect for property, and maintenance skills to manage a home and a career; the son gradually must earn money to cover his own expenses, leading to the establishment of an independent household. The domestic unit serves, then, to reproduce the primary structures and values of the social environment.

Because of the close connection between subsistence activities and the transmission of values and culture, one might expect societies and cultures to reproduce themselves without significant change in successive generations. Such a view is too simplistic, failing to recognize the dynamic characteristics of domestic units and social environments. In actuality, the members of any given family unit monitor the success or failure of their subsistence activities and use that feedback as information from which they learn and plan future activities. Success affirms domestic authority and activity, while failure usually provokes participants to reassess and sometimes to refocus or reorganize so as to meet their domestic needs. One of Jacob's sons, Joseph, learned the structure and social environment of Egyptian culture and adapted effectively to it. We read in Genesis that when Joseph met his brothers on a much later occasion, he greeted them and interacted with them, employing the values of the Egyptian world and culture rather than those of his own family unit. Seeing Joseph's success and their own failure during this famine period, the whole family decided to follow Joseph into Egypt. After Jacob and his family settled there, they began a process of interaction with Egyptians, leading to new experience, feedback, and subsequent changes in their values, family structure, and social environment. The high group orientation of Israelite families upon their leaving Egypt stands in marked contrast to the autonomous individualism (low grid/low group) of the brothers who entered Egypt.

Members of domestic units in every society in the world participate in an ongoing process of activity and feedback from those activities into values and structures. The Deni Indians, who interact on a regular basis with Brazilian families, gradually adopt values from their Brazilian cohorts. I have personally observed one of the Deni chiefs adapting the role of patron in relationships with his fellow villagers. Learning this role in association with peasant farmers just a few miles away on the river, he has gradually adapted their patterns to relationships in his own village.

Brazilian families have a much more authoritarian structure. Brazilian fathers keep their sons dependent upon them, participating within their domestic community. A man keeps his sons in his own household and gives his daughters to other households, reversing the Indian pattern of residence at marriage. In 1977 during our study, we observed Deni men assuming the patron role but not adapting that relationship to their sons. Perhaps after another decade of interaction, some Deni men will be keeping their sons at home as do their Brazilian role models.

The domestic unit is crucial in every society because it provides the adaptive structure by which people survive and perpetuate themselves for succeeding generations. As members of these units find new ways of accomplishing these objectives, they will adjust their activities and ultimately their structures to accomplish this goal. They change their culture and adapt to their circumstances because they see change of direct relevance to their survival and to the perpetuation of their domestic unit.

The following case studies from the Old and New Testaments show how family structures varied through time in the life and culture of the Hebrews. Their domestic relationships reflect the larger economic organization of the society around them.

Jacob

The case study of Jacob is presented in Genesis 25–31. The biblical account does not provide all of the ethnographic details of the life and family relationships of people at that time in Hebrew history. However, many of the domestic details presented in the text provide interesting

insights into the nature of marriage, domestic labor, parent-child relationships, and aspects of family authority.

The story begins with an account of the births of Jacob and Esau. At
their birth, the boys are described as having distinct personalities. As
they grow up, Esau chooses to spend his early life with his father in the
open country, while Jacob lives with his mother among the tents. Esau
becomes a skilled hunter, while Jacob learns to care for the flocks and
cook. Jacob and Esau are described as competitors. Jacob, relying on
his skill as a herdsman and a cook, succeeds in negotiating from his fam-
ished brother Esau the rights to inherit the property of the firstborn
from their father. Jacob and Rebekah use the skills of slaughter, cooking,
and sewing to disguise Jacob. He deceives his father Isaac, and steals
the blessing of the firstborn from Esau. From the moment of their birth,
the text describes these two men as competitors, and the social environment in which they were reared encourages that competition and
independence.

Both Jacob and Esau spent forty years with their parents, living and
working as members of their household. Esau arranged his own marriages with local Canaanite women. His choice was not pleasing to his
mother and father, and he did it without their permission or support.
Jacob, who was more easily influenced, obeyed his father Isaac's direc-
tive to go to his uncle Laban's home in the hills of Syria, and find a wife
among his kinsmen there. When Esau heard of this, he took a third wife,
the daughter of his uncle Ishmael, his father Isaac's half-brother.

While the text tells us nothing about Esau's relationship to his wife's
parents, the story of Jacob is much more detailed. Laban offered to pay
Jacob for working with the flocks. Jacob requested marriage with
Laban's daughter, Rachel, and agreed to wait for seven years of bride
service. Laban exercised his authority as father-in-law over Jacob for the
total seven years. When the time was completed, Laban gave his oldest
daughter, Leah, rather than the girl he had promised. Laban had the
upper hand since he was the father of the girls and controlled their marriage. Jacob agreed to work seven more years and a week later he was
allowed to take Rachel as his second wife. After almost twenty years of
working for his father-in-law, Jacob negotiated a share of Laban's herds.
Laban agreed to give Jacob the speckled and spotted lambs and goats,
and Jacob used selective breeding to enhance his own personal wealth.

The patterns in Jacob's family of birth are continued in his relationships with his wives and his children. Rachel and Leah engaged in competition with one another over who could bear the most children.
Rachel used Jacob's love for her to keep Leah from having sexual access
to her husband. Leah used her son, Reuben, who brought to her man-
drakes, a fertility plant, to bargain with Rachel to gain sexual access to
Jacob. The boys served as co-laborers with their mother and their

father. Jacob gave his sons responsibility over his speckled herd while he took care of Laban's flocks. As we follow Jacob and his sons in later chapters in Genesis, we find the sons exercising much independent power, making their own decisions as Jacob and Esau did before them.

Jacob planned an escape from his father-in-law (Gen. 31). When Laban discovered that Jacob had departed with his wives, children, and herds, he set out in pursuit with his sons and a small army. Once again, Jacob engaged in a process of negotiation to placate his angry uncle and defended himself against the accusation that one of his party had stolen Laban's gods. Rachel, Laban's younger daughter, was the one who had stolen the idols, yet was successful in hiding them in her saddle bags from the discovery of her father.

Zachariah and Elizabeth, Mary and Joseph

The most extensive data available in the New Testament on family life come from three accounts in the Gospel of Luke: Zachariah, Elizabeth, and the birth of John the Baptist; Mary, Joseph, and the birth of Jesus; and the parable of the prodigal son. While the intent of these texts is not to portray an ethnographic account of family life, the details in them provide data from which we may answer questions about the structuring of authority, the organization of labor, and regulations surrounding marriage in first-century Jewish families.

The importance of genealogy for Jewish families is illustrated in both the Gospel of Luke and the Gospel of Matthew. Elizabeth and Zachariah are listed as descendents of Aaron (Luke 1:5) and Mary and Joseph as descendents of David in the tribe of Judah. The genealogies recount a line of patrilineal descent, and the text portrays the men as having primary authority in family relationships. Zachariah is the one who decides what his son is to be named (Luke 1:57–63). Joseph makes key decisions—whether or not to marry his betrothed, Mary; where they should go when threatened by Herod; and where they should ultimately settle.

While little information is given on the relationship between parents and children, the few clues that we find show children clearly subject to the authority of their parents. When Jesus is discovered in the temple by his parents (Luke 2:48–51) he accepts the rebuke of his mother. The text says, "He went down to Nazareth with them and was obedient to them" (v. 51). At the wedding at Cana in Galilee, Jesus' mother asks him to assist the host when the wine is gone, and Jesus responds to her request. Jesus illustrates obedience to the Jewish custom of lifelong subjection to parents. Yet this subjection was not always consistent with the calling that Jesus had from his Father. At the marriage in Cana, Jesus gently rebukes his mother: "My time has not come" (John 2:4).

With regard to family decisions and economic relationships the extended family appears to play an important role in first-century Jewish society. This is illustrated most graphically in the story of John the Baptist. Mary came to see her cousin Elizabeth and spent significant time with her before the birth of her baby. After Elizabeth gave birth to John, the neighbors and relatives attempted to influence Elizabeth's apparent decision to name the boy John. The relatives, who appealed to Zachariah with regard to this decision, were astonished when he wrote "his name is John." The third incident that shows the importance of the extended family is when Mary and Joseph took Jesus to Jerusalem. As they were returning to Nazareth, they thought that Jesus was in the company of their relatives who were traveling with them. These cases suggest that the role of the extended family was to provide mutual support and to give input on decisions that affected individuals within the group.

With regard to economic affairs in the family, Jewish families gave priority to the eldest child. This is most graphically illustrated in the story of the prodigal son (Luke 15:11–32) in which the younger son sought his portion of the estate and his father granted the request. The estate was held jointly by the father and the elder son (Luke 15:31); the younger son was given a designated share of the inheritance (v. 12). After the younger son squandered his portion of the inheritance, he was welcomed back to his father's house as a member, rather than a slave, much to the displeasure of his elder brother. At the same time, the father did not further divide the inheritance; he affirmed the rights of the elder son to all of his property. The younger son was welcomed back to the family, but the inheritance that he had squandered was not restored.

The concept of duty is often used to characterize relationships in Jewish family and society. Zachariah is described in Luke 1:8–10 as a man who had assigned duties in the temple because of his particular place in the genealogy of the family of Aaron. Joseph, as he considered the untimely pregnancy of his betrothed wife, decided to do his duty and set her aside quietly until he was persuaded otherwise by the Holy Spirit. In the story of the prodigal son, the elder brother became angry because he had been a model son, always performing his duty to his father; his father's welcome for his profligate brother offended his sense of justice, an insult to one who had been obedient and responsible according to the expectations of the culture (Luke 15:28). From this evidence we may characterize relationships between parents and children in these Jewish families by a sense of duty, obligation, and reciprocity.

These first-century families were very careful to do everything according to Jewish law. Luke records how Joseph and Mary took the child Jesus to the temple on the eighth day to have him circumcised and to go through the purification rituals for Mary specified in the law of Moses. Luke is careful to point out that only after they had done everything required by the law of the Lord did they return to Galilee in the town of Nazareth (Luke 2:39).

Marriage in first-century Jewish families carried many of the same attributes described in the Old Testament historical books. Luke records the fact that Mary was pledged to be married to Joseph, an arrangement typically made between families in preparation of the marriage of their children. Mary and Joseph and Zachariah and Elizabeth married members of their tribe. Arranged marriages remained a typical pattern among New Testament Christians as is evidenced by Paul's instructions in 1 Corinthians 7:36–38. The role of the family in the matter of marriage is evidenced by the practice of widow inheritance, illustrated in the discussion between the Sadducees and Jesus in Matthew 22:23–33.

To sum up, the authority structure of Jewish families in the New Testament period shows a strong commitment to corporate family relationships. The father in the family had ultimate authority. Family activities were regulated by the Mosaic law and by formal duties spelled out in customary practice. The eldest son was the heir of the family estate and held the right of succession to the role of his father. Marriages were arranged and the corporate family had a long-term interest in the activities of the children. Once a woman married into a family group she belonged to that group. Should she become a widow, men in the group had the responsibility to provide for her—even to the point of producing children.

Domestic Authority and Family Sins

Jewish family structure at the time of Christ is best characterized as a C-Corporate social environment. This type of social environment is neither unique to the Jewish people nor especially endorsed by Scripture. The features of Jewish family life described in the Gospels can be traced directly to the tribal and kingdom periods of Jewish society and culture. Similar family structures are typical of other pagan cultures scattered widely throughout the Middle East, Africa, Asia, and around the world. We can draw many parallels between the Jewish families and Yapese families described in this book, for example.

Following upon the presupposition stated in the first chapter of this volume, we shall consider each type of family structure in some way or another in conflict with the redeeming work of the Lord Jesus Christ. No family structure is God-given or biblically endorsed; families are human institutions that may be transformed through the redemptive work of Christ.

The question then becomes not which of these family structures have a correct biblical frame, but rather what sins are typical of each of these social environments, thereby creating a need for the redemptive work of Christ. Table 6.2 details the distinctive sins of parents and siblings that may commonly occur in each of the four distinctive social environments.

We only need to reflect briefly on the case study of Jacob to identify sins typical of the A-Individualist social environment. The behavior of

Table 6.2
Domestic Authority and Typical Sins
of Parents and Siblings

B-Bureaucratic (Faculty-CC)	**C-Corporate** (Yap)
(high grid, low group)	**(high grid, high group)**
Disciplinarian without love	Property used to control children
Separation, independence leads to isolation, loneliness	Love conditional, based on obedience, submissiveness
Self-fulfillment more important than siblings	Elders humiliate, use younger for corporate family interests
Parental rules have priority over child's needs, interests	Respect-avoidance more important than tenderness, compassion
Parents pressure for marriage to enhance career and status of child	Parents reject marriages of "wrong" family or village
A-Individualist (Deni, Jacob)	**D-Collectivist** (Aukan)
(low grid, low group)	**(low grid, high group)**
Parents create amoral atmosphere	Family interests become moral duty
Advancing self and family is highest goal	Nonconforming are "rubbed" until blended or excluded
Sibling rivalry leads to deception, hostility	Sisters ridicule husbands, men play sisters against wives
Family members run away from family problems	Problems addressed by collective force, divination, ritual coercion
Father uses daughter, son-in-law for his interests	Mothers manipulate daughters and their husbands

Rebekah, Jacob, Esau, Laban, Leah, and Rachel showed something of an "amoral familialism" practiced among these people. Their primary objectives were to advance self-interest and their particular family interests in opposition to those of their other relatives. They sacrificed principles for the sake of personal gain and did not hesitate to use deception and intrigue to meet personal or family objectives. Jacob's attitude reflects the ideal that "doing for oneself" is the primary goal, and his economic practice suggests that the "ends justify the means" (bargaining for his brother's birthright, stealing his brother's blessing, breeding his father-in-law's flocks to produce for his own flocks, etc.).

Members of "typical" evangelical middle-class American families are quick to see and criticize the behavior of Jacob, Rebekah, Rachel, and

Laban. However, to see the sins that typify their own B-Bureaucratic social environment is much more difficult. Because it is appropriate for B-fathers to be disciplinarian, discipline may become more important than love. In their struggle to make children independent, they may fail to see how their strategies to create separation and self-sufficiency often yield loneliness and isolation as well as independence. While teaching their children the value of independent property and the necessity to care for their own things, they may fail to see that they are also teaching that "self" is more important than "others," and that self-interest is more important than sharing with those in need. The emphasis on good grades may press a child toward achievement at the expense of honesty. Parents may also teach that the rule is more important than the person.

The case studies of the prodigal son, David's family, and the Yapese illustrate that parents and siblings of the C-Corporate family also have their own unique sins. In these corporate family groups, property becomes exceedingly important to the members. Parents may typically use property to control their children. Jesus uses the parable of the prodigal son to perhaps refute the commonly held conception of a "just" father, and to illustrate the will of his "Father in heaven." The father forgives the son who dissipated his inheritance, and restores him as a member of the family. This is highly uncharacteristic of C-Corporate parental behavior. Parents in this type of social environment often hold their children in a lifelong dependency relationship, which may lead to immaturity and irresponsibility. David's sons are a prime example. C-parents often extend conditional love in return for obedience and submission on the part of their children. The obedient son in Jesus' parable complains to his father because he had always been submissive and served his father, whereas the other brother had been disobedient; the sibling's conclusion is that love for his wayward brother should be withdrawn and that he should be excluded from their family relations. Younger children may be humiliated by their older siblings and may be exploited for the "good" of corporate family interests. Finally, C-parents and siblings often avoid showing tenderness and compassion; the criticism of the elder brother in the parable of the prodigal son stands over against his father's tenderness and compassion. Family authority and public reputation may be more important than tenderness and compassion in the C-Corporate environment.

The D-Collectivist social environment often produces parents who seek total control over their children. Aukan parents threaten their children with random malicious acts of ancestral spirits if they fail to support the interest of the collective group. Nonconforming Aukan children are pressured socially and "rubbed" ritually (literally with herbal washes to purify them), until they are blended or excluded from family relationships. This pattern of pressing for conformity is not unique to the Aukan. A Chinese proverb says that a nail that sticks out must be pounded until it is even with the rest of the surface. Aukan families pound and rub their members until they are like everyone else. Parents may manipulate their children in marriages, and may force them to break up a marriage if it does not meet parental interests. The collective group seeks to control individuals for good or evil interests.

In conclusion, each social environment has its own unique forms and expressions of oppression and sin in the relationships between parents and children. The sins of the parents and the sins of the siblings arise not only out of their private interests, but also out of the social environments in which they are participants. The individualist and collectivist social environments produce sins of excess in which either the individual or the group manipulates others to achieve selfish ends. In high grid social environments where rule has much greater priority over social behavior, legalism and the abuse of authority are much more common. People use law and authority against others rather than for just and compassionate ends.

The Gospel, Marriage, and Domestic Authority

How does the gospel challenge each of these social environments? In what ways are family members called to be transforming agents within their social environments? To what extent does Scripture address their specific sins?

The story of the prodigal son is an excellent illustration of how Jesus addressed the sins of a particular social environment. The father's sons are more important to him than his property. When his younger son requested his share of the inheritance, the father released that inheritance rather than holding his son in a dependency relationship to him. The father was unconditional in his love for his son, accepting him back even when he had dissipated all of his inheritance and lived a life of complete and utter disgrace to the family. The father rebuked the elder brother for his conditional love for his younger brother and denial of compassion when his brother pled for mercy. At the same time, the father did not betray his elder son by dividing the property again. The younger had lost his property, and the consequences of that act remained. Forgiveness entailed restoration of relationship in the family and provision of food and clothing, but not a restocking of his former wealth.

The theme that is taught so profoundly in this parable and repeated throughout the New Testament is that of "the loving father." "For God so loved the world" (John 3:16); "God demonstrates his own love for us in this: While we were still sinners, Christ died for us" (Rom. 5:8); "how great is the love the Father has lavished on us" (1 John 3:1). The theme of the loving father is not only appropriate for this C-Corporate environment, but can be expressed in unique and appropriate ways in each of the four contexts. One might ask the reader to recreate the story of the prodigal son in each of the other three social environments. What would the son seek in each of the other three family types? How would the elder brother respond? How might the father manifest the love of God and deal with two sinning sons as Jesus did in his parable?

A second major theme that we see in the Scriptures is love of God and of one's neighbor (Deut. 6:5–6; Matt. 22:38–39). Loving one's neighbor as oneself takes different forms in each of the four social environments. Jacob and Esau would have behaved differently if they had practiced this principle of loving each other as they loved themselves. American siblings who do not have contact with one another for years would make a greater effort to keep contact and support one another if they practiced this principle. Yapese parents and siblings would be able to show more tenderness and compassion for one another and forgive the unsubmissive and the disobedient. The Aukan and Chinese would not be so insistent upon pounding in the nail that sticks up or rubbing to exclusion their family members who find it difficult to fit in.

A third theme repeated in several places in the New Testament is the loving husband. Ephesians 5:25 challenges husbands to "love your wives, just as Christ loved the church and gave himself up for her." Peter tells believing husbands to "be considerate," and to treat their wives "with respect as the weaker partner and as heirs with you of the gracious gift of life" (1 Pet. 3:7). Psychologists tell us that many family problems are generated from the strained and broken relationships between father and mother in a family unit. How a man expresses love as a husband will vary in each social environment. Yet, in my experience observing families in diverse parts of the world and in each of these social environments, I have seen loving husbands who have fulfilled these New Testament commands within the context of their own culture and social environment. A loving husband can be a transforming power in family and society. If Jacob had treated Leah with the same respect and love that he gave to Rachel, the conflicts between these two women could have been largely resolved, which in turn would have had a transforming power upon their children.

Finally, the Scriptures challenge women to be wives worthy of respect (1 Tim. 3:11). In each of the social environments described above, authority is allocated in a particular way within the family unit. In some social environments the husband and father has more exclusive authority than in other social environments. It is, however, true in every social environment that husbands and wives share authority within the domestic family in socially prescribed ways and husbands/fathers always have some interest and authority in relationship to their children. The biblical command is that wives should submit to their husbands (Eph. 5:22; Col. 3:18). Families cannot operate effectively without the allocation of authority among the members. Women who live lives worthy of respect and who are submissive to their husbands in their particular social environment are promised that their lives will have a transforming power and influence in society. Peter says, "They (unbelieving husbands) may be won over without words by the behavior of their wives, when they see the purity and reverence of your lives" (1 Pet. 3:1–2).

To sum up, the diverse and varied forms of family found around the world are part of the creative genius of human life and culture. The Scriptures do not prescribe a single family form or a single social environment by which people may be identified as followers of Christ. Rather, the message of the gospel specifically to husbands, wives, parents, and children, calls for transformed relationships within the social environments and domestic groups of culture. The commands given to us in Old and New Testament alike lead us to transformed relationships and domestic groups that have a powerful transforming impact on the society at large.

The Aukan

The basic theme running through this book is that all peoples are in their prison of disobedience and the gospel will bring conflict and change into the lives of each and every group. The gospel creates significant conflict for Aukan marriages and families. Malachi 2:16 states clearly that God hates divorce. Jesus speaks openly against divorce (Matt. 5:31–32; Luke 16:18). Paul repeats a similar message in his letter to the Corinthians (1 Cor. 7). The sanctity of marriage is attributed to the created order (Gen. 2:24; Mark 10:6–9). While the issue of multiple marriages is more complex since they were obviously permitted in early Hebrew history, the Epistles state clearly that church leaders have only one wife.

Some may question the Aukan practice of granting a maternal uncle more authority for the instruction of a child than they give to the father. While at first glance this seems unusual and inconsistent with some biblical texts (see Prov. 13:24; 19:18; Eph. 6:4), parental authority is a more important issue than the specific role of the father. In fact, the Aukan separate the role of nurture and care from the role of authority and instruction. The biological father is the one who provides nurture and care for the child, while the maternal uncle, serving as lineage-father, exercises authority and instructs the child in appropriate social behavior. One might argue that it is easier for Aukan men to hear, understand, and receive the message of God as "the loving Father" than for many men in Western societies, who have been reared in homes where fathers are harsh, distant authoritarian figures, who show little if any love and affection for their sons. In fact, Aukan men are much more receptive to the gospel than Aukan women.

The strong Aukan emphasis on brother and sister relationships is sustained in the Gospels (Matt. 23:8; Mark 3:35; John 21:23) and the Epistles (Rom. 8:29; Heb. 2:11). The Scriptures also support the Aukan belief that women exerting authority over men is bad. Aukan men find comfort in biblical passages that admonish women to submit to their husbands in the Lord since the collective power of women in Aukan villages can be abusive and destructive to men.

The case study of Asoinda, a Saramaccan believer, illustrates the power of women in these societies. When Asoinda accepted the message of the gospel and proclaimed publicly his faith in the Lord Jesus Christ, all three of his Saramaccan wives rejected him. They refused to receive him into their homes and provoked their fellow villagers to reject him from the village and to keep him from seeing his children. Asoinda became an outcast in his own village. All of his wives divorced him and remarried. Since these women and their brothers control the children, Asoinda has had almost no contact with them since his conversion.

Over the last ten years Asoinda has dedicated himself to evangelism, teaching new believers, and working to translate the Scriptures into his mother tongue. He has rejoiced in his opportunity to suffer for the gospel's sake, giving up wives and children, brothers and sisters as Jesus proclaimed in Luke 14:26. He is praying that God might one day give him a Christian wife and children who know the Lord and follow his leadership.

The Aukan and Saramaccan converts recognize that a new set of brothers and sisters in Christ supersede their clan and lineage ties. In their local churches in the city of Paramaribo, these believers have formed a new clan, the local church. The elder men and women work together to teach the younger men, women, and children the words of Scripture, and the rules for life that come from being followers of Jesus Christ. Men and women still look to their elder brothers and sisters for help in training their children in the Lord. Christian families emphasize the authority of the senior generation and relationships of brothers and sisters more than they emphasize the authority of father over child or the authority of husband over wife. At the same time Christian Aukan men and women have committed themselves to one husband and one wife, to a lifelong marriage in Christ, and to the rule of elders in their family and in their church relationships.

The Yapese

Economic changes introduced by American post-World War II occupation have significantly undermined the economic contribution and authority of women in Yapese families. Women, reduced to the status of house-keepers, are often no longer respected by their husbands. Many have lost their self-esteem and respect within their family and community.

As a careful observer of Yapese society I believe that wage work has not improved Yapese marriages, but has produced conflict and increased abuse of wives in the marriage relationship. The respect and economic reciprocity between husband and wife characteristic of the Yap subsistence society provide a striking parallel to the "wife of noble character" in Proverbs 31. The pattern of relationship described by my friends Tamag and Rungun for the ideal Yap man and the ideal Yap woman requires mutual support, honor, and submission. That is not to say that the Yapese practiced the ideals of their own culture; in fact Tamag was very candid in his comments about his own life, stating that he only did this when he became old and wise.

Perhaps our best insight into the significance of the gospel for Yapese marriage comes from a Yapese believer. In 1980 I interviewed an old man by the name of Fiithingmew, who because of diabetes had lost one of his legs. His father had been something of a scholar of Yapese culture and had passed on that gift and interest to Fiithingmew. As a believer, con-fined to his house for most of his days or to moving about on crutches, he had become a student of Scripture. He accepted the Scriptures as the source of authority and truth, yet he had the unique ability to reflect on his culture and discover analogies that provided a clearer understand-ing of Scripture.

In our conversation, Fiithingmew said that the Yapese word for mar-riage, *mabgol*, had hidden meanings that cast light upon the relationship of a Christian husband and wife, and upon the relationship of a believer with God. Part of the word for marriage, *mab*, is the Yapese word for "door." The Yapese may use the word as either as a noun or verb. To say, *ka mab*, is to say, "It's open." The second part of the word for mar-riage, *gol*, is the word for "generosity." A *bagol* gives to others whatever is asked and more abundantly than has been requested. Yapese honor men and women for their generosity. To be called *bagol* is one of the finest character traits that one can have in Yap.

Fiithingmew said that the ideal marriage is one characterized by *mab-gol*, "open generosity." He said that a Christian husband and wife should be completely open to one another, withholding nothing, giving what-ever is asked and more. A man and a woman should share without reservation their labor, their material goods, their love, and their respect. Giving should be without consideration of return, and a mar-riage partner should seek to give more than the other could ever return.

Fiithingmew likened this to Paul's instructions to believers in Ephesians 5. He noted how Paul commanded wives to submit to their husbands and husbands to love their wives as Christ loved the church.

He said that Christ's love for the church was *mabgol*. Christ withheld nothing of himself from the church; he gave himself to his disciples, and to the people he taught and healed during his ministry on earth. He laid down his life on the cross for all who would believe.

Fiithingmew suggested that even now Christ extends to us, through his relationship with the Father in heaven, open generosity. God has promised to show the incomparable riches of his grace and to provide all of our needs according to his riches in glory (Phil. 4:19) through Christ. He noted that we believers, members of his church, as the bride of Christ have a marriage partnership with Christ. We are to give him whatever is asked. All of the good gifts that we have—our labor, our goods, our thanksgiving, our love, our respect—we should return to Christ, just as he has extended to us all that is available to him in his relationship with the Father.

I came away from this conversation with Fiithingmew deeply touched by his understanding of the Scripture, and the analogy of Yapese marriage to the relationship between Christ and the church. As he articulated his thoughts, it became clear to me that I could learn much from the concept of *mabgol*, not only for my relationship with Christ, but also for my relationship to my own wife. The wonder of the gospel is that it not only redeems people, it also redeems their creativity, enabling them to articulate their understanding of their relationship with God and to create distinctive and unique avenues of communication. Through these creative insights, believers from distinctive cultures may help one another, as members in the body of Christ, to comprehend the joy of deeper relationship with God and redeemed relationships with members of family and society.

7
Authority and Community

The Context of Local Churches

Case Studies

The Javanese Pastor

A large population of Indonesian Javanese came a century ago as immigrants to work on Surinam plantations. Many of these people stayed after their labor term was completed, and today form a population of around 60,000. Living in and around the city of Paramaribo, they for the most part practice the Islamic faith, blended with Javanese animism. In the last ten years many have responded to a significant movement of the Spirit of God, and the Javanese evangelical church has grown rapidly.

One young pastor stands out in the church movement among the Surinam Javanese. This man became a believer in the early 1970s and, under the discipleship of a missionary, studied the Scriptures and committed his life to preaching the gospel to the Javanese. His success as an evangelist and church planter was recounted in the first chapter. He also served as the primary mother-tongue translator for the Surinam Javanese language.

As the church grew and the pastor's responsibilities became increasingly demanding, his Bible translation associates began encouraging him to delegate some of his responsibilities to younger men whom he had been discipling. They were concerned because the work of Bible translation had nearly ceased. After some months the pastor recruited another man to help him in the translation program, but he refused to allow this young man to do any translating of Scripture, limiting him to transcribing old Surinam Javanese stories. A frustrated translation team encouraged the pastor to release some of his trainees to carry on the Javanese work, arguing that he had many capable men working under him. They pointed to several lay leaders whom he had been discipling and encouraged him to allow them to take more responsibility for the total church work. They suggested that a co-worker with the Bible translation organization might begin translation drafts that he then could revise at a later time.

The pastor resolutely refused to follow their counsel, explaining that these men were not ready yet to carry on the work of the ministry. Citing their lack of experience and training, he refused to give responsibility to them until he was confident that they were truly qualified. The translation team argued that the men would grow and mature. Further, the amount of work to be done was so great, more workers were needed. Even immature men could help to carry more of the load.

The disagreement that ensued between the missionary leaders and pastor, while not one of open conflict, created tension and frustration. The missionaries, who were financially supporting the translation work, were discouraged at the rate of progress. At the same time they were very positive and excited about the growth in the Javanese church, and were stymied as to exactly how to proceed without retarding that growth. To them, the pastor held the key, if only he would release more of his leaders to carry on the work of the church, while he concentrated on the Bible translation work. The pastor, unwilling to release his workers, delegated to them a limited amount of authority. These men carried out their responsibilities effectively. The pastor's presence and leadership assured strict control over the total church activities, building a community that was rich in its depth and responsive in every way to the needs and concerns of its members. The pastor's lay leaders held an intense, deep loyalty to him, and submitted readily to his leadership, following him in the work of the church. Likewise, the members of the church expressed open and affectionate loyalty to him; the group was very strong in its corporate and worship activities. In fact, one of the most appealing aspects of the church to new believers was the strength of the community and its genuine warmth and love for them as they entered it.

The tension between mission and church leaders arose from their conflicting expectations regarding work productivity, and their rules of authority and responsibility for leaders and supporting workers. They had contrary solutions on how to manage an increasing work load.

The Deni Chief

When Gordon Koop first began to work with the Deni he needed a great deal of help from the people in various labor activities. They helped him build his house and settle into the community. They transported his goods on the river, and he traded with them in the village. The Deni were very happy to have him in their village because he provided material goods and supplies.

After the completion of a jungle airstrip, my friend needed their assistance on a regular basis for maintaining the airstrip. One of his greatest frustrations was the inability of the Deni chief to organize the work and make payments to the people. Koop sought to hire a local foreman who might supervise this work, and turned to the Deni chiefs as potential foremen for the job. The two men in the village, recognized as chiefs, were not able to fulfill his expectations. Neither paid people appropriately for their labor, and neither organized the work project to his satisfaction.

As long as Koop directed this project, they were able to work to his satisfaction, since he could show them exactly what he wanted. When he was not there, however, his radio message to the villagers was insufficient. Relying on the chiefs to pay workers inevitably resulted in conflicts. People complained that they were not paid, or they were frustrated that Koop was not happy with the job they had done and expected them to work again.

Koop hoped to find someone who could act as a supervisor, direct the routine maintenance, and pay people fairly in terms of the amount of labor that they had contributed. The Deni chiefs had no experience with supervision, and had never had the responsibility, nor even observed someone paying in the manner that Koop expected. In their relationships with the Brazilians they merely asked for certain material goods that were generally given. Sometime later the Brazilian patron demanded that the Deni come and work for them until they had satisfied their debt. The pattern was cyclical. After an Indian had paid off his previous debt, the patron allowed him to take more material goods and establish a debt again. Through this method of continuous debt the Deni obtained an irregular supply of material goods and the Brazilians an irregular supply of labor.

Koop did not want to want to employ the debt-labor model. He preferred to pay people immediately for their work, thereby avoiding debt himself and also teaching them the privileges of a cash economy. To do so, however, required a different set of rules and procedures; in effect the chief must supervise the work and pay people fairly. The Deni chief was at best an influential man among equals. Without significant authority in the community, chiefs acted as cheerleaders, mobilizing people to accomplish things at times when they were disposed to follow. They had no power to coerce or control people in the community; they employed influence, or persuasion, with more or less success, and people did what was in their best interest. As a consequence, Koop's expectations were unrealistic; the chiefs failed totally in the task of administering either the work or payment of the workers.

Authority and Power

To understand authority it is useful to focus specifically on the issue of power. In every society the question of the allocation of power illustrates the authority dimension of relationships between individuals, and between individuals and groups. In the case study above, the Deni chiefs did not have power over villagers to make decisions about labor, nor to enforce the particular distribution of goods. The Javanese pastor, in contrast, had a great deal of power over his congregation and co-workers, and refused to relinquish it to others who were working under him.

The Deni Indians have a low grid social environment in which the chief has very limited power over others. Villagers grant power to the chief on a personal reciprocal basis, and may readily withdraw that power if and when the chief fails to please them. Each individual in Deni society holds independent power in relationship to livelihood and to membership in the village. People may come and go as they please, and leaders have limited ability to coerce them or to induce them to participate.

The Surinam Javanese differentiate relationships within and outside the church in a moderately high grid environment. The pastor has been allocated power by the people who have joined his congregation, and they allow him to speak for them and make decisions on their behalf. The pastor, in turn, has delegated power to some of his lay leaders who then conduct different aspects of the ministry under him.

The Javanese social environment may be characterized by centralized high grid relationships, and the Deni environment by an aggregated low grid relationship. The Deni and the Javanese cases are also different in terms of their commitment to group. Among the Deni we see fragmentation and a low commitment and orientation to group. The Javanese, in contrast, demonstrate a high degree of coordination and commitment to group.

The fragmentation of the Deni village is evidenced by the historical relationships of families within the villages. In his historical study of the Deni village Koop found that they averaged about two years in any village settlement. Some settlements, which endured for a longer period of time, grew larger than others, but inevitably some disaster or illness caused the village to split and fragment into smaller groups. Koop documented this process of fragmentation and coordination through the residence histories of the elderly people in the Marrecao Creek community.

Linkages in Deni villages are primarily based upon weak ties of kinship, marriage, and reciprocity. When the people find reasons to dispute with one another, a household or family unit may break from the village, move to another place, and align with other households. The history of household alignments and realignments into small villages is one of constant fragmentation and change.

The Surinam Javanese who are members of the city church do not live in coordinated village settings. While some live in villages in surrounding districts, most are residents of the metropolitan area of the city of Paramaribo and live in scattered Javanese neighborhoods. Their relationship as a group has little to do with residential proximity, but rather is generated from their commitment as new believers to the Surinam Javanese congregation. Organized activities encourage unity and fellowship in the group. The most important activity is a region-wide service held every Saturday evening. This is a service of celebration, worship, and fellowship, rather than a service of teaching. During this time people gather from all over Paramaribo and spend the evening together, enjoying each other's company and celebrating their unity in Christ. On other days members gather in four distinctive areas for Bible study, prayer, and small group fellowship. Bible studies are also social times in which people eat together, and work together for their fellowship in Christ. The pastor tries to be at all of these. He has lay leaders who lead these small group fellowships. On Sundays large group activities, such as soccer games or other events, bring people together for fun and fellowship. Coordination among the Surinam Javanese is based upon social and worship activities rather than geographic proximity. These activities create the links between people that emphasize group participation and group membership. The pastor has made a considered effort to celebrate the collective joy of Christians and the fellowship that people have together in the church of Christ; their meetings create a sense of joy, celebration, and unity, as he disciples them and trains them in the Scripture.

Authority and Community

Power authority is the legitimate right, held by a social elite, to control people and/or resources in a given social setting (Adams 1975). An individual may gain power authority by the mere ownership of significant resources or by controlling the access of others to those resources. When resources are held or controlled by individuals independently of others, they have "independent power." Power authority may also be allocated by a group of people to their leaders, who then act on their behalf; having gained authority by consensus or majority support from members of the group, these leaders have "allocated power." Power authority may also be delegated by leaders to subordinates; these subordinate leaders hold "delegated power," often legitimized by an institutional structure, in which the locus of power is held by leaders at the top.

Skill authority refers to control of information or technology derived from the mastery of particular technical skills, and occupying a role assigned to people who hold such skills. Teachers have particular skill authority related to the subject matter that they have studied at great length. Mechanics have skill authority based upon their ability to repair automobiles or other kinds of machinery. Individuals who hold skills, such as carpenters, plumbers, dentists, chemists, and computer technicians, have authority that derives from their mastery of that skill and is based upon the needs of others in their society for their expertise.

Table 7.1 illustrates how power and skill authority are elaborated and applied for community leadership in four distinctive social environments. In the high grid social environments, power authority is elaborated and expressed in all of its forms. In the C-Corporate social environment, the consensus interests of the group place significant constraints upon leaders. Seniority has greater value than skill for the selection and legitimacy of leaders. Leaders have little if any independent authority; group dialogue and consensus dominate the decision process. Authority is allocated by the group, leaders hold specific titles, and authority is elaborated in specific role expectations for group members. In the B-Bureaucratic social environment, the top leaders have independent power and exercise significantly greater control over subordinate roles through delegated authority. Skill authority is a primary factor in role differentiation, and skilled leaders play significant roles in administrative structures.

In low grid social environments power authority is limited to the reciprocal granting of power between individuals, and the allocation of power from a group to its collective elders. Skill authority confers little more than prestige and personal advantage to those who have it. In the A-Individualist social environment individuals grant power reciprocally, but no further elaboration occurs. Individuals play out personal dramatic roles in the life and work of the community, to the admiration or scorn of others around them. Skill confers prestige, but not authority over others. In the D-Collectivist social environment, members of the group allocate authority to either elders or skilled members, but retain strict control over them through the demands of consensus. Positions and privileges of authority are few and unelaborated, and an ethos of egalitarianism pervades group life.

Table 7.1
Social Profiles: Community Authority

B-Bureaucratic (Christian College)	C-Corporate (Yap, Javanese)
(high grid, low group)	**(high grid, high group)**
Task orientation	Person orientation
Skill authority (expert/trainee; specialist/support)	Skill authority—traditional focus (craftsman/apprentice)
Power authority	Power authority
independent (CEO, executive board)	allocated (chiefs, pastors)
delegated (manager/staff; supervisor/worker)	delegated (councilor, associate) seniority (elder/younger)
A-Individualist (Deni)	**D-Collectivist** (Aukan)
(low grid, low group)	**(low grid, high group)**
Task orientation	Person orientation
Power authority	Power authority
(individuals grant reciprocal power)	allocated (elders speak for group)
	consensus, egalitarian ethos
Skill authority—technical focus (prestige based on skills)	Skill authority—traditional focus (craftsman/apprentice)

Christian College: B-Bureaucratic (High Grid/Low Group)

Task orientation is a key factor in the assignment of authority in the Christian College setting. People hold specific jobs with carefully defined authority, and have power delegated to those roles because of particular tasks that must be done. A resident director has the responsibility of managing a particular dormitory for the college. Each job is assigned on the basis of skill and expertise. An employee who has no training in the management of a residence hall would not be considered qualified to serve in that capacity and, in all likelihood, would not be given the job.

Because of its task orientation Christian College assigns authority to its personnel on the basis of skills. Individuals may be specialists and serve the college in their specialized roles with others, assisting them as supporting staff. The faculty are considered experts in their fields; students are apprentices who are studying with these experts. The organization of authority in the Christian College setting emphasizes specialist/support and expert/apprentice relationships.

The governing power in Christian College is based upon power authority. Governed by a board of trustees, which holds independent power, the board delegates full executive power to the president of Christian College, who is the chief executive officer. In such a role the president has independent power to the extent that it has been granted to him by the board. All who report to the president have power that has been delegated to them, and they are accountable to him on a day-to-day basis. These people operate in a management or staff relationship. Each supervisor is accountable to a higher supervisor, and workers have a supervisor to whom they must report and from whom they receive their directions to work.

Most Americans who join the missions task force to serve overseas come from communities in which Type B social environments predominate. Most American businesses and government agencies operate on the same basic structural premises as does Christian College. Americans educated in public schools are familiar with a Type B social environment, and most have learned to work within and conform to the demands of this type of administrative social environment. The training for mission and ministry in any of the major theological seminaries in America prepares pastors to operate in Type B social environments. The organization of authority through the reciprocal statuses of expert/apprentice, specialist/support, and supervisor/worker pervade American society.

When pastors and missionaries move out of the American society and begin to serve in the two-thirds world they experience significant value and authority differences. The following cases illustrate some of the cultural diversity with which these cross-cultural workers must cope.

The Yapese: C-Corporate Environment (High Grid/High Group)

The people of Yap discuss authority in terms of land and people who speak for the land. Individuals hold authority because of their inheritance and identity in a specific village and corporate family estate, and because of their ability and character as persons to meet the expectations of Yapese society. Some individual Yapese have inherited land rights to authority in their communities, but they do not have the personal qualities necessary to earn corporate support to exercise those inherited rights. As a consequence, someone else in the community is given authority in their place. The quality and character of the person are essential considerations. A man who does not manifest these qualities will not be accepted as a leader, even if he has all of the formally prescribed requirements.

The Yapese community operates on power authority very much like the Christian College community. However, power authority in Yap is allocated by the community rather than delegated by a group holding independent power. The Yapese people, in their villages or regions, allocate power to men who hold titles through inheritance of particular estates, and who show competence and reliability to exercise the authority of those estates in a manner satisfactory to the people.

The hierarchy of age and the seniority of generation are fundamental in the assignment of authority in Yapese communities. In all Yapese activities elder men are in authority. One becomes an elder after one's father dies; as long as a man's father is living he is considered to be a junior member of society and has no right to speak in public meetings. If a man has an older brother in his family estate, he likewise keeps silent, allowing his elder brother to speak on his behalf.

Both men and women in Yap have authority. The men hold public authority, overseeing village activities that affect both men and women in the community. Women, on the other hand, exercise authority over domestic labor and women's activities. Men and women alike serve on the basis of their relative age and generation. Female leaders in Yap come from titled estates as do their husbands. Usually the wife of a titled man serves as village leader of women, provided she has the character and capability of exercising this authority adequately.

The Yapese emphasize the importance of titled individuals, called *pilung,* or "those who give the word." The people who carry out their instructions are called *pimilngay,* or "those who run to do it." The speaker/follower relationship is one of delegated authority. The Yapese council of elders and chiefs in the village delegate specific authority to certain individuals within the group. If, for example, the leaders of the community wish to organize a large labor project, they must first mobilize the men and women of the village to gather food and fish to feed the laborers. Summoning the senior working men in the community, they ask them to organize a major fishing expedition. These elders appoint certain individuals within the community to organize the young men to fish. The appointed expedition leaders bring the catch back to the council of elders, who distributes it appropriately. A similar process is employed in the mobilization of women to harvest and prepare yams and taro.

Prior to World War II, a few Yapese men were skilled craftsmen; these experts included house builders, canoe builders, and men skilled in the magic for planting crops, controlling the weather, and assuring success in war. All technical skills were associated with magical and supernatural power; the skilled carpenter knew how to build houses, and also how to make appropriate magic so that the structure was secure, the ropes used to tie the timbers strong, and the spirits who undermine the work of the carpenter and his crew thwarted. A Yapese craftsman passed his skill on to apprentices very slowly and with great deliberation. A man did not become an apprentice until he reached middle age; and at that time he began a long process of study with the expert, paying fees in traditional shell and stone valuables as he learned. The wise craftsman retained significant parts of his knowledge until the time when he was on the threshold of death. At that particular moment he gave his final treasures of knowledge and skill to the one he had chosen to be his successor. For Yapese, skill authority was highly treasured and exchanged only after a long and trusted relationship between the craftsman and his apprentice.

The Aukan: D-Collectivist Environment (Low Grid/High Group)

The Aukan society, like the Yapese society, places a strong emphasis on persons. However, Aukan villages are low grid, having limited hierarchical power arrangements in their social organization. Each Aukan village has a *kabiten* and several *basia,* men and women who serve the *kabiten* as his delegated agents within the local village. These positions, however, are not indigenous to Aukan society, but are paid positions in the external government hierarchy. While the government holds the *kabiten* and the *basia* accountable to the regional district official, the actual authority in the local community is given to them because of their role as elders rather than because of their formal government positions.

Aukan leadership operates on the basis of consensus support from the members of the society. When the *kabiten* calls a meeting, young and old, men and women come. They come, not because they are commanded, but because they have an interest in the decision and their input is considered important. The men and women who act as *basia* in the community have been chosen to serve on the basis of their loyalty to the community and their willingness to work hard on behalf of the whole.

Both men and women may serve as *basia* in the community. Men and women come to the meetings and participate in the discussion. Men and women have an equal voice in the public affairs of the community and an egalitarian ethos pervades their relationships to one another. Women often have more influence in public affairs than men because they are the permanent members of the village, while men tend to travel up and down river. The women in the community have enough power that if they together oppose the activities of men they can control public decisions.

People in the Aukan villages appeal ultimately to their ancestors for authority. Compelled by their expectations of how the ancestors will evaluate their behavior and by their fear of supernatural retribution for inappropriate behavior, they make public decisions to satisfy the ancestors who have gone before. To violate that code is to invite disaster of the greatest kind.

The Deni: A Individualist Environment (Low Grid/Low Group)

The Deni are much more like my colleagues in the colleges than they are like the Yapese or the Aukan. Their orientation is toward tasks and the motivation to achieve in those tasks in such a way that they gain prestige and recognition in the local community and in the larger world around them. Deni applaud their leaders for success in mobilizing people for tasks that are of interest to them. If a Deni chief does not stimulate and encourage people to hold feasts at least every five to seven days, the people begin to complain that the chief is weak and ineffective. Men expect their chief to lead them on extended hunts, so that they may kill game for larger celebrations. A public goal of Deni society is to engage in periodic rituals of feasting and good talk.

When we interviewed Deni informants about succession to office, they said that their fathers were chiefs. When we asked why their older brothers were not chiefs, they said their brothers were not interested in being chiefs. One of the chiefs living in the village at the time of the study acquiesced to serve because the prior chief had died and the people wanted someone to lead them in feasting. Because he was so busy with his own activities he was not interested in feasting and did not call them more than once every two or three weeks. This was not satisfactory, particularly to some of the women in the community who enjoyed feasting because it gave them access to more meat. As a consequence, people grumbled and complained about this man because he did not act like a chief.

The second man in the community who was chief at the time of the study decided on his own that he wanted to be chief. Upon returning to the village after a period of time laboring for his Brazilian patron, he announced to the people that he wanted to be chief. After an early morning public discussion, they agreed to have two chiefs in the village. Being more aggressive than the other man and more interested in group activities, this man satisfied the people by calling more frequent feasts and by organizing public activities that provided entertainment and other benefits for them.

Each of these men became chief because of a negotiated agreement between them and the people in the community. When the second man began to exercise his leadership, the first man accepted this fact without grumbling and continued to pursue his own personal activities with greater freedom. Not feeling pressured to lead in public activities, he could go about hunting, fishing, collecting latex, and other personal business.

The primary source of recognition and authority in a Deni community is that of skill. If a man is ineffective he is criticized and even scorned within the community. In contrast, people express admiration for an individual who is skilled as a hunter or who can organize people to get things done that benefit the whole. Authority is a matter of reciprocal granting of power among people. Individuals participate when they desire to do so and refuse when they have other interests that are of higher priority to them. Each individual maintains independent authority over fields and other resources. The people individually give their loyalty to the chief when they see it is to their advantage to do so. They can just as easily withdraw that loyalty, move to another village, or just refuse to participate in his activities, if they are dissatisfied with his leadership.

Mission/National Conflicts

Corporate versus Bureaucratic Decisions

The chapter opened with a case study of the Surinam Javanese pastor in conflict with his Bible translation co-workers. The pastor's missionary colleagues questioned his leadership, suggesting that he was unwilling to delegate authority. At this point we can see readily that the conflict arose between people who come from two distinctive social environments. The guest leadership operates from a weak B-Bureaucratic social environment, in which task orientation and skill authority are the primary basis for organizing work. The Javanese pastor, in contrast, is operating in a C-Corporate environment, in which authority based upon power given to him by the members of his congregation and upon a hierarchical structure that concentrates power in that leader is delegated only with great care and caution. The Javanese pastor recognizes that the unity of his group depends very much upon the loyalty of the people to him, as well as to one another. As new converts, who for the most part did not have extensive social ties before they joined as believers, their relationships formed around a nucleus of fellowship activities and pastoral leadership.

The corporate solidarity of the new church grows out of expectations spawned in the villages from which most of the members originate. Outside of the city, villagers see themselves as a corporate group, with a high degree of commitment to one another. The whole village attends a funeral. To build a house, the men gather to work and the women prepare food to feed them. Families share food from their respective gardens, and mutual labor and support at births, marriages, and other key family events. Village Javanese emphasize harmony, togetherness, and commitment to group goals.

Members of the city church struggle with the tensions created by their conversion to Christianity. By the mere fact that they live in the city, they have broken from the corporate villages of their childhood. Yet family and village ties remain as strong pulls upon them. Acceptance of the Christian faith has created further strains with family members, and some have been ostracized for their public baptism and proclamation of faith. The church provides a new corporate community, a new group of "kin" with whom they may express harmony, loyalty, and mutual support.

The pastor, taking the power allocated to him by these people, has built community through the many celebrations and social and spiritual events that are part of their worship and fellowship. At the same time, he is very careful not to delegate too much power to individuals who represent segments of the larger group. These younger men, who are his disciples and future co-leaders, are not in his estimation ready to take over the major responsibility of molding this group into a cohesive whole. A perfectionist in personality, he retains tight authority over the whole and carefully supervises the work of each of these individuals. The corporate values and needs of these Christian converts are well served as he creates a tightly knit church community, united through his personal control.

Whereas the pastor is preoccupied with the corporate unity of the church, training the persons who work under him and nurturing them to assume positions of leadership, his guest colleagues are task-oriented and concerned about getting the job of translation done on a time schedule that they themselves have determined. These different presuppositions have led to tension between the pastor and his missionary colleagues. They work from an expert/trainee model, whereas he operates on the basis of a senior pastor/junior lay leader framework. The elder/younger dichotomy in Surinam Javanese culture sustains the pastor's leadership. He holds authority and the younger men serve in positions of prolonged subordination to his leadership and control. The guest staff, in contrast, working from the expert/trainee model, see the training as just a matter of time. Once completed, the individual should be released to do the job. Training in the Type B society takes a limited period of time, after which the student assumes a role at least of some equality with the master teacher.

Delegated versus Granted Power

The conflict between Koop and the Deni chiefs involved different understandings of power and administration. Koop was working on the supervisor/worker model drawn out of his North American social environment. The Deni chief, in contrast, recognized himself as a spokesman for his peers. He understood that the power that he had was granted to him by the good will of his villagers and that if he did not provide the resources that they demanded he would lose that good will and his power. Koop, in contrast, was looking at the Deni chief as his delegated supervisor to oversee the work. He expected that as supervisor the chief would pay according to the amount of labor that the workers had completed and that he would treat them fairly so that those who did not work, or those who worked only to say they had contributed, would be given less pay.

The Deni chief was unable to understand or to operate upon the supervisor/worker model. He took the goods given to him by Koop and as peer spokesman he presented them to the people. They in turn took what they liked and as much of it as they could, according to their own personal wishes. This became a source of frustration for Koop and those Deni who had not received anything in the distribution.

Technically Qualified versus Corporately Qualified

The final case study in this chapter is that of another translation team working with a team of Aukan mother tongue translators. In this situation the leaders of the translation team desired to get support from the local church in Paramaribo for the Aukan Bible translation. More specifically, they asked these churches to provide partial support for the salaries of these mother tongue translators. The elders of these churches resisted the missionary proposal. They complained that the young men who were working for the translation organization were unproven as leaders. They said that they had not worked for or contributed to the continuing ministries of the local congregations.

As the translation team explored the opposition to these young men they discovered that the pastors themselves were not paid by members of the local congregations. Only the senior pastor in the First Church in Paramaribo earned a salary. All of the other pastors gained their income through full-time jobs in other sectors.

The elders saw themselves as committed workers. They saw these younger men as only casually interested in the ministry of the church, and primarily interested in gaining a salary. They recognized that these young men were educated, bilingual, and able to do the translation work. However, they did not see them as committed members of the church who were worthy of earning a salary. Further, comparing their own ministries to that of these younger men, they asked why it was that these men could not contribute their time for Bible translation as they contributed time for church ministry.

The conflict between the translation staff and the Aukan pastors was based upon different assumptions about authority. The translation organization was employing these young men because of their skills and expected that the church would be willing to help support them for the contribution they were making to the future of Aukan churches. The pastors, in contrast, saw these young men as part of their congregations and as part of a larger group of people who were participating in a total ministry. Since only the senior pastoral staff received salaries, to pay these young men for church work seemed totally out of line. Furthermore, they believed the mission organization should pay these men on the same basis that the government paid people for labor. If the church were to support such projects, they would do so only after the young men had earned their trust and support. All of the leaders in the church had received their assignments because of their faithfulness and long-term (ten-year) commitment to the group. These young men had not demonstrated either faithfulness or long-term commitment and were therefore not qualified for the support of the church community.

The conflict between these two groups of people grows from distinctive social environments and expectations regarding authority. The mission organization operates from high grid, B-Bureaucratic social assumptions, whereas the Aukan church operates from low grid, D-Collectivist assumptions. For the Aukan technical qualifications carry little weight, whereas technical skills are mandatory for translation work. The mission felt that the Aukan church should support the translation project because it was for their benefit; the Aukan measured benefit primarily in terms of evidence of commitment to group goals.

But Doesn't the Bible Say? . . .

When I have presented this material to missionary candidates, or in workshops with missionaries in the field, someone inevitably raises the question, "But doesn't the Bible say some very specific things about leadership and the church?" My response to this is "certainly." The Bible says very much about leaders, about the church, and about authority. The question is, what does the Bible say about leaders and authority? Should churches be organized according to a scriptural model, and if so what is it? Is there a "correct" structure taught in the Scriptures?

The first important fact for us to understand is that the church is always founded in an existing social context. The church in Jerusalem grew up in the midst of rabbinic Judaism and as such reflected much of its social context. The churches in Antioch, Ephesus, Corinth, and Rome were established in very different social and religious contexts from that in Jerusalem. It is evident as we read the letters of Paul that each of these social and religious contexts exerted significant pressure on these newly founded churches. Paul's discussion in Romans of the plan of God for Gentiles and Jews concludes that "God has bound all men over to disobedience so that he may have mercy on them all" (Rom. 11:32). Paul then admonishes the Roman Christians not to "conform any longer to the pattern of this world." What does it mean to not conform? If we are not to follow the pattern of the world, is there a pattern we are to follow? Is that pattern elaborated in the Scriptures?

Through the grid/group model we are able to identify four distinctive patterns of authority that are found typically around the world. If we can interpret Paul's comment universally, then Christians are "to be not conformed" to any and all of the social environments that we find in the world. From the evidence presented thus far, it should now be clear to the reader that a social environment exerts significant pressure on individuals in any given society. Individuals are pressed by people around them to conform to the values and relationships that are approved in that social setting. From the cases that we have just examined it is evident that both missionary and national operate in conformity with their own social environments. Their frustrations with one another grow out of their inability to break out of their own social environments. They are unable to accept the values and patterns in the differing social environments where they work. In fact, conflicts between missionaries and nationals arise because each brings to their relationship values and authority expectations that arise from the context in which they have lived for much of their lives. In spite of Paul's pleas that Christians should not be conformed to the pattern of this world, Christian leaders, missionary and national alike, have difficulty thinking about relationships in any other terms.

What does the Bible say about social environment? First, Scripture focuses not on factors of social environment, but rather on the motives and actions of people within social environments. Jesus illustrates this most graphically in his dialogue with the Pharisees about their customary eating habits (Luke 14). Noting that the guests picked the places of honor at the table, Jesus did not criticize them for having high and low places, but rather criticized their motives to obtain public honor. He did not criticize his host for having friends, relatives, and rich neighbors over to dinner, but tells him that in so doing, he has already achieved his social reward. Jesus did not criticize the high grid social environment, but rather challenged these Jews to live within that environment in a unique and different way, having a humble attitude and compassion for the helpless at the bottom of the grid.

At the same time, Jesus and the apostles taught members of the new church to submit to the existing authorities. Jesus commanded his disciples to pay taxes to Caesar and he himself submitted to the authority of the chief priest and the governor, Pontius Pilate. Paul commands Christians to submit to governing authorities (Rom. 13:1) and to pray for all secular authority (1 Tim. 2:2).

What does the Bible say about leaders and authority? David W. Bennett (1990:169–83) notes that the terms "leader" and "leadership" do not appear in the Gospels. Rather, the profound emphasis in these texts is on "following" rather than leading. The terms that Jesus used to describe his followers, such as "witness," "servant," "salt," and "disciples," expand our understanding of the nature of leadership in the Christian church. Jesus was very clear in stating that his kingdom was not of this world, that his disciples were in the world but not of it. His disciples were called out of their social environment and, after an extended period of training, sent back into it to be "salt" and "light."

It is clear from the references to authority in the Gospels that Jesus had special authority from the Father. The Jews noted that he taught as one having authority, and he proclaimed himself to have the authority to forgive sins and to cast out demons and unclean spirits. In Matthew 28:18 Jesus proclaims that "all authority in heaven and in earth has been given to me." Paul picks up the same theme in Ephesians 1:21 and Colossians 2:10, proclaiming Christ head over every authority and power.

"Independent power" in the church belongs exclusively to the Lord Jesus Christ. The apostles had no power of their own, but only that which was been delegated to them by the Lord himself. Jesus gave the Twelve authority to drive out evil spirits, to heal disease and sickness, and to make disciples and teach. The Lord appeared directly to Saul, and then through a messenger, Ananias, commanding him to carry his name before the Gentiles and their kings and before the people of Israel. Paul declares that his authority as an apostle comes directly from Jesus Christ (Gal. 1:1). The leadership of the apostles in the church is thus characterized as "followership," men who have been touched directly by the Lord Jesus Christ, who have been called to follow him, and who have received "delegated authority" to lead others to become followers of Jesus.

The Gospels record the process by which Jesus discipled the Twelve as "apostles in training," and the Book of Acts documents how these apostles provided leadership for the early church. The sense of "delegated authority," evidenced by the filling of the Holy Spirit (Acts 2:4; 6:8; 10:47) and witnesses of the fact of the resurrection of Christ in fulfillment of the Scriptures (Acts 1:4; 2:32; 5:29–32), pervades the Book of Acts. The apostles were Christ's emissaries, teaching new believers and further delegating authority in the growing church to mature believers, "full of the Spirit and wisdom" (Acts 6:3), to serve the leadership needs of the local fellowship.

The "delegated authority" for church leaders in Acts 6 was derived from their relationship with Christ, the Holy Spirit, the Scriptures, and the apostles. Mature men, filled with the Holy Spirit and wisdom, were selected by the congregation and anointed by the apostles (Acts 6:3, 6) to carry out the work of overseeing the distribution of food. The source of "delegated authority" in the church is universal, and constitutes a kingdom principle for leadership in the universal church, but the process employed to confer that authority grows out of the social environment. In Acts 6 the church was suffering growing pains, and the D-Collectivist social structure was unable to cope with the strain. The act of the congregation, selecting among its members and allocating authority to them, was routine social process and the only legitimate way in that social context to select new leaders.

Should churches be organized according to a scriptural model, and if so, what is it? Is there a "correct" structure of authority taught in the Scriptures? Many books have been written on this subject and it would be extremely naive to think that we could address this issue in a substantive way in just a few short paragraphs. Many of the arguments for church structure and authority come from texts in the Book of Acts and in the pastoral Epistles. Many books have been written on pastoral leadership and new studies appear each year. Rather than attempt to address the vast literature on this subject, I will present my position on the issue briefly and wait for another time and place to elaborate more fully.

I believe the Scriptures teach kingdom principles that apply to the structure of the church in any social environment. The first of those principles is that "independent power" in the church belongs to Christ, and to him alone. No church leader has independent power and authority to control knowledge, people, and resources. The second is that Christ delegated to the Twelve "apostolic authority and power," from which they led the early church and, empowered by the Holy Spirit, gave to us the New Testament Scriptures. These same apostles delegated authority and power to subsequent generations of leaders, "full of the spirit and wisdom," to serve the needs of the local fellowship of believers. This "delegated authority" is always subject to the prior authority of Christ, of Scripture, and of a living senior generation of mature leaders whose lives have evidenced "the spirit and wisdom" of servant leadership.

At the same time, I see around the world pervasive evidence that the pattern of leadership and authority in the church always reflects the social context in which the church is planted. The plurality of elders model taught in some seminaries works well among the Aukan people, who have a social environment that "allocates power" and authority to elders in their community. The episcopal model, with the bishop and council or presbyters, works well in the social environment of the Yapese, where high grid and high group are key features of their traditional social organization. Yapese have little difficulty adapting the council of presbyters, holding both "allocated" and "delegated power," since such councils are a common feature of their own social organization.

The authoritarian pattern of leadership common in Pentecostal groups, emphasizing "independent" and "delegated power," has fit well with the authoritarian pattern of Islamic societies such as the Surinam Javanese. Each of these patterns fails when people grasp social power, implicit in the relationships, rather than working in submission to the authority of Christ and the Scriptures.

In brief, a review of the history of the church with its many divisions and splits into denominations and subgroups illustrates the adaptability of the church to diverse variations in social environment in human societies. The argument here is that, beyond the kingdom principles outlined above, there is no "correct" structure of authority taught in the Scriptures. No single organizational model is mandated or taught in Scripture. To the contrary, the organizational structure of the early church adapted to changing social needs.

Beyond the issue of structure, many texts in the New Testament address very specifically the qualities, character, and expectations of church leaders. In Matthew 20 and Luke 22 Jesus discusses the issue of leadership with his disciples, noting that great men exercise authority over others, calling themselves "benefactors." Jesus declares (Luke 22:25–27) that "you are not to be like that. Instead, the greatest among you should be like the youngest, and the one who rules like the one who serves. . . . I am among you as one who serves." In the cases presented above the missionaries all too often appear as "benefactors" rather than as those who serve. This penchant grows not from an inherent carnality, but rather is derived from the structure and values of their B-Bureaucratic social roots, and the position of economic power that they so often have in relation to their national co-workers.

Obviously, Christian leaders must also exercise authority in the church. As we have illustrated in the cases above, there are many different forms in which this authority may be exercised. The critical issue regarding authority in the church is not the form that that authority takes, but rather the manner and the motivation by which the leader exercises that responsibility. As Bennett (1990) notes, the disciple is *under* authority rather than having authority *over*. Paul proclaims his authority as one for building up the brethren, not tearing them down or lording it over them. Paul calls Christians to be transformed by the renewing of their minds. Jesus calls disciples to identify with him, in his pattern of life and in his suffering. He does not impose a particular social system upon the church, but rather calls his disciples to follow him, the good shepherd who cares for the sheep.

8
Disputes, Conflicts, and Communication

To Command or to Serve?

ettling disputes is perhaps one of the most crucial areas for break-down in communication. All people have unwritten procedures for settling disputes, defined by their cultural context and prior experience. As a consequence, missionaries often find themselves in conflict with nationals over issues that are not clearly defined and for which neither the missionary nor the national clearly understands the cause or the consequence.

Case Studies

A Water Tank in Yap

During my field work on Yap I became involved in a dispute with the Yap Trading Company about money and labor on my water tank. In the initial plan to build a house, I contracted with the Yap Trading Company to hire a group of men to construct the house. That job proceeded well and both the laborers and I were satisfied with the arrangement. They completed the house within the time schedule that we had agreed upon and the money I paid was precisely stipulated in the contract.

Shortly after we moved into the house we decided to construct a water tank to provide a reliable supply of fresh water. The Filipino who was the head contractor for the Yap Trading Company agreed to construct a water tank for me. This time the men were paid by the hour rather than through a labor contract. This proved to be a disastrous mistake.

The two men assigned to build the water tank were clearly in no hurry to complete the job. From my perspective they took much too much time to bring the materials. When they actually began to work, they worked two or three hours during an eight-hour day. Of course, when the bill came for their labor I was charged for a full eight hours. I discovered, much to my chagrin, that it cost me more to have a water tank constructed than to build the whole house!

Being a graduate student at the time and working on a very limited income, I was furious. I went to the foreman at the Yap Trading Company and complained bitterly about the performance of these two men on this job. When I refused to pay the bill, the foreman told me I would have to talk to his boss.

The manager of the Yap Trading Company was a Yapese man who had earned his B.A. in business and who had returned to assume this management position. He was a man approximately ten years older than me, from a middle-level village in the Yap social structure.

I was angry and self-righteous. I believed that the laborers intended to cheat me and that the men in management were happy to let them do this so long as they were paid. Entering the manager's office with an aggressive, confrontive attitude, I approached his desk and after his courteous "What can I do for you," I unleashed a verbal barrage of indignation and anger at the work of these two men and the audacity of the Yap Trading Company to bill me for labor that they had not done.

The manager sat quietly and listened to my tirade. When I was finished he reviewed silently some figures on his desk and then offered me a price for their labor that was half of that which they had originally charged. When he asked if that would be agreeable to me, I was, of course, delighted. I had not anticipated such a reduction and was ecstatic to see this problem resolved so readily. I quickly wrote a check for the balance due and we agreed that the bill was paid in full. I left the office victoriously.

Nearly a year later, after I had mastered the Yapese language to the point where I could work without interpreters, I attended the annual sessions of the Yap district legislature. The manager of the Yap Trading Company was a member of the legislature and participated in the meetings that I was actively observing. At the end of these legislative sessions the legislature had a party and I was invited to be their guest. During this party I had the occasion to sit next to the manager.

Since parties of this kind generally involve the consumption of rather large quantities of beer, the manager had drunk enough to allow him to lose his ordinary caution and restraint. As I sat next to him he turned to me and began asking me questions. "Why do you Americans come here to study us?" He suggested that I was arrogant to come there, demanding my way and expecting that the Yapese should bow and scrape, doing what I pleased. He made it very clear that I was not the kind of person that he wanted to have visiting on Yap, and he would be very happy if I would leave. They had helped me in the legislature, not because I deserved it, nor because I was a good person, but rather because of my American status and my association with that power structure in their midst. He concluded that I was a typical American who came uninvited, pushed the Yapese around, insisted that things be done my way, and had no sincere interest or concern for the people themselves.

At that moment I realized that the confrontation nearly a year before had produced an enemy and stimulated significant animosity and hostility toward me in the society. My behavior in that setting had not been appropriate, and had generated strong negative feelings toward me. By this time, having learned more about Yapese society and social relationships, I recognized that I had indeed been pushy and aggressive, and merited all of the negative approbation given to me. When I tried to apologize, it was of no avail. My character was evident and any excuses could never make up for my behavior on that occasion.

Only years later have I fully understood the significance of my actions and the inappropriateness of my behavior. The manner in which Yapese settle disputes and the manner in which they conduct themselves in conflict with one another are extremely different from that of my own social environment. My behavior on that occasion, no matter how justified in my own eyes, was totally inappropriate and unacceptable to the Yapese. The manager's judgment of my character was consistent within the context of his own culture.

Disputes among the Deni Indians

Upon arriving in a Deni village in the Purus River region of the upper Amazon in Brazil, I took up residence in a thatch-roofed house in the center of the village. The second night I was awakened at about four o'clock in the morning by loud shouting that seemed to be inside my house. I sat upright and, as I became oriented to my surroundings, recognized that the voice was coming from the neighbor's house just behind me. He continued to speak in a loud, argumentative voice for the next ten minutes. When he finally stopped talking another man responded from a house across the village plaza. His voice was much quieter but I detected an intensity in his response as well. Over the next hour I listened to people speaking back and forth from their hammocks in the early morning darkness.

At daybreak I left my house and walked across the plaza to the Koops' house. I asked him what all the commotion was about that early in the morning. To my dismay, he had slept through the whole thing and told me that he had long ago learned to ignore these early morning discussions. My curiosity would not rest, however, and I asked him to discover the explanation for this rather vehement early morning conversation.

Later in the day he told me that the man speaking right by my house was one of the two village chiefs. He was complaining about women in the village who continued to pester him for a black sticky substance used to glue feathers in their traditional headdresses and to manufacture other craft items. Frustrated that these women sat in the village while he worked in the forest, he resented their frequent requests to him and his wife for something they could collect themselves. He angrily refused to give any more glue to those who asked him. The other man in the village echoed his complaint and criticized those who had taken his things without asking.

After several days in the village I discovered that this early morning public confrontation was not at all unusual. One afternoon I observed a man sitting on the top step of his house, shouting vehemently at another man across the village plaza. Beginning as a monologue, soon the object of his scorn responded to him, and both of them carried on a loud public debate over the next hour. The first man accused the other of having an affair with his wife. The other man denied the accusation and they battled openly until both were exhausted from the dispute. During their argument others in the village from time to time gathered next to them and participated in the shouting match. The argument continued until all parties tired and disappeared into their houses.

Confrontation and Confrontation Avoidance

The two case studies above illustrate two distinct methods of handling social conflict. In the Yapese situation my open confrontation not only offended my Yapese host, it totally destroyed any possible relationship with that particular individual. My style of handling a dispute and managing interpersonal conflict was so offensive that I have not to this day been able to rebuild that relationship. In stark contrast, the Deni Indians in Brazil not only engage in open confrontation and conflict, but expect outsiders as well to express their frustrations and their grievances publicly. How can we explain such drastic differences in procedures for settling disputes? What is the nature of the social environments that characterize each of these societies, and what can we learn by a comparative study of such social environments?

The first obvious distinction in the two case studies above is the difference in the management of confrontation. Open confrontation is unacceptable in Yap society. The manager of the Yap Trading Company not only resented my open confrontation but was unable to respond until he was under the influence of alcohol. This is a common pattern in Yapese society; people avoid confrontation as much as possible until or unless they are drunk. To confront others when one is sober is inexcusable. People recognize that drunks cannot control themselves, and therefore excuse them when they do what is otherwise socially unacceptable.

The Deni, in contrast, handle conflicts by open confrontation. When individuals find fault with others in the village they demonstrate their displeasure publicly in face-to-face conflict. This conflict is not without rules; to the contrary, there are many social conventions that govern this confrontation.

These differences in approach to confrontation reflect differences in emphasis on the importance of the group as opposed to individuals. Yapese value the dignity of other persons, and seek to maintain good relationships within the group. The Deni are strongly individualistic and openly promote individual interests and rights.

Each of these societies takes a significantly different approach to individual vulnerability. Yapese people see vulnerability as a weakness (Lingenfelter and Mayers 1986:106); they exercise extreme care to protect the vulnerability of individuals and to avoid behaviors that provoke interpersonal conflict within the group. This is not to say they do not engage in conflict; clearly the Yapese have a long history of extragroup conflict. However, relationships within the group are carefully regulated and unity and solidarity of the group have extremely high value for Yapese.

The Deni, in contrast, do not hesitate to expose the vulnerability of others. Openly critical, they are willing to expose vulnerability (Lingenfelter and Mayers 1986:107–8). They denounce individual failures publicly and criticize one another in open debate over issues of importance to them.

The second key difference between the Yapese and Deni is the distinction between working through channels and engaging in face-to-face resolution of conflict. The Yapese define relationships hierarchically and manage disputes through the hierarchy. The Filipino foreman could not make a decision about the bill for my water tank. Instead, he asked that I go to his manager. My later understanding of the situation suggests that I should have sent a mediator to conduct my case with the manager. Such a person could facilitate a decision on my behalf without the intense alienation produced by my own open confrontation. Yapese pursue appropriate channels to achieve a favorable decision, applying pressure from the hierarchy to prod someone who may be obstructing, or to enlist support of someone who has the power to make a decision on another's behalf. Going through channels is the appropriate means of managing conflict in Yapese culture and society. A mediator works through those channels to bring about a favorable decision.

The Deni, in contrast, engage in face-to-face confrontation and negotiation. The concept of channels is completely alien in their social environment. Deni operate in a "web" of personal relationships and influence. Motivated primarily by their personal interests and guided by shared values of what constitutes public good, individuals negotiate their own disputes and draw upon the support of family, friends, and neighbors. When one's "web" of influence is weak, the individual may choose to flee from a conflict, rather than risk prolonged harassment by a stronger opponent.

These communication procedures and emphases reflect once again the influence of hierarchy and group in the social environment. The Deni value individual autonomy rather than group solidarity. The Yapese, in contrast, place every person in an elaborate hierarchy, and assert the importance of group conformity. These contrasting values are reflected in the procedures that are acceptable to these societies for communicating in situations of conflict and dispute.

High Grid: The "Chain" and the "Net"

At the top of the grid/group matrix we find B-Bureaucratic and C-Corporate environments, which emphasize hierarchy. These social environments have certain features in common and also significant differences between them. The case studies that we have considered earlier in the text once again provide a useful framework for exploring communication, decision making, and the settling of disputes.

The social environment of the universities in which I have worked is fairly typical of B-Bureaucratic settings (Table 8.1). The organization of the hierarchy is conceptualized as a "chain of command." Most organizations of this type have as a significant part of their organizational structure a hierarchical chart showing the offices that are at the top of the command structure, and all of those reporting to them in a continuously expanding chain of subordinate relationships. The chain is pyramidal in structure; a central office at the top has power over all of the offices beneath. Authority in this type of social setting is vertical. Information is passed through certain channels. If someone should have the audacity to go around the link that is above, people occupying the intermediate levels will become angry and frustrated with both the individual avoiding their authority and the higher officials who have allowed that person to engage in such practice. The integrity of the chain is based upon each link fulfilling its obligation to be subordinate to the link

Table 8.1
Value Profiles: Communication and Conflict Resolution

B-Bureaucratic (Faculty-B)	C-Corporate (Yap)
(high grid, low group)	**(high grid, high group)**
"Chain" of command	"Net" of command/consensus
Vertical authority	Vertical and horizontal authority
Support by authority/majority rule	Support by obligation, tradition, consensus
Conflict addressed by formal confrontation	Conflict avoidance or indirect confrontation
Adjudication, arbitration, win/lose result	Mediation/plea, restore peace result

A-Individualist (Deni)	D-Collectivist (Aukan)
(low grid, low group)	**(low grid, high group)**
"Web" of influence	"Hive" of consensual authority
Support by public good and individual interest	Support by obligation, tradition, consensus
Conflict an open confrontation	Conflict avoidance or ritual confrontation
Weaker party withdraws or submits	Divination, spirit sanction, offerings

above and superordinate over the links below. Individuals who consistently refuse to go through channels may be subjected to severe social criticism and punitive action by other members of the system.

Individuals who occupy offices in the chain of command gain support from the authority figures over or under them, or by appealing to a decision of the majority of those who are part of the structure. The concept of "authority rule" refers to how people in the structure legitimize their actions by reference to their job descriptions and to the rules and procedures by which the chain structure operates. The concept of "majority rule" refers to how people within a structure support and act upon decisions made by a majority of the group; the majority carries power and legitimacy for the structure. People will justify changing a rule of authority on the basis of the decision of the majority.

In a college setting conflict is most frequently addressed by formal confrontation. Individuals who have grievances take them to officials within the chain of command who have authority to arbitrate. Usually individuals who engage in conflict desire a win/lose decision. Each individual attempts to gain a favorable decision and feels that they have lost if the decision is made against them. A faculty member who desires promotion must apply according to structural rules: the power to make that decision, however, lies with someone in the vertical hierarchy who has the authority to promote or to deny promotion. Those individuals and committees arbitrate such decisions and their ruling either confirms the faculty member's decision to apply, or rejects that decision and thereby makes that person a loser. People who feel they have been treated unjustly may appeal their decisions and seek further arbitration.

While Yapese society shares the preoccupation of hierarchy and channels, the importance of group in its social environment creates a significantly different version of communication and decision-making processes (see Table 8.1). The Yapese hierarchical structure is more like a "net" than a "chain." While a net has some of the characteristics of the pyramidal chain structure, cross-linkages yield distinctive variations. In the overall structure of the Yap Islands there are approximately one hundred villages; fourteen villages occupy the top rank in a parallel structure. Underneath these fourteen high villages are another twenty or so villages of noble rank, which are also key players in political relations. Underneath these noble villages are approximately fifty more common villages. Beneath them are chief servant and serf villages. The "net" organization operates on parallel as well as vertical relationships. The parallel or horizontal links bring together villages and leaders of the same social and political rank.

Authority on Yap, then, is one of both vertical and horizontal relationships. The Yapese describe the links between these different communities and leaders as *tha* or strings. These strings link villages and titled estates in both vertical and horizontal planes. Unlike the chain concept in American bureaucratic organizations, information in the Yap system can travel both vertically and horizontally. The Yapese find it not only appropriate to go around someone who is blocking them, but have in fact appropriate means of circumventing individuals and offices that are obstructing them. Going through channels on Yap means utilizing both vertical and horizontal relationships to accomplish objectives.

The mechanisms that govern relationships in this society are primarily the obligation of hierarchy, the traditional relationships between villages and local estates, and the desire that people make decisions by consensus within a group. Each of the titles in a Yapese village has certain traditional obligations and authority. Individuals who hold these titles are expected to fulfill their obligations and abide by the traditions that they have inherited. Leaders and elders make decisions for the community and for the settlement of conflicts by consensus; without consensus they delay or defer decision. As a consequence, people in

Yap rarely make decisions in public meetings. Almost all decision making follows lengthy periods of informal discussion within the community. When the leaders sense that the people have reached consensus on the matter, or that they have support of a large enough group so that those who disagree will not voice their objections, they bring the matter to the public. Once an issue is raised in a public meeting only the most indiscreet individual or a public drunk would dare to object to the decision of the leaders. It is because of this that leaders very carefully seek the support of the people, and have assurance of consensus before they bring matters to the public.

This pattern of indirect discussion and communication is particularly important in the settling of disputes. Yapese will avoid open conflicts with people in their own group at almost any cost. When conflict does erupt it is usually between people who are in the same village or in neighboring villages who do not belong to the same family groups. People will not often directly confront those with whom they are in conflict. Instead, they will send word by a relative or by a friend that they have been injured and intend to pursue this matter until it is resolved. Such an announcement cues the other parties that mediation is necessary. When conflict occurs within a village or another social group on Yap, mediation is almost always the tactic taken by people within the group. Not all individuals wish to have a conflict mediated because the process generally leads to restoration of peace in which everybody and nobody wins. The purpose of mediation is to allow the guilty party to plead for mercy from those who have been offended. People exchange traditional shell or stone valuables and the injured party must accept the shells or stones and the apology or plea of those who have caused the injury. While mediation restores peace and maintains the unity of the group, individuals suffer loss, usually without restitution.

Low Grid/Low Group: The "Web" of Influence

The Deni reflect a low grid/low group social environment in which hierarchy and regulated communication of information to others are insignificant. The Deni Indian chief has no hierarchical influence, but rather is first among equals. Lacking authorities, and anything resembling either a chain of command or net of consensus, Deni operate upon a "web" of relationships and face-to-face negotiations. The best that a Deni Indian chief can do is to acquire authority through personal influence.

Individuals gain support for personal goals and interests through kinship relationships with others and through relationships of mutual interest. Individuals who engage in regular economic and social exchanges often support one another during situations of conflict.

In spite of thoroughgoing individualism the Deni hold common beliefs about the public good. These ideals define appropriate behavior for people within the community, and people use them as standards of measurement against which the behavior of others in the community are judged. The Deni value "good talk," and sharing that which they have gained through hunting or farming in the community. When individuals violate these standards of public good people exert social pressure upon them to conform.

Conflict in the Deni community is carried out by open confrontation. People do not hesitate to vocalize their personal interests and to attack those with whom they have disagreement or dispute about violations of their personal interests. In such open confrontation very often it is a matter of the strong overpowering the weak. Strength may be demonstrated by a person standing behind someone and arguing on that person's behalf in a public dispute or by a show of public support because an individual's case represents the public good.

Deni conflict is governed by significant rules of procedure. To keep the conflict from erupting in violence individuals take positions at some distance from one another. If a man wishes to fight with his wife he will leave his own house and go across the village plaza to a friend's house, stand on the top step of his friend's ladder, and shout at his wife across the plaza. The wife, in turn, will shout from the top step of their house. The argument will proceed back and forth across the central plaza. Individuals in the community who support either the husband or the wife will come and join in chorus with them. A man may join the husband on the steps and shout across the plaza at the wife. Other women in the community may join the wife, walking up into her house and standing with her, or sitting on the steps and taking her part.

After a public shouting match individuals may challenge one another to a ritualized wrestling match in the village plaza. This is particularly common between people of the opposite sex, but may also happen between people of the same sex. I have observed Deni husbands and wives putting stinging ants in one another's hair, wrestling with one another in the village plaza, and working out their frustrations through ritualized conflict where everyone in the society can observe and protect them from excessive violence.

The resolution of such conflict is always face-to-face negotiation. Individuals fight to the point of exhaustion or until they agree to establish "good talk" once again with one another. If the conflict cannot be resolved the weaker party may withdraw to a safer place some distance from the village. Deni involved in conflict may travel an hour down river to take up residence with a large extended family of Brazilian peasants. These people feed them and incorporate them into their work force for as long as the Deni wish to stay.

We observed that people who withdrew from the village returned after several days, when they were certain that the intensity of the conflict had died down. The runaways came quietly back into the village and sought to establish peaceful relationships with the person in conflict. To accomplish reconciliation, they first communicated their desire to reestablish "good talk," and then resumed ordinary social and economic activities.

Low Grid/High Group: The "Hive" of Consensus

The Aukan are unlike the Yapese in that they do not have significant hierarchical relationships, and unlike the Deni in that they place strong emphasis on the group at the expense of the individual. Their social environment is analogous to a bee hive, in which everyone has similar work, individuals are not distinguished from one another, and the collective has far greater value than the individual. The ancestors constitute the ever-present "queen" of the hive.

Unlike the Deni, Aukan elders are recognized as social leaders. These senior men and women hold the knowledge and traditions of the community and act as defenders of the communal good. As we have discussed in earlier chapters, the Aukan have an authority structure based upon a coalition of consensus among the members of the society. No one individual has the power to command or direct. However, those individuals who are the captains and the elders articulate the consensus decisions of the group.

Like the Deni, the Aukan have a strong sense of public good. They have clear standards as to what is desirable and appropriate for the good of the community. These ideas of public good are much more carefully defined than in Deni society, and the boundaries and interests of the group are more clearly articulated. Among the Aukan, people subject individual interests to the control and over-riding interest of the group. Those who choose to violate group norms may be excluded permanently from the group. Unlike the Deni who come and go, settling with one local group or another at their personal pleasure, the Aukan have a clear, strong identity with their local community and must abide by the standards of public good to continue their membership within it. Individuals gain support for their personal interests by demonstrating their commitment to the public good and to the interest of the group as a whole. Decision making is based upon group consensus and individuals are expected to conform to these group decisions.

The Aukan, like the Yapese, avoid conflict as much as possible. Confrontation occurs through the mediation of diviners. An individual Aukaner will not directly confront another Aukaner in a public dispute. Instead, people allow social insults and injuries to lie below the surface of relations until they experience bad luck or illness. At that particular point in time the person who has experienced a disaster or illness will seek the counsel of a diviner to find out what or who is the cause of that particular problem. It is the diviner who is the broker for the settlement of conflict and dispute in Aukan society. The diviner determines through ritual what wrongs the person has done and which of the spirits or ancestors or the living are punishing this individual for wrongdoing. Illness, disaster, and other misfortunes are all punitive actions from the perspective of the Aukaner.

Biblical Perspectives on Situations of Social Risk

When missionaries leave their homes to serve in cross-cultural settings, they inevitably encounter people and cultures in which the patterns of decision making and the processes of communication and settling of disputes are significantly different from those in their home cultures. When missionaries move out of their social environment into a new one the differences of structure and relationships are certain to provoke conflict and stress. We have already seen that distinctive social environments carry with them very specific expectations, procedures, and processes for decision making and settling disputes. The case studies with which we opened this chapter illustrate how Westerners fall into significant misunderstandings in their relationships with non-Western people. Does Scripture provide guidelines by which we can approach the resolution of conflict?

Many missionaries with whom I have worked in the third world context derive their structures for communication and processes for handling disputes from their personal, cultural background and through interpretations of Scripture derived from those roots. The typical pattern for conflict resolution is the high grid/low group interpretation of Matthew 18:15. The missionary interprets this text as a universal process without reference to the social environment in which the command was given or to the social environment in which it is to be applied. Usually the command, "If your brother sins against you, go and show him his fault, just between the two of you" is interpreted as a command to confront, face to face and privately. No other passage of Scripture is relevant, no other references are considered, and the missionary attempts to put this into practice in any social environment encountered. When the personal confrontation fails, the "authority rule" strategy implied in the statement to "take one or two others along so that every matter may be established by the testimony of two or three witnesses" is employed. The final step is to bring the full authority of the church to bear on the matter in a public and confrontational way.

Most evangelicals fail to see that this text is written to a specific group of people in a specific social environment applying universal kingdom principles for specific social action. Confusing procedure with principle and form with meaning, they attempt to resolve all situations of conflict with a culturally specific formula.

What are the key principles implied in this text that may be extended to any social environment? Is the form prescribed appropriate to the social environment in which the conflict occurs? How can a missionary or a national believer live a transformed life, consistent with this text, within the local social environment and culture?

The first kingdom principle is to exercise caution and wisdom in situations of conflict by restricting the scope of the disagreement to "just between the two of you." In the Old Testament Wisdom Literature, we find many proverbs instructing people to exercise caution. "Do not accuse a man for no reason" (Prov. 3:30); "It is to a man's honor to avoid strife" (Prov. 20:3); "What you have seen with your eyes do not bring hastily to court" (Prov. 25:8).

The second principle is to restore relationships with those with whom we have disagreement. Later in Matthew (22:39) Jesus affirms the centrality of the Old Testament command to "Love your neighbor as yourself." This command is repeated numerous times in the Epistles, and Paul reminds us to "Do nothing out of selfish ambition or vain conceit, but in humility consider others better than yourselves" (Phil. 2:3).

The third principle is to humbly rely on the counsel of others, rather than on personal judgment. The effect of bringing "two or three witnesses" is to invite their counsel as well as their support. James writes that we are to be quick to listen, slow to speak, slow to anger (James 1:19). Paul admonishes us to "Be completely humble and gentle; be patient, bearing with one another in love. Make every effort to keep the unity of the Spirit through the bond of peace" (Eph. 4:2–3). We are warned against quarreling about words (2 Tim. 2:14) and that jealousy and quarreling are products of worldliness (1 Cor. 3:3).

As I have illustrated in the opening case study in this chapter, face-to-face confrontation, even done privately, destroys the unity of the spirit and the bond of peace in Yapese society. In Yap to use the literal social procedure defined in Matthew 18 accentuates quarreling and strife rather than eliminating it. Certainly I did not consider the Yapese manager better than myself and I obviously failed to exercise caution and wisdom in that social environment. The outcome of my behavior was a relational disaster.

A classic illustration of mediation techniques for restoring peace is described in 2 Samuel 3. Abner first sent a messenger to David asking him to make an agreement of peace. David responded that he was open to such a measure, but only if Abner returned his wife Michel to him. David sent a messenger to Ish-Bosheth demanding Michel, and Abner saw to it that Michel was returned to David in spite of the weeping protests of her second husband. Once David had received his estranged wife, he sent a messenger to invite Abner to his palace. David prepared a feast for Abner and his twenty men and a contract of peace was confirmed between them. David sent Abner from his presence with a commitment to continuing cooperation and political support.

The three ingredients in restoring of peace between Abner and David are the use of messengers, the presentation of gifts, and the feast of peace. Similar factors are present in the story of Abigail, who acts as mediator between Nabal and David (1 Sam. 25). David sent messengers to Nabal requesting a share in the harvest feast. Nabal rejected them and David declared war. Abigail discovered Nabal's stupidity and collected two hundred loaves of bread, two skins of wine, five dressed sheep, five seahs of roasted grain, a hundred cakes of raisins, and two hundred cakes of pressed figs; she then sent these presents to David. When she met him she bowed down before him and begged forgiveness for the wickedness of her husband and pled for peace between David and her family. David accepted the gifts and granted her request for peace.

Numerous other illustrations of mediation occur in the books of 1 and 2 Samuel. Jonathan acted as mediator for David to Saul; Joab acted as mediator for Absalom to David; and the wise woman of Tekoa acted as mediator for Joab to David. Even God used the process of mediation when he sent Nathan to David to confront him on the matter of Bathsheba. Nathan did not confront David openly, but rather told him a story, following the same pattern that the wise woman of Tekoa used on behalf of Joab (2 Sam. 14).

As we explore New Testament passages, seeking guidance for the management of conflict within the church and between church and society, it is essential that we understand the social environment of the early church. The management of conflict in the Jewish and Greek worlds described in the Book of Acts is characterized by formal confrontation, majority rule, and arbitration/adjudication of disputes. These features grow out of a rather classic B-Bureaucratic, high grid/low group social environment that typified the expanding, dispersing church.

The case of the conflict in Jerusalem, described in Acts 15, is a classic illustration of conflict management techniques. Following a public debate in Antioch with regard to whether Gentiles should be circumcised, a delegation was sent from Antioch to the apostles and elders in Jerusalem. Paul and Barnabas were part of this delegation. When they arrived in Jerusalem they gathered in a large assembly in which the opposing parties engaged in a discussion of the issues. The arguments were heated and the parties divided. On this occasion, Peter, the leader of the church over the first decade in Jerusalem, addressed the assembly and argued on behalf of Paul and Barnabas. Following his address

James, the formal leader of the council in Jerusalem framed the solution and articulated the conclusion. James was the arbitrator of the dispute on this occasion. He concluded the argument with a statement, "It is my judgment." His decision was written down in a formal letter and a delegation was appointed to carry it to the Gentile churches announcing the decision.

The process described in Acts 15 is one in which there is formal, open confrontation on an issue. People publicly criticized one another and argued openly about the issue. Mediation was not part of the process. Confrontation continued until objections were silenced and no further argument was allowed. James had the authority to arbitrate the solution, which was not questioned. While the objections were silenced, the conflict did not end. Many dissidents carried on their crusade for circumcision and adherence to the law throughout the Gentile world.

Those who desire to be effective Christian leaders must understand the social environment in which they practice ministry. The question of whether to confront, whether to use indirect or direct modes of decision making, or whether to define channels of authority or webs of relationship must be ascertained on the basis of social environment. Once the social environment is understood, Christians must examine how they may live a transformed life, employing kingdom principles, renewing the quality of relationships, and engaging the people in that society to discover the unity of the spirit and the bond of peace. Further, we must understand that the Book of Acts and the Epistles were written to people in a high grid/low group social environment, so that we are better able to distinguish process and procedure from moral value and ethical principle. It is not a procedure that produces transformed lives, but rather a relationship to Christ and the moral and ethical transformation that follows a commitment to him, to his teaching, and to his church.

Case Studies

To Confront or Not to Confront: The Missionary in Deni Society

Early in their ministry with the Deni, the Koops found that the Indians were extremely curious about the sexuality of their children. When their children went out of the house to the nearby toilet, Deni men and women often followed them and touched their private parts. This created a great deal of concern and tension for the parents. Anxious about their children's safety, they decided that the children must not go out alone. From that time on they confined the children to the house during the months of village living, and allowed them to go out into the public places only when accompanied by a parent.

This limited interaction between the Koops and the community was deeply distressing to the Koops. They found it hard to keep their children confined to the house for long periods of time, and yet were anxious about them being in the village. Concerned that their Christian testimony would be lost if they confronted the Deni, they resigned themselves to isolation, knowing no other way to resolve the problem.

The solution to the Koops' problem lay at their doorstep, but because of their own cultural values they were unable to utilize it. When I asked Gordon Koop why he did not confront the Deni openly and shout at them from his porch step about these matters he could not imagine that such behavior would be accepted nor was it in any way appropriate from his point of view. From his own culture of origin in Canada displays of public anger are un-Christian. However, this display of public anger was necessary to deal effectively with Deni. As long as he was unwilling to confront the people openly and to publicly declare his concern, they had no idea that their behavior was offensive to him. To get their attention he must stand at the top of his ladder and shout openly across the village at those people who had offended him.

Seeing that they were not able to bring themselves to shout at their neighbors, I began to look for an opportunity where I could illustrate the power and effectiveness of using this strategy for settling disputes. One afternoon we had been working on the airstrip. Nearly exhausted from the heat, I decided to go to a nearby stream and bathe. When I reached the bathing area nearest to our house I discovered that several women and children were already bathing. Since Deni women bathed in the nude, Gordon and I did not feel comfortable entering a stream where they were bathing. I turned around and crossed over the airstrip to find a more distant stream where I could bathe in peace. As I neared the second bathing area I heard the voices of women and children coming from the water. In my frustration I decided that this was an opportune time to test my hypothesis about conflict resolution. I began to shout at the top of my voice in English, which of course the Deni did not understand. I complained that the women were lazy, that they spent hours in the afternoon bathing while the men were hard at work on the airstrip. Feeling gratified with at least the opportunity to shout in my frustration, I began a lengthy exhortation in English. Within two or three minutes, a Deni woman and her children hurried toward me on the path. In quick succession several others followed. Within minutes I had the stream all to myself, and sank with great pleasure into the cool refreshing water.

That evening, one of the women came to visit us. She recounted to Gordon the afternoon's incident with great delight and humor. As she told him how I scolded and scolded, she related how everyone laughed afterward and how at last they had begun to understand this foreigner. As Gordon related the story to me, it was clear to both of us that my shouting had not in any way damaged our standing in the community, but rather it had enhanced it.

Indirect Decision Making: The Power
of Contextualized Behavior in Yap

Mediation is a key process by which Yapese settle disputes. However, similar principles operate for routine decision making in Yapese society. A few years ago I received a letter from one of my missionary friends on Yap who asked how he could be more effective in drawing Yapese men into leadership and decision-making roles in the local evangelical church.

I related to him an incident that I had experienced back in the late 1960s. I had not yet learned the Yapese language and was dependent upon my language teacher to translate for me. We were sitting in his home village in the local men's house where the men engaged in extended discussion.

One of the elder men initiated the subject by saying, "I have an idea but it will take a lot of tin." Another man in the meeting responded by saying, "It takes a lot of money to get tin. Only a few of us are working in town. Can you young guys help us buy tin?" The discussion then progressed around the subject of money, wage work, and buying tin. After more than a half-hour of dialogue on this subject, they concluded that they could not afford a lot of tin and that ended the discussion.

I asked my Yapese interpreter to explain the meaning of the conversation. He said, "Oh, it's very simple. The first man wanted to build a community house, but he couldn't say it. If he had stated that he had an idea of building a community house, no one in the meeting could have disagreed with him." He explained that everyone knew that the village needed a community house; it was humiliating to be without such a building. If he had stated this openly, the others could not disagree with him. The word would have immediately spread that the leaders in the village had decided to build a community house. In fact, they were not ready to make such a decision and if they had said "no" they would have been humiliated publicly. They would be further humiliated if they had said "yes" and did not build it.

I then suggested to the inquiring missionary that the standard operating procedure of Western missionaries is to present their agenda in public to church leaders. In the Yap evangelical church these leaders come from the same cultural background as those men in the men's house. They are extremely reluctant to disagree with a missionary, and feel embarrassed to reject what they know are worthy ideas for the church. As a consequence, they readily agree with the missionary's agenda, but often fail to support its implementation.

An alternative approach to decision making is to follow their example. For example, suppose the Yapese church was in need of a new paint job. The missionary might suggest that the church is looking shabby in comparison to the other churches in town. He can make this comment to several of the elders on a one-to-one basis rather than in a public meeting. As he makes his comment and listens to their feedback the idea is sown as a seed for them to think about and to discuss independently. If they themselves begin to see that this is a problem and decide they want to do something about it they will raise the issue at some future meeting. At that point, however, the decision will already have been made. When the elders raise an issue in a meeting they have already discussed it with one another and are ready to move ahead and mobilize the people to accomplish what they have proposed.

The inquiring missionary accepted my suggestion and began to try to work with Yapese leaders using this indirect decision process. After just a few attempts to implement this strategy he was sharply criticized by another missionary colleague. The colleague told him that he was being devious and dishonest. The critic argued that talking to people individually he was setting up a situation so that a decision would be made in his favor. The indirect strategy denied the Yapese a fair opportunity to disagree with him and to object to his point of view. The critic felt that the indirect process was a dishonest one and objected violently to my friend's proceeding in this way.

The disagreement between these two men reflects a basic misunderstanding of the issue. The critic accused the inquirer of predetermining the decision. In fact, the strategy of the critic had precisely that effect: by bringing an issue to the attention of the Yapese congregation in a public setting, their own cultural rules forbade disagreement and therefore assured an affirmative decision. Private dialogue allows them to think, talk, and even disagree with the missionary on a one-to-one basis.

The key to this behavior in Yapese society is the importance of consensus decision making in the group. Individuals may disagree with one another on a one-to-one basis, but when they are in a setting where the group process is at work, the desire and need for consensus are so great that individuals who have dissenting views will be silent, rather than risk the disfavor of the group.

Missionaries must be willing to risk their own values and concept of process. To follow Western ideas of process in Yapese society is to result in the breakdown of decision making and the loss of public support. To win the support of these people it is necessary to use the indirect decision model that they utilize for their own public process.

The Power Encounter: The Missionary in the Aukan Society

Louis Shanks relates this story of a particular event in the village of Manlobi in Surinam in which a young woman was confronted by members of the society for her antisocial behavior. Aki harbored bitterness against her mother, who she felt was responsible for the death of her sister by sorcery. Aki expressed her emotions in violent and disruptive behavior toward her mother and toward other people in her matrilineage. People in the lineage began to fear that the lineage ancestral spirits had reached their limit of tolerance for these continued outbursts of anger and antisocial behavior. One day they decided to exorcise the spirit inhabiting Aki.

Aki had earlier in the day thrown large rocks at her mother and expressed fury and rage in the community. In response the elders of the lineage section and the local priest determined to hold the exorcism at the foot of a newly constructed shrine. They dragged Aki to this place and the priest in an ecstatic frenzy encircled the young woman, castigating her about the evil she had done earlier in the day. Other lineage members also rebuked her and threatened her for this antisocial behavior.

Suddenly Aki broke away from the growing crowd and ran to the foot of the stairs going up into the Shanks' house. The Shanks felt deep sympathy for her and allowed her to enter their dwelling. At this, the priest and the crowd dispersed to plan the next stage of the exorcism.

That evening Louis walked to the residence of a Baptist Aukan evangelist and asked him to come to pray for Aki. The evangelist already knew Aki and had intensive conversations with her earlier about her relationship with Jesus Christ. When he returned to the Shanks' residence, Aki asked if she could pray to *Masaa Yesus*. Following prayer, Aki fell asleep in their cramped room, and enjoyed a calm and peaceful night.

At 5 A.M. the next morning everyone was awakened by a cry demanding that Aki come out and be ritually washed. The people claimed that an evil spirit was inhabiting her and the only solution was that she be ritually cleansed. At this point the Shanks pleaded with the presiding elder, asking if Lisa might accompany Aki as she underwent the ritual.

The priest agreed and so they all proceeded from the house to the bathing site where most of the villagers had already undergone ritual washing. The people stripped Aki to her underclothes and elaborately washed her body. After her ritual cleansing she was led to the newly erected shrine. Her hands were tied to the pole of the shrine. The priest warned her that she must undergo an ordeal to ascertain her guilt or innocence. Although she resisted violently, the priest forced her to drink an herbal concoction that would reveal her guilt or innocence. The priest then led her away to a house where divination continued to determine the will of the spirit with regard to Aki's antisocial behavior. After several hours of divining Aki was placed under "house arrest."

In the next few weeks Aki's emotional and physical health degenerated dramatically, to the point where she finally suffered a mental breakdown. At this point in time, since village remedies had provided no measurable success, the lineage head agreed to allow Aki to fly with the Shanks to the capital city for medical help. For several months both Aki and her mother lived in the city of Paramaribo, where they were nurtured and cared for by members of the Christian Aukan community.

When they returned to the village of Manlobi both were professing Christians. Aki's mother maintained a courageous and sincere testimony of what Christ meant in her life. Aki's mother died several months after her return to the village and Aki died approximately a year later.

The key expectation of the village community is that people will worship the village ancestors and perform the rituals necessary for their veneration and appeasement. The missionary strategy in this case was to remove Aki from the village and take her to the city for medical care and assistance. However, this did not settle the dispute or ease the pressure of the group upon Aki to conform to group standards and group values. As long as Aki was away from the group she and her mother were able to respond to the nurture and care of the Christian community. However, once they returned to the village they were again subjected to the intense pressure of the village society to conform to village expectations and values.

This situation seems certainly to be one of those in which a Christian "power encounter" may have been as appropriate a response as a visit to the Western doctor and a prescription of medical drugs for a cure. Antisocial behavior in Aukan society is always attributed to demon possession or some other form of social deviance. Individuals who do not conform must be cured of their ills and cure resides in supernatural events and procedures. The use of medicine and removal of the person from the social environment in which the problem is generated may provide temporary relief. However, the real cause of the conflict and stress resides in the social environment of the village and that social environment dictates the nature of the conflict and conflict resolution.

This is not to say that the Shanks could have done anything more than they did in those circumstances. They were not prepared by their own culture for power encounter of this kind, and they had not spent enough time in the village to know how to manage such power encounters in an Aukan way. Further, their biblical/theological training had not addressed such issues, or prepared them for such open spiritual conflicts with unbelievers. As a consequence, they would have been extremely ineffective in attempting to respond in any other way to the situation.

The point of this illustration is that the missionary must learn the context in which disputes occur, and must understand the social and spiritual dimensions of social conflict. Strategies for conflict resolution should grow out of the social environment in which the conflict occurs and the worldview of the people participating in the conflict. As Christians we may draw upon the social strategies that exist within that environment, but we must also bring the transforming message of the gospel and confront the worldview conflicts head on. To provide a medical/social solution from outside without the truth confrontation with those who are agents of the group results in only temporary pauses in the conflict and will not resolve either the conflict or the crisis for the individual member of the society. Such encounters require a biblical truth/power response, such as that employed by Paul against Elymas the sorcerer (Acts 13:9–11). After the church takes hold in such a community, the first major change will occur in the worldview of the people, as they respond to the gospel. That response in turn will bring about a restructuring of the social environment, along with new ways of managing social conflict.

9
Eating

A Window into Social Relationships

How should a missionary or cross-cultural field worker begin the process of learning a new social order? After grasping the basic skills of language, the field worker faces the more subtle yet challenging task of learning to understand the social structure of a community or neighborhood. All human societies and cultures define patterns of social identities and relationships that are foundational for interpersonal relations in each social context. Whether a society is rural or urban, people agree upon certain standards for social behavior and share patterns of structure and value that extend from family relations to public life and include the church as well as other kinds of social groups.

In order to study and understand the social order, we must identify social behaviors that yield insights into the structuring of social relations. One universal human activity that inevitably leads to understanding the basic structure of relationships is that of public eating. In every human society individuals must eat, and in every part of the world people engage in this activity on a daily basis. No social activity is more foundational and fundamental than the gathering, preparation, and consumption of food.

While people in every society and culture eat on a daily basis, their eating habits do not necessarily reflect larger aspects of social structure. However, in most societies public eating provides the observer with important information about the nature and structure of social relations.

Public Eating in Hong Kong

Hong Kong is a city of literally thousands of restaurants and the vast majority of these restaurants are Chinese. The people of Hong Kong spend a significant amount of time in any given week eating in public places. Each central shopping area in the cities of the New Territories, the British-ruled zone on the mainland opposite Hong Kong island, has at least one very large Chinese restaurant and some have two or more. Seating hundreds of people, each restaurant caters primarily to a local clientele, which returns quite frequently in family groups. A key social activity in these restaurants is *dimsum*, the Chinese version of American breakfast and British tea.

Outside observers may begin a study of Hong Kong society by observing restaurant clientele and behavior. If we begin our survey at one of the government low cost housing complexes in the New Territories, we find that the price and the atmosphere vary distinctly from restaurants that cater to a higher class clientele. For example, the table cloths in this restaurant are significantly worn, stained, and even torn. Customers dress poorly in contrast to those in the other high rise housing areas such as in the middle-class city of Shatin, and the price of food is significantly cheaper than in the Treasure Restaurant in the New Town Plaza in Shatin. This restaurant caters to poor people who must live in government housing. Social behavior in this restaurant is lower class social behavior. The management of the restaurant does not provide napkins. People who need to wipe their hands, do so on the table cloth.

Hong Kong people select different restaurants for different social occasions. My Chinese hosts, for example, took my wife and me to a variety of different eating places during our stay in Hong Kong. The type of restaurant chosen served as a social indicator. When we were welcomed as guest lecturers for the summer courses we were to teach, we ate in a very fine restaurant at one of the major hotels in Kowloon, one of the central shopping and commercial districts. The Chinese guests joining us for the meal were men with doctoral degrees who were significant leaders in the Christian schools of Hong Kong. The place chosen for our meal catered to people of similar or higher social class than our party.

The students in our classes took us to a Chinese restaurant to thank us for our contribution to their summer courses. This restaurant, while of a significantly higher level than the one in the New Territories at the lower class housing complex, was more modest than the restaurant chosen by the host principal and board members. While the students apologized for the patrons in the restaurant playing mahjong very loudly behind a screen near our table, they explained that the restaurant, reasonably priced, fit their particular financial abilities, and had a social atmosphere of quality, so that they felt comfortable to entertain us there.

Some of our Chinese colleagues took us to restaurants with lower class constituencies. They explained that they ate at these restaurants from time to time for financial reasons, ignoring issues of social class and structure. All of these men, involved in Christian service, spent their financial resources carefully, and chose very inexpensive eating places chiefly to save money. One of our hosts, introducing us to the wide social variation in Hong Kong, took us to Temple Street, known for its open air market and poor clientele, to a restaurant where we rinsed our bowls and chopsticks with hot tea, and the prices clearly catered to the poorest of Hong Kong. We were the only representatives of the upper middle class present.

The significantly different levels of social class in Hong Kong may be clearly seen in the constituency of public eating places. People who are laborers or street people with low incomes frequent the street restaurants in areas such as Temple Street. While poor people are not the only ones who eat at these places, they may not frequent restaurants of a higher class. Likewise the poor in government housing areas eat at the restaurants provided in the nearby shopping plazas. Wealthy or higher status people may come to these restaurants, but only on occasions when they are either looking for a cheap meal or showing visitors the diversity of Hong Kong's cultural and social life. People with small businesses or laborers with a more secure income eat at moderately priced restaurants in which social activities, such as mahjong, are encouraged and permitted. Upon formal occasions, such as weddings, people eat at the highest level restaurant they can afford. Upon our arrival in Hong Kong, our hosts took us to a restaurant that represented the level of prestige thought appropriate for visiting professors.

Public eating places in Hong Kong show very significant distinctions in social class and social relationships. To understand how Hong Kong people relate to one another, and with whom one can relate readily and freely, one needs only to examine the diverse eating places and identify with some degree of care and accuracy those people who frequently eat in these public places. These eating places allow the observer to identify the particular populations present, to determine the target population, and then to begin to formulate a ministry strategy.

Participant-Observation of Eating

The field worker whose objective is to learn the social order of a community may begin by seeking to identify the hierarchy and group expectations for eating establishments, situations, or contexts in the target culture. Once these factors are known, it is possible to investigate how people in the society participate in these different settings at particular times. Some useful questions include the who, what, when, where, and how of public eating activities that occur on a daily or weekly basis. What are the public eating customs and places for special family celebrations such as a marriage feast or some other lifecycle event? Where and how are distinguished guests from other places entertained?

As the observer explores patterns of public eating, the presence or absence of class and other factors of social difference will emerge. In hierarchical societies, people will move out of their class relationships only on special occasions when they seek either to impress those of the same class or to be hosts to guests who they feel are of a higher status than themselves. Generally, when people move outside of their own social setting they experience discomfort and feel intimidated by their surroundings.

The missionary who ignores issues of social class when targeting populations for evangelism and church planting invites frustration and even failure in those activities. Mixing people from different social classes and backgrounds is indeed the ideal for the church of Jesus Christ, but in the secular world people mingle across classes only when individuals themselves choose to do so. The high class professor may choose to eat in a street restaurant, but he does so primarily because it is economically in his best interest. He is not likely to sit down at a table with lower class individuals and socialize with them. He will separate himself from these people, being there only to obtain the food at the price he desires, and then moving back into his own social network.

The same principle applies to church planting and evangelism strategy. To ask a lower class person to teach people who are in upper class positions creates stress and conflict for both the teacher and the students. Just as the upper class person chooses to avoid lower class clients at a street restaurant, so will higher class people avoid church situations when lower class members are leaders.

Eating and Social Structure in the Gospels

The who, what, when, where, and how applied to texts on eating in the New Testament yield some fascinating insights into the social structure of Galilee and Judea at the time of Christ. In Luke 4:38–39, we find Jesus in the home of Simon, a member of the synagogue. Simon's mother-in-law is ill and Simon calls upon Jesus to help. Jesus rebukes the fever, and she is healed. She immediately waits upon Simon, Jesus, and others in the house. It is reasonable to assume that her waiting upon them included food.

The Gospels imply that Jesus was a frequent guest at Simon Peter's house and that the relationship that Jesus had with Peter, James, and John was a rather intimate one. Eating at someone's house in first-century Judea identified the guests socially with their host. Jesus, a guest by the mere fact of his presence, acknowledged that he was accepting the social class of his hosts and participating in their activities.

When Levi decides to follow Jesus, he invites Jesus to come to a great banquet at his house (Luke 5:27–30). The crowd that gathers at Levi's house are members of his social group, including tax collectors and others that the Jewish leaders labeled "sinners." The complaints of the Pharisees and teachers of the Law against Jesus are clearly related to his public eating practices. They ask, "Why do you eat with tax collectors and sinners?" Jesus' eating with these people implies his acceptance of and identification with them. Those of the ruling class are offended, since such an action is unacceptable in terms of their social norms and their religious doctrines and practice. The mere fact that they ask the question signifies the extreme importance of eating for social and religious identification.

Jesus provokes the Jewish leaders further by making it very clear that he has not come to associate with the ruling class, but rather to minister to those in need. Because of his desire to see these men and women repent from their sins and be restored in their relationship to God, he makes a conscious choice to eat with them.

Eating in the house of Levi makes a significant social statement to the Jewish leaders. The reaction of these leaders to tax collectors and sinners identifies a clear sense of hierarchy in Jewish society. The text is noticeably silent about Jesus eating with Simon Peter and spending time in his house. When Jesus goes to Levi's house, leaders respond in public outrage.

The pattern modeled by Jesus in the Gospel of Luke is instructive for the Christian worker. Jesus eats with a variety of people. We find him in the house of Peter, in the house of a tax collector, and in the house of a very important Jewish leader. How was it possible for him to move across such a wide spectrum of society? The teachers represented the highest level of the social structure. The teachers and religious leaders had Jesus in their home because he was equal to them and one with them. It was his stature as a teacher that opened to him this highest level of the social order. At the same time he was not bound, as they were, by the constraints of the social order, and thus they complained about him. He moved freely through the social order, eating at the highest and at the lowest social levels. Often a "holy man" or "holy woman" status will allow a person to move freely in the social structure, without assuming the social trappings of any level. However, the "holy" status has particular social and cultural expectations associated with it. Jesus knew what was expected, and lived that role, even while challenging beliefs, social values, and relationships.

In spite of the status that Jesus had as a teacher and a prophet, he rejected social privileges and trappings. He did not have a house, an income giving him prestige and power, or a position in the religious hierarchy. Jesus, like John the Baptist, chose to separate himself from the social trappings of his status, yet he retained the role of teacher and prophet. This is an important lesson for those in mission ministry. Oftentimes people confuse the social trappings of status with the reality of status. It is not necessary for the field worker to have an extremely expensive house and car to have high status. High status may be due to knowledge, reputation, and skill. A field worker may choose to live at an economic level that is distinctively different from others with the same status. This is possible in both the secular world and in the religious world. I have known individuals who have had very high status in American businesses, but have chosen to live in modest homes and follow a modest lifestyle because of their commitment to use their income wisely for the Lord Jesus Christ. Missionaries who feel that it is necessary to have social trappings confuse status with material holdings. Jesus was never denied his high status as master and teacher because he lacked material wealth. In fact, the rejection of that material wealth gave his message greater impact.

Luke 14 provides a rather lengthy discourse on eating, and a commentary by Jesus on eating in relationship to the structural arrangements of Jewish society. The passage opens with Jesus invited as a guest for dinner at the house of a prominent Pharisee. Jesus observes the behavior of other guests, and notices a general scramble among them to occupy seats of honor near to the host at that gathering.

As a participant-observer, Jesus carefully watches what people are doing and assesses the implications of their behavior. The example that Jesus provides in Luke 14 is absolutely crucial for effective cross-cultural ministry. Missionaries must be participant-observers, carefully studying events around them and assessing critically the meaning of social behavior for ministry.

In this particular setting Jesus observes the social relationships in the dining room. He identifies the fact that some seats are more highly valued than other seats. While this was not the first time that Jesus had observed such behavior among the religious leaders, the point is that he understands the social significance behind their actions. A missionary who goes into a cross-cultural setting can be no less observant and astute. We must have a basic understanding of social space, know how people allocate it for prestige and power, and understand when people are competing for places in those settings. The commentary that Jesus makes here would have been completely irrelevant if he had not diagnosed correctly the model of social space being utilized by the Jews and the interpersonal competition motivating guests at the dinner as they vied for seats of honor.

The parable that Jesus tells is a critique of personal motives and behavior, not of social structure. The text shows clearly that Jesus does not judge the social distinctions of seats of honor and seats with less honor. He does not reject the system as invalid; rather, he questions people's personal motivations. He teaches that they should not strive for the seats of honor, but should in humility take seats of lesser honor so that others present and in authority might honor them if they so desire. The message given to these people is not a message of change in their culture, but rather a message of transformation in their attitudes and relationships within that culture. Jesus calls them to actions motivated by humility and the esteeming of others better than themselves. He challenges them to take the low place, the humble place, rather than to exalt themselves above others in the social hierarchy.

Customary patterns of honored places at feasts is not unique to Jewish culture. Public banquets or dining rooms for mission organizations may have seats set aside for recognized leaders, or special services rendered to individuals in authority. For example, at a recent conference at which I was the speaker, the organizer of the conference insisted that my wife and I should not go through the line with other participants in the conference. Rather, we were instructed to take seats at the table and one of the hostesses prepared our plates and brought them to our table. The leader explained that we were so busy talking with people, they were afraid we would be left out and be the last to make it through the line. Therefore, to insure that we were fed appropriately they made these arrangements to serve us. Interestingly enough, we were not the only ones served in this way. Other leaders had the privilege of going directly to a table, and a hostess provided them with table service. Hierarchy and eating are social facts in many cultures in the world, including mission organizations.

In the same way, if we are to understand the instructions of Jesus in this text, we must recognize that the attitude of those who are being honored is the point of his message. He points to fundamental motivations; if their objective is to be recognized they are rebuked. If their goal is to follow the path of humility, then they have taken the Christ-like path.

Recognizing that eating customs make profound statements about social relationships and moral values, Jesus addresses the more routine public eating of people in Galilee and Judea. Luke 14:12 details the ordinary custom of Jews to invite friends, relatives, and rich neighbors to social banquets. Such social behavior is not unusual; in most societies a social gathering of people includes those who are kin and of the same social rank. More rarely people will invite the rich and prestigious, but seldom do people invite those of a lower social class. In societies where social ranking is important people love name dropping. It is much more advantageous to invite someone to your home or have a public dinner with someone who has a significant name than to have dinner with someone who is a criminal or homeless, or in some way or another a ward of society.

Jesus' instructions to these Jewish leaders reverse the common pattern and social practice; he challenges them to invite the poor, the lame, the blind, the lower ranking people in society. While such people cannot repay their hosts, Jesus promises that they will "be repaid at the resurrection of the righteous." Jesus contradicts the social practice and social expectations of these men. The advantages of inviting someone of a higher social status to a banquet are obvious. Clearly Levi benefited by inviting Jesus to his house. To have someone of Jesus' stature attending a banquet served to legitimize, or at least to enhance, the reputation of the host offering the dinner. It was for this very reason that the "righteous" leaders were so disturbed; in their eyes the behavior of Jesus diminished their reputation and stature as religious teachers and leaders.

In this particular text we discover the bottom—the other end of Jewish society: the poor, the lame, the helpless, and the blind. We have now reached the level below the tax collectors and sinners, people with whom few desire to associate. The circumstance in which Jesus makes these comments is significant; he is in the house of a very prominent Pharisee, at the top of society. While he accepts the social hierarchy, he pinpoints the callousness of these men, the hardened condition of their hearts, exposing their concern to retain power and the trappings of power over the command of God for compassion and mercy to those in need.

In Luke 14:21–23 Jesus returns to the same theme in the parable of the great banquet. A great man invited many guests—people of standing, of the same or a slightly lower level of social status, but who would be respected guests at his dinner. Several excused themselves, concerned about property, or engaged in business transactions, or preoccupied with the social transactions of marriage. When the servant of the master planning the banquet reported that many of the invited guests had declined, the master in anger sent the servant to invite the lowest strata of society—the poor, the lame, and the blind. After these came, and finding there was still space for more guests, the master sent a servant to bring in the poor and the lame from the country roads and the poverty-stricken areas outside of town.

Luke outlines for us, through Jewish eating customs, the key features of Jewish social structure. At the top are the religious and secular leaders, the teachers, and the Pharisees. Underneath this high strata of society we find the smaller property owners—the ones who own land, buildings, oxen, boats, and other economic resources. Below the landowners are the businessmen in disreputable professions—wealthy, but through means unacceptable in society, such as tax collectors, prostitutes, and others of ill repute. Another segment of society are bond servants or hired laborers who work for prosperous landowners. As members of their masters' households, they acquire a certain degree of standing and recognition because of the prestige of their master. Finally, at the bottom level are the urban and rural poor—the lame, the helpless, and the blind. They are the social rejects, the lepers, the discards of society.

The lesson of the parable in Luke 14 is that preoccupation with the economic and social demands of social life to the exclusion of fellowship with "the master" will result in the withdrawal of the invitation and giving it to those who are socially "less deserving." Jesus does not call for an overthrow of the social hierarchy; nor does he ask that the rich and the landowners abandon their lands and give them to the poor. He provokes them to question the values that lead them to an endless round of dinners for social ambition and reward, or to expend their energies for land, business, and social transactions. Rather, he calls upon them to pursue higher priorities—humility within the social order, compassion for those less fortunate, and attention to fellowship with the Father in heaven and with the people on earth for whom the Father has a heart of compassion.

The Social Environment of First-Century Jewish Society

The teachers and Pharisees of Jesus' day formed a well organized, cohesive power group in Jewish society. Throughout the Gospels we read of their regular meetings with one another, their public discussions, their public power, their eating with one another in private homes, and their organization of the final confrontation with Jesus that resulted in his crucifixion. In the Book of Acts they systematically organized opposition to the growing church. Nicodemus came to Jesus by night because he feared the group pressure that would be leveled against him. The evidence suggests that the rulers and the Pharisees had a strong, cohesive, high group society, and played high grid hierarchical roles within the group; they constituted a C-Corporate social environment. Throughout his ministry Jesus addressed many public sermons against the abusive power of this group (see Table 9.1).

The second major segment of society were the townspeople and property owners of Galilee. Peter, James, John, and Andrew came from lower ranking property owning families. They and their fathers owned houses and fishing boats, and they acted as masters with servants or hired men. Their family business was fishing, and they apparently

Table 9.1
The Social Environments
of First-Century Jewish Society

B-Bureaucratic	C-Corporate
(low grid, high group)	**(high grid, low group)**
Roman administration	Leaders, teachers, Pharisees
Roman legions	Property owners (Peter, James, John)
	Bond servants, hired laborers

A-Individualist	D-Collectivist
(low grid, low group)	**(low grid, high group)**
Low professions (tax collectors)	Jewish Zealots
Urban and rural poor (lame, lepers)	

worked jointly in support of their family interests. These men lived in the town of Capernaum, along the Sea of Galilee. They attended the local synagogue and their lives were integrated around the synagogue and the economy of the town of Capernaum. While these men do not appear to constitute a tightly integrated power block, as did the teachers and the Pharisees, they clearly worked together on a day-to-day basis and knew one another intimately from their daily economic life. The group cohesion among these property owners was probably as important and as strong as that of the Pharisees and teachers of the law, and they shared in the hierarchy of town and religious life. Perhaps because of the nature of their small town living they were even more intimately involved with one another in daily life than the religious leaders in Jerusalem, thus sustaining a C-Corporate social environment. When one of their group became acquainted with Jesus, the news about Jesus spread quickly to others in the community.

The bond servants and the hired men also belonged to the C-Corporate environments of their masters or employers. The bond servants lived with their masters, and served as integral members of their households. They participated in both the public and private lives of their owners. The hired men lived in the same communities, and while they were poor, they retained their freedom and lived as commoners in the community.

The fourth segment of society was the tax collectors and sinners. There was little group cohesion. These people were typically entrepreneurs who worked to become wealthy in their own right. While they recognized a certain amount of grid within their organization, tax collectors in general seemed to be independent entrepreneurs, willing to risk the displeasure and the criticism of the larger society.

These people were apparently unconcerned about public opinion and willing to risk the judgment and scorn of other members of society. Other people—prostitutes, thieves, and sinners—had relationships with the tax collectors, and perhaps took the same kind of risks. In fact, the tax collectors were considered thieves because they often extracted more from the people than they were legitimately entitled to take. These people did not conform to the pressure of the larger society, but rather stood apart, flaunting their personal autonomy and independence. In this sense they constituted a subsocial environment in which people valued individual freedom and the autonomy to become wealthy by "illegitimate" means. The other "sinners" in these categories probably had the same sort of independent lifestyle, and therefore they were rejected by the legitimate larger structure of society. More interested in forwarding their own individual careers than belonging to a group, they constituted an A-Individualist social environment, and were outsiders to both the Jewish and Roman societies.

The final segment of society was the rural and urban poor. These people had no external or internal hierarchy and formed no significant cohesive group. Isolated individually and collectively from other members of society, they lacked resources that might allow them to form a corporate identity, and competed with one another for the meager offerings obtained through almsgiving or other kinds of beneficence in the larger society. This is illustrated by the parable that Jesus tells of the owner of a vineyard who hired laborers to assist him. When he paid the workers equally, regardless of the time they had worked, they were frustrated and angry because they felt they had not been treated fairly. Having individual rather than group interests, they competed with one another for scarce income. Like the tax collectors, the poor survived in an A-Individualist environment. Without family or other support groups, the poor depended upon the charity of people coming to the temple or others who might have pity upon them.

The examination of eating practices and the analysis of data through the concepts of grid and group provide insight into the internal structuring of a society and its social environments. The practice of public eating allows the outsider to see the distinctions of hierarchy and group in action. The social setting of eating, the frequency at which individuals gather together for public eating, the social distinctions made between those with whom one eats and those with whom one does not eat, and the recognition given to individuals within the group when they eat together are all key factors in understanding grid and group interests.

10
Church Planting

A New Social Order?

One of the things that I have observed in visiting church-planting teams overseas is that new converts bond quickly to the evangelist but often fail to form relationships with one another. As a consequence, the problem of establishing a church becomes not only one of helping new believers mature, but also guiding them to discover one another and to build relationships. At times friends come to know the Lord together or a whole family responds to the gospel. On rare occasions large groups of people or a whole community embrace the gospel at one time. However, in urban settings very often it is individuals who respond to the gospel, and these individuals must somehow be molded together to form a church. How do we bring together people who may have been strangers and help them form the fellowship of a local church? By examining the life and ministry of Jesus, we may gain some insights into the strategy that he used to bring believers together.

The Social Context of Making Disciples

Jesus chose his disciples from diverse backgrounds, from both the C-Corporate environment of the larger society of property holders and the

A-Individualist environment of tax collectors and sinners. Jesus did not choose the Twelve from among the teachers and the leaders, the elite of that society. He knew that these people opposed everything that he had to say; his message challenged and contradicted their assumptions and worldview. Further, because of their group cohesion, social power, and commitment to their cultural system, they strongly resisted his message. The Gospels record that Jesus selected his disciples from other segments of society. The masters of knowledge rejected the call to become his disciples.

Peter, Andrew, James, and John were property owners. While they were not the least in the society, neither were they at the highest level of the hierarchy. They were people whom others in the society would not scorn or reject, yet people who were open to his message. He also chose tax collectors and sinners—people open to his message, who were also prosperous. Because they were social outcasts, their calling provoked much criticism against Jesus. Jesus did not select the Twelve from among the poor and the downtrodden in the society, perhaps because these people had no social power from which to serve as leaders. Acts 4 records how the believing landowners mobilized great support to carry on the ministry of the church after Jesus had departed into heaven.

While Jesus chose to devote his time and ministry to the Twelve, people selected from the middle strata of Jewish society, he did not reject people from other strata of society. He received Nicodemus, a Pharisee, readily when he came to inquire about Jesus' teaching. He accepted the rich young ruler, the teachers of the law, the Canaanite woman, the Samaritan woman and her townspeople; he was open to all who would receive his message. He fed the people, healed them, and had compassion on them, as sheep without a shepherd. However, it was neither the poor nor the Pharisees who were his choice for future leadership.

The example of how Jesus Christ selected and trained his disciples must be given serious consideration as church planters think about and plan discipling strategies. The men who were chosen as Jesus' disciples had to make significant changes in their lives. Peter, James, and John left their boats and followed Jesus. From that time on fishing was no longer their primary occupation or preoccupation; they had become followers of Jesus. Levi abandoned tax collecting for the higher calling, Simon left his political activism. For nearly three years these men committed themselves to a new group—a group of men who had no property and who depended upon several generous women to provide their meals and to pay for their general expenses. They became students in the traveling school of Jesus, the master teacher, as he went from town to town preaching, teaching, and ministering to those who were sick and helpless.

In essence, Jesus pulled these men out of their everyday social and economic life and drew them together into a completely new kind of group, a different social order. They gave up their property, their social standing, their security, and their family relationships, and for a period of time lived with him on a daily basis. They traveled together, ate together, and slept outside or in homes of friends. Their lives became totally entangled during this time period. Jesus created a temporary, but significant D-Collectivist social environment. His close followers gave up their previous status, their occupations in society, and committed themselves totally to being disciples.

Jesus understood an absolutely crucial fact of social life. He could not make these men into his disciples unless he took them out of their social structure and brought them into an intensive new kind of relationship with him and with one another. By encouraging them to leave their familiar surroundings and move out with him in his itinerant ministry, Jesus began the process of retraining them by modeling for them the life to which he was calling them. Only through this kind of intensive relationship was it possible to produce the kind of disciples to whom he would entrust his ministry.

People in diverse cultures in the world have accomplished the same goal in many different contexts and settings. A similar process is commonly employed in the training of missionary candidates before they go overseas. Often mission candidate schools require a similar separation and commitment, although most training programs are much shorter than the one that our Lord instituted in his ministry.

Eating together was part of the daily life of Jesus and his disciples. The Gospels record a few of these occasions. They also report the miraculous feeding of thousands. The account of the Last Supper is described in all the Gospels and in varying detail, as Jesus ate a final meal together with his disciples. The significance of that event was its finality; it represented the end of what had become a very ordinary part of their lives together.

To Make Disciples

The church at Pentecost was formed from the same dynamic as the group of disciples that Jesus drew to himself. The Twelve were drawn from the middle sectors of Jewish society, yet were divided in their economic and political interests. As they joined him and began to walk with him on a day-to-day basis, they discovered not only the Teacher, but they also discovered one another. Jesus taught them to love one another, to share with one another, to sacrifice for one another, and to minister together. After two and one-half years of walking with him, eating with him and ministering together, they were left to carry on his ministry. Taking the mantle of leadership from the Master, they preached and taught, and drew together people from all sectors of society. Those at the top of the social strata were most resistant, but people from every segment of society responded to Peter's message at Pentecost. These people were drawn into a cohesive, integrated group, where they shared their material goods, their faith, their fellowship, and their deep concern and prayer with one another. Out of this God again molded a new body—a new group of disciples, who then were scattered out of Jerusalem in great power to bring their influence to the world.

This dynamic of making disciples provides some practical insights for Christian missions. As the church grows the diversity of factions and interests emerges again to become an important part of the dynamic spread of the church. These differences remain even today. However, the church can tolerate diversity and opposing interests and viewpoints because of the unity of discipleship that emerges in the initial phase of commitment to Jesus Christ.

A word of caution is necessary. What we have discussed here does not provide a formula upon which church planting should be modeled; rather, it is a provocative set of issues and ideas that we must consider creatively in thinking about how to bring together people to make them disciples of Jesus Christ. The social setting in which we work defines the parameters around which we are to adapt our ministry and strategies.

In the previous chapter, I used the illustration of eating in Hong Kong as a means of communicating the significance of eating in human society. If I had the opportunity to make disciples in Hong Kong, I would begin by bringing together the new believers in a Hong Kong restaurant and spend time with them eating, drinking tea, and having prolonged conversation. It is an ideal setting for Bible study, fellowship, and prayer.

The Growth of the Early Church

In Acts 2: 41–47, we have the record of a dramatic growth in the membership in the New Testament church. In just one day thousands were added to the number of those who were believers, and the apostles were faced immediately with how to disciple these new believers and to lead them to an understanding of their new relationship to Jesus Christ. The text tells us that these new believers "devoted themselves to the apostles' teaching and to the fellowship, to the breaking of bread and to prayer."

In the contemporary church new believers are introduced to the gospel as a fundamental part of the discipleship process. However, the other three elements identified in this text are sometimes neglected. Fellowship, eating, and prayer are also important in the mentoring process. Lest one confuse the breaking of bread with communion, verse 46 tells us that "they broke bread in their homes and ate together with glad and sincere hearts." Eating together and fellowship were integral elements of the new relationships being built in the rapidly expanding Jerusalem church.

The economic dimensions of discipleship and the growth of a new community of believers have, in my estimation, been greatly neglected by evangelicals. In this text we see clearly that becoming a believer in Jesus Christ had significant economic as well as spiritual implications. We find that believers had everything in common (v. 44), that they sold their possessions and goods and gave to anyone as they had need (v. 45). These behaviors contributed to the growth of community and commitment to Jesus Christ. They formed for a period of time a D-Collectivist social environment.

The pattern that the apostles encouraged among new believers in this brief period following Pentecost was a pattern that they had already practiced with Jesus. Peter left his boats, Levi left his tax collecting, and they and the other disciples followed Jesus in an itinerant training program over the next two and one-half years. Significant economic changes characterized their lives. They became dependent upon a group of prominent women, who provided food for them and ministered to them. In Acts, people gave possessions and goods, serving one another as they had need, just as the disciples had learned in their relationship with Jesus. When thousands of believers joined the church in just a matter of days, this same practice became part of their daily activities.

The particular community that we see emerging in Acts 2–4 is one in which the believers emphasized group identity. Acts 4:32 tells us that "All the believers were one in heart and mind. No one claimed that any of his possessions was his own, but they shared everything they had." The unity of this community is profound. The submission of personal desires and needs to the group is illustrated repeatedly in these texts. The leaders did not coerce contributions. People identified with the group voluntarily, and contributed out of their desire to serve one another.

Leadership in this group was focused exclusively on the apostles, who derived their authority from their relationship with Jesus. The text clearly emphasizes unity and oneness. Acts 4:13 reports that Peter and John were unschooled, ordinary men. At this opening moment in the history of the church hierarchical distinctions were unimportant. All external symbols of hierarchy and status were rejected and the primacy of the group and their identification with Jesus Christ were their foremost concerns. The movement operated by consensus, and converts granted the apostles authority over their collective and personal lives.

I am convinced that the practice of eating together by new believers after Pentecost had a profound effect upon the unity and cohesion of the early church. These people, converts from different nations, even speaking different languages, joined together in a short time to become a dynamic, unified body of believers committed to Jesus Christ. Eating together provided the social milieu in which relationships were built and solidified, and through which the fellowship, prayer, and teaching ministries of the church could flourish.

Harold Dollar (1990:264) notes that table fellowship distinguished Jews from Gentiles, and became a major theological hurdle for the unity of Jew and Gentile believers. Luke first addresses this issue (along with circumcision) using the story of Cornelius and Peter in Acts 10. Peter went to Cornelius' house and ate with Cornelius while he shared the good news of Jesus Christ with him, knowing that Jewish law prohibited associating with Gentiles. When Peter returned to Jerusalem the news of the Gentile conversion had already preceded him and Peter was publicly criticized. Acts 11:3 reports the nature of that criticism: "You went into the house of uncircumcised men and ate with them." Once again we see the profound importance of eating in Jewish society, and the importance of eating with new believers. Peter defended himself, relating the vision that he had been given from God before going to Cornelius. His explanation satisfied the critics in Jerusalem at least temporarily. The issue arises again in Acts 15. Dollar argues that the decree framed by James to the Gentile churches addressed the theological barriers that stood in the way of table fellowship between Jew and Gentile believers (pp. 279–84).

In my exposure to mission candidate schools one of the most important activities that I have observed is that of group eating. Missionary candidates eat together, serve one another at tables, and commit themselves to general service and communion around the meals of the school. They are not permitted to eat alone as families, or to keep themselves separate from the general work and service of eating activities. One of the most important byproducts of such practice is that people who have no relationship to one another and who have no reason to share together as a community become not only friends, but people who have a common concern and commitment for one another.

In one particular mission candidate school that I attended the eating arrangements were such that people sat with those who were not part of their own family, and interacted with people from outside of their own particular social setting. Missionary candidates came from different parts of the country and had not met one another before. As a consequence, the eating time was a time of learning to know one another, a time of fellowship with one another, and a time of serving one another around the table. Not only did we eat together—we moved from one table to another during the training program, so as to become acquainted with all the members of the community. In a very short period of time people attending the school began to know one another intimately because of the daily practice of eating together. Yet, often these same missionaries fail to connect this experience to later ministry, and neglect totally the eating experience as part of their discipling strategy in the field.

The central significance of social eating for building relationships is one of the most profound social and spiritual truths about life. If missionaries neglect this fact in their ministry, they do so at that ministry's peril. One of my mission friends shared that the most significant event in his twelve-year ministry was the time period in which a national family lived with his family in their home. He confessed that this time was a great trial to him and to his wife, as they had to learn to adjust to another family and to include them in every part of their daily life. However, that opportunity provided the most profound discipling experience in all of his ministry, and the man who lived with him has now assumed successfully the responsibilities of leadership.

Growth and Change in the New Testament Church

As the church continued to grow in numbers, the D-Collectivist social environment collapsed. The increasing numbers of believers in the church made eating together a much more difficult and cumbersome task. As the church grew to include more than seven thousand people, the problem of fellowship, eating, and prayer groups reached unmanageable proportions, given their "collectivist" low grid organization. Ethnic diversity reared its head and factional conflict about food distribution divided the growing church.

The division came between Grecian Jews and Aramaic-speaking Jews, and the dispute focused on the distribution of food to widows (Acts 6). At that particular point in time the process of sharing goods, and particularly sharing food, had become cumbersome and difficult to manage. The apostles recognized that some hierarchy was necessary to minister to the needs of the expanding church. The Twelve determined that it was not right for them to "neglect the ministry of the word of God in order to wait on tables" (Acts 6:2). They decided to choose seven men to organize the distribution of food to the widows. These men were appointed and delegated authority for the ministry of food distribution, and also the ministry of preaching and teaching.

The factions of Greek-speaking and Aramaic-speaking Jews signaled the inherent diversity in the growing New Testament church. The large size of the Jerusalem church was clearly a factor in this process. After the appointment of the seven and the sermon of Stephen (Acts 7), the unbelieving Jews intensified persecution against the believers and the Greek-speaking believers scattered through the towns and cities around Jerusalem. Although scattered like seeds at planting, these Christians, nurtured in the intense, open-sharing community of Jerusalem, remained faithful and proclaimed the gospel as they moved from place to place. Instead of disintegrating, the church dispersed began the process of multiplying itself with hundreds of local congregations.

Perhaps if the church had been scattered shortly after the day of Pentecost, it would not have survived. Instead, God protected his church for a period of time, allowing it to grow and to be nurtured in a cohesive community, unified by the sharing of material resources, by daily fellowship, by eating with one another, and by being nurtured by the Word of God and prayer. As these new believers became one in mind and in spirit, and committed to one another in body and material life, they developed a spiritual maturity enabling them to stand the most intense persecution. Without this level of spiritual maturity and commitment to unity in the body of Christ, the church may have been crushed.

The lesson for missions and church planting is that small collections of believers, churches established in areas of great spiritual opposition, must be nurtured to form community through fellowship, prayer, eating together, and sharing basic resources. Discipling on a one-on-one basis, working separately with individuals in hostile urban and anti-Christian environments, leads to bonding with the missionary, but not with other believers. Unless we help believers form a community, the sense of oneness in the body of Christ will not happen. Believers without the experience of the unity of the body of Christ may fall away under persecution.

As the church in Acts dispersed from Jerusalem and factions within the church gained strength due to the ethnic and theological conflicts about the traditions of the Jews, the social organization of the church shifted to "C-Corporate" social structures. The apostles delegated authority to the seven to oversee the Greek-speaking congregations, and to other emerging leaders, such as Barnabas (Acts 11:22), among the Aramaic believers. Given the linguistic differences, theological differences, and the loss of commensal unity, we should not be surprised at the growth of factions and the separation into distinct communities of believers.

The execution of James and the exile of Peter in Acts 12 spelled the end of Peter's leadership in Jerusalem, and the subsequent diversification of the church. The third phase in the growth of the church is reported in Acts 15. By this time the church had expanded into the Gentile cities of Asia Minor. Many Gentiles had accepted Christ. The Jews, adherents to tradition, insisted upon their circumcision. The evangelistic fervor of certain Jewish Christians for their traditions stirred great controversy, leading to the council at Jerusalem where the hierarchy of apostles and elders was called upon to arbitrate the dispute. The C-Corporate social environment now governed church process and relationships.

Members of local churches continued to have fellowship with one another at the Lord's table, and in many places people shared their resources as did the church at Pentecost. However, the Lord's Supper was transformed into a public ritual rather than a communal meal, and the practice of eating became a symbolic act of occasional performance rather than a daily event communicating cohesion and group commitment.

This is illustrated in Paul's letter to the Corinthians. In 1 Corinthians 11:33 Paul instructs believers that they should eat at home, complaining that some come to the Lord's Supper to eat and drink to satisfy their own selfish interests rather than to commune as members as the body of Christ. He is particularly critical that some go hungry while others gorge themselves and get drunk. The sense of community that characterized the church in Acts 2 is completely missing in Corinth. Eating no longer serves to build community, but merely provides an opportunity for people to pursue selfish interests. This case may be a commentary about the membership of the church at Corinth, but it also reflects something of the changing composition of the growing church at large, which by this time had developed into many diverse local groups.

During this period of church history, the making of disciples followed the model established by the Lord and followed by the apostles after Pentecost. Paul traveled with companions, selected to be his disciples and fellow workers. They joined new believers in their homes, ate with them, and lived with them for the period of time—weeks, months, even years—that they ministered in a particular town or city. Through this daily interaction, eating and working together, Paul discipled those who became the local leaders when he left to continue his missionary journeys.

In the later chapters of Acts the church as a whole changes in its dynamic organization. The body of Christ now is a diverse community with many different parts. Delegated authority has become a significant part of the leadership structure. However, local communities of believers have a greater integration than the whole and discipleship groups continue the intensive person-to-person relationship illustrated in the Lord's ministry and in the church at Pentecost.

The final phase that we see in the development of the overall social organization of the New Testament church shows a clear emphasis on grid (delegated authority) and only moderate group integration. The Jerusalem church seems to have stabilized as a C-Corporate structure, with a formal council and James as the leader. The local church at Ephesus seems to have a collective body of elders (Acts 20:17), reflecting a D-Collectivist organization similar to the early church in Jerusalem. As Paul continues planting churches at various places he appoints his lieutenants to identify and train leaders for the new churches. Titus is given the responsibility of appointing elders in Crete. Timothy is given the responsibility of instructing and directing the development of leadership at Ephesus and resolving issues among congregations in various cities where Paul and others have preached. In these broader activities we see the seeds of the modern B-Bureaucratic administration of national and denominational churches. The decision of the Jerusalem council in Acts 15 and Paul's subsequent directives to the churches in Antioch and Asia show a drift toward centralized, as opposed to consensus, decision making.

The one fact binding together these diverse churches is the unifying ritual of worship, the Lord's Table. Whereas the churches in Jerusalem continued to require circumcision and the observation of Jewish law, the churches in Asia Minor had none of these requirements; however, the churches in Jerusalem, Judea, and Asia Minor observed baptism and the Lord's Supper. Baptism served as the ritual of entry into the Christian community, while the Lord's Supper, repeated on a regular basis, provided one means through which believers reaffirmed their common community of faith.

The Changing Social Environments of the Church: Unity and Diversity

The church is a growing structure, a changing dynamic environment that responds to the diverse conditions and tensions of the communities in which it is planted. Not only does the church at large change but the local church changes. In the earliest phases of church planting, the sharing of resources and intimate relationships around the table may serve to promote the growth of fellowship and disciples. However, as these disciples expand their ministry into the community and many respond to the gospel, the bond and unity of a small group cannot be sustained; hierarchy and adjustment to the pressures of a growing, diverse community must follow.

The review of the dynamic growth of the New Testament church suggests that the church planter must anticipate many phases, and prepare disciples to help the church grow and become a vital force in the secular community in which it lives. When a church clings to any phase of growth, it may lose its spiritual power and strength to influence the world. Some contemporary Christian churches have focused so intently on sustaining the face-to-face community (D-Collectivist) that they have lost their capacity to be salt and light or to evangelize the world. Emphasizing low grid collective leadership, they usually do not grow much over two hundred members. If they do the group frequently fragments, then splits as the dynamic unity of community cannot be sustained. This is particularly true when people do not share material resources and eat together on a regular basis.

C-Corporate church communities have a greater capacity to reach out and incorporate others into their net. Because they have a leadership hierarchy they are able to encompass groups that are different, to coordinate and mobilize them for joint activity and interests that are beneficial to all. The hierarchy that emerged in Acts 6 was a hierarchy that sustained the unity of the church in the intense persecution that followed Stephen's death and the scattering of the disciples across Palestine.

The decentralized church, acknowledged formally at the council at Jerusalem in Acts 15, accepted diversity, recognizing the distinctiveness of the different subjects within it, and the loss of the unity that had been present in the D-Collectivist environment surrounding Pentecost. The dispersing church (some central authority but diverse local groups) allowed the maximum impact for evangelism and church growth.

Church planters must recognize that if the church they establish is to be a dynamic, growing, mission-minded church, it must go through these phases and processes of structural change so that the end product is a church that is diverse but reaching out to bring those who have not heard the good news of the gospel.

II
Transforming Culture

Recapitulation: The Gospel and Culture

This book has focused on the issue of social environment. Beginning from the work of Mary Douglas, I have argued that the social environment exerts decisive pressure upon individuals, and that these individuals resist this pressure at great personal and social cost. One important contribution of this work is the elaboration of the features of four distinctive social environments as they affect economic and power relationships and produce definitive patterns of social values.

This book is also distinctive in focusing on the pervasive and central importance of economic and power relations in the social environment. Recent missiological literature has concentrated almost exclusively on the ideological aspects of worldview and has given relationships of economy and social power only minimal attention. While the spiritual battle relating to conflicting ideologies is crucial for the propagating of the gospel, the truth is that oftentimes the ministry of making disciples and planting churches is thwarted by conflicts that reside primarily in the spheres of economic and power relationships. The purpose of this volume has been to bring to the foreground discussion of how economic and power relations affect the ministry of cross-cultural workers.

A third key contribution of this volume is to challenge the romantic idealism that pervaded the functionalist missiology of the 1960s and

1970s. In an effort to compensate for the unmitigated cultural colonialism of the 1940s and 1950s, missiologists of the 1960s and 1970s tended to overidealize traditional cultures and encourage an almost uncritical acceptance of other cultural systems while trying to communicate the gospel. This book is an appeal once again to critical realism, in which sin is seen as the pervasive corrupting force presented in Scripture, and culture is regarded not as a neutral objective entity that can be accommodated readily to the gospel, but rather a corrupted order that is inextricably linked to the unbelievers who participate in and perpetuate it.

The perspective taken in this book is what Niebuhr has called a "conversionist" view of the gospel and culture. Christ is the transformer of culture through his body on earth, the church. The conversionist themes are the wonder and glory of God's creation, the tragedy and corruption of the fall and sin, and the incarnational work of redemption through the virgin birth, the holy life, and the sacrificial death and resurrection of the Lord Jesus Christ. Through the redemptive work of Christ, the Word made flesh to dwell for awhile among us, persons and cultures can be restored to fellowship with God and to relations on earth that glorify him and bring joy and fellowship to his creation.

The Duality of Culture

One of the most important advancements in contemporary social and anthropological theory is the movement away from unified theories of culture, as symbolized in the concept of worldview, to theories that emphasize the "duality of culture." British sociologist Anthony Giddens (1979) proposes that structure and interaction must be addressed as separate levels for analysis. The structural dimension focuses on the systemic factors that define the enduring cultural components of relationship, the features that are reproduced over time and provide meaning for the participants. Interaction, on the other hand, focuses on the actors engaged in communication within the institutional framework, yet with the freedom of individual choice characteristic of social behavior. Actors in every social situation formulate an interpretive scheme, a modality of the structural and interaction systems available to actors.

Margaret Archer (1988:134) defines the constituents of culture in similar dualistic categories: the cultural system and the sociocultural level. Cultural system comprises the knowledge, beliefs, theories, and conceptual schemes, that is, the sum of knowledge and the logical relations that persons bring to social interaction. The sociocultural level, in contrast, focuses upon people and the causal relations between groups and individuals in the social context. Archer insists that cultural system and sociocultural level be held conceptually distinct from one another. If we are to understand culture adequately we must examine the logical properties and the causal processes of both the cultural system and the sociocultural level. Each aspect is independent of the other and an adequate understanding of them will arise only out of the careful assessment of each as separate components.

In reflecting upon the history of missiology, most students of culture have combined or conflated these two distinctive levels into one unified system, generally referred to as worldview. The error in conflating these levels is that one becomes epiphenomenal of the other. In other words all behavior is reduced to worldview or to the sociocultural level. In missiology the typical error has been reductionism into the concept of worldview. Missiologists have defined the concept of worldview as the all-encompassing cultural frame through which behavior is interpreted and understood. This perspective arises from a long-held anthropological "doctrine" of the unity of culture, which Archer terms the "myth of cultural integration" (pp. 1–21). Critiquing the versions of this "myth," including the functionalist version, the structuralist version, and more recently the Marxist version, Archer argues that all fail to recognize the recurring inconsistencies within every cultural system, the inherent differences that exist in every population, and the volatility and unpredictability of human behavior.

The point of Archer's discussion is that by maintaining a clear conceptual distinction between the cultural system and the level of sociocultural interaction, we are better able to understand the dynamics of human behavior and to address the presence of cultural contradictions and complementarities as they interplay in sociocultural affairs. With regard to our discussion of culture and the gospel, this distinction allows us to examine much more carefully the interplay of these two and the transforming processes that occur when the gospel brings contradiction into the life of the individual and into the systems of cultural and social relationships.

The idea of "cultural system" is an old one in the study of culture. We see within a cultural system the symbols and beliefs that are fundamental to members of a society. People generally see their symbols and beliefs as having logical relationships to one another and providing a reasonable explanation of their world and their relationships. The cultural system, or "worldview" in missiological terms, provides the theories and beliefs upon which people attempt to order their lives and explain their relationships with others. Out of this cultural system people define values that establish priorities for their action and from which they formulate their arguments to explain and justify their actions and their relationships with others.

The sociocultural system, as described in this book, grows from distinctive social environments, producing values and behaviors that may be contradictory to beliefs held in one's "worldview." We see this repeatedly in cases of Christians who have acted in ways contradictory to their Christian beliefs, but in accord with values typical of their social environments. These social values arise from causal relationships between groups and individuals, described in terms of the concepts of grid and group throughout this work, and have their own independent dynamic force apart from the cultural system or "worldview." We have seen in other places in this work the significance of social environment for issues of property, labor, and exchange relationships. In spite of ideology present in a cultural system, the pressures of the social environment produce relationships that often contradict it. An illustration is the ideal of equality in American society, stated in the Declaration of Independence and the Constitution, which was contradicted by the founders in the practice of slavery, and by their descendents in the social rules of high grid and low group that create inequality in property, labor, and reward within the sociocultural system.

The relationship then between cultural system and social environment is neither unified nor integrated as anthropologists once thought. On the contrary, the interchange between social environment and cultural system leads to contradictions as well as complementarities. Archer proposes that participants in a social environment engage in dialogue and/or debate about their competing interests and their alternative interpretations of the cultural system. The connections between the cultural system and the social system occur in the process of communication and social interaction. Richard Adams (1988) argues that all social behavior ultimately connects in some way to the dissipation of energy. Human interest in land, labor, and the exchange of goods pervades society and culture. Adams argues that social relations are ultimately focused on power in relationship to economic resources. Both the social system and the cultural system ultimately address issues of economy and power. As people engage in social relations, they commit resources to social activities and dissipate energy for personal and social ends. People appeal to propositions in the cultural system to justify their activities or to criticize the activities of others. Information provides a trigger mechanism upon which social and economic behavior follows. Communication and social activity define the arena in which social environment and cultural system interact. Archer argues for a clear temporal sequence in these arrangements: cultural system has a prior temporal existence and exerts influence upon the activities that occur in the context of a social environment. Yet, these very activities feed back into the cultural system, provoking adjustments in current logical relationships and the addition of new ideas and a reordering of relationships.

The dual theory of culture provides a powerful framework from which to consider the mission of the church and the communication of the gospel of Jesus Christ. From this theory we are now able to ask questions about the direct impact of the gospel on specific issues of belief and social action, and to explore the ramifications of the gospel for both cultural system and social environment. Working from this theory we are able to assess the distinctive roles of theology and the church, which are, respectively, the cultural system and the social order components of the gospel. The local church provides the social environment in which theology is lived and experienced. By examining the beliefs and the practical life of the local church, we may evaluate the power of the gospel to transform both the cultural system and the social environment of people engaged in dialogue and debate with the gospel message. The separation of these two concepts also allows us to investigate economic and power relationships essential to life in the world, yet which create contradictions and tension for believers and the local church. Finally, we are able to evaluate the experience and the agenda of the cross-cultural missionary.

"The Corrupt World" and the "Love of God"

The theological motif of a corrupt world is an ancient one in Christian theology and is found throughout the Scriptures. H. Richard Niebuhr (1951) has identified three particular viewpoints that have placed great emphasis on the corrupt character of the world: "Christ against culture," in which the world is utterly pagan and the source of evil; "Christ and culture in paradox," in which sin is all-pervasive and "the whole edifice of culture is cracked and madly askew" (p. 155); and "Christ the transformer of culture," in which "culture is all corrupted order rather than order for corruption, as it is for the dualist" (p. 194).

This work is a modification of the "conversionist" paradigm described by Niebuhr. I have encouraged the missionary to be empathetic to the social environment and cultural system of the national, recognizing that it is corrupted order, but not the order of corruption. Being corrupted order it can by no means be viewed as neutral. Every social system reflects the ordering of power relationships to sustain the interests of corrupt people, and through these relationships and their companion "worldview," people serve their private or group interests and attempt to contain the aggressive and sometimes hostile activities of other individuals and groups. While these corrupted systems organize labor and relationships of exchange for unbelievers, yet in themselves they do not constitute an order of corruption. It is possible for Christians to work within these systems and to transform them to reflect kingdom principles through the power of Christ and the gospel.

Likewise, each cultural system is constituted of beliefs and values that are framed in rebellion against God. Each cultural system has substituted human creations for the revelation from God. In the Gospel of John we read that the ruler of the world is not the Word (Logos), but rather the devil. Jesus says that the world obeys the will of its father, the devil (John 8:44; 12:31).

The Epistles pick up the same theme of the corruption of the world and the depravity of humanity. Paul cites the wrath of God against the world for its pervasive corruption and unrighteousness (Rom. 1:18), and states that God gave up human beings to the depravity of their actions and their minds (Rom. 1:24–25). Paul describes the flesh as a corrupt element in human spiritual life from which humankind must be redeemed (2 Cor. 5:4, 6). The institutions of culture prevent sin from becoming as destructive as it might otherwise be. Paul advises Gentile believers to marry to avoid immorality and to submit to the governing authorities since they are servants of God against wrongdoers. Yet he is aware that these same governing authorities are ruled by the powers of darkness and are a threat to the Christian community (Eph. 6:12). The struggle with sin is an ongoing battle for believers (Rom. 7:7–25) and victory comes only by the gift of the Spirit who provides new life in Christ (Rom. 8:1–4).

The second major theological theme in relationship to the world is that of the love of God. This theme is found throughout the New Testament but is most thoroughly developed in the Gospel and First Epistle of John. The love of God for the world seems rooted in the creative work of God. The Gospel of John begins with a poem celebrating the creative work of Christ in the world (John 1:1–3), followed by the proclamation (John 3) of God's love for the world, and his intention not to condemn but rather to redeem the world. Nature and culture are part of God's creative work. We see early in Genesis the development of distinctive social environments and cultural systems. God provides livestock and seed-bearing plants for food (Gen. 1), and we find Abel keeping flocks and Cain working the soil (Gen. 4). The descendents of Adam who are farmers live in cities and those who raise livestock live in tents. The creative work of God provides the energetic resources for human survival (grain and livestock), language enabling human beings to communicate with God and with one another in a cultural system, and a social environment within which individuals and groups order their lives.

The Gospel—Redemption of Persons, Transformation of Culture

The transforming work of the gospel begins with its active challenge to the existing cultural system, or worldview, which is carried by each individual. This is illustrated most graphically in the sermon that Peter addresses to the crowd on the day of Pentecost (Acts 2). Working from their known history and identifying specific texts from the prophets that proclaim the coming of salvation to Israel, Peter challenges and contradicts the accepted view of Jesus Christ, proclaiming that Jesus of Nazareth was the one that God had sent expressly to fulfill his promises. Peter recounts how his listeners, with the help of wicked men, put Jesus to death, but God raised him from the dead. Calling upon the authority of the patriarch David to substantiate his assertions and quoting from the Psalms, Peter concludes that "God has made this Jesus, whom you crucified, both Lord and Christ" (Acts 2:36). In a matter of days thousands of people accepted this new information, revised their theories about the Messiah and Jesus, and were baptized. These same people also committed themselves to new social relationships, which produced a significant transformation of values. Accepting the authority of the apostles, they devoted themselves to this new teaching and they committed themselves to a life in which "all the believers were together and had everything in common" (Acts 2:44).

Once these believers had accepted the new information about Christ and made significant adjustments in their cultural system, they began to make changes in their social system. The "words of life" incorporated into their beliefs became trigger mechanisms for action in their social environments. Whatever power relationships they had before their conversion, following it they submitted to the authority of the apostles and the collective will of the *ecclēsia*. Many relinquished control over their material resources, selling possessions and goods to share with one another in ways unusual and different from their economic behaviors prior to their conversions. There was a significant restructuring of their social environment as they formed a new body, the church of Jesus Christ.

The Book of Acts presents a similar pattern in the conversion of the Gentiles. The details of Paul's sermon to the Greeks at Athens show a pattern similar to that used by Peter. Paul placed his message in the historical, social, and economic context of the Greeks in Athens (Acts 17), yet at the same time provocative and contradictory to their existing belief system. Some Athenians accepted this new information and joined with other believers to sit under the authority of the teaching of Paul and his companions. While the text does not provide the details of the sociocultural changes in Athens, Paul's letters to the Thessalonians show that Greek converts responded in a manner similar to Jewish converts; they submitted to the authority of the apostles (1 Thess. 1:6–9) and established new patterns of communication, sharing, and consumption that served the new community, the church. Some believers abused the new order, prompting Paul to remind them in a second letter that "If a man will not work, he shall not eat" (2 Thess. 3:10).

The gospel's transforming power operates at two distinct levels of cultural life, and in a particular time sequence. First, the gospel addresses the cultural system—the values, beliefs, theories, and arguments that make up the logical worldview from which people order their lives. The gospel contradicts that worldview, challenges those beliefs, and, once it is received by a new believer, results in a rethinking and reintegration of those theories, beliefs, and arguments. Second, this new information in the cultural system becomes a "trigger mechanism" for new social action in the believer's social environment. As people commit themselves to new power relationships and to alternative means of controlling their sources, the relationships between individuals and groups are transformed.

However, people restructure from the original cultural system and the original social system. The old system of Jewish beliefs was not erased on the Day of Pentecost, but rather was reformulated and reinterpreted in terms of the new gospel message the people had received. Likewise, the cultural system of the Greek believers was not eliminated, but reformulated in terms of the new information and beliefs provided in the gospel. As people reflect upon and receive this new information they must rethink to achieve a new logical consistency in their knowledge, eliminating those things that they perceive as contradictory and retaining that which they see as complementary to their new beliefs. The tension between the Jewish Christians and Greek Christians described in Acts 15 grew out of their different integrations of the gospel message into their preexisting belief systems. In the same way, both Jews and Greeks adapted and revised their social relationships in a new social context, the church.

The Church—A Transformed Sociocultural System

The church is the social body within which theology and social environment combine to create a dynamic living group. The church grows out of the process of making disciples, "followers" of Jesus Christ, described in the Gospels and the Book of Acts. The first phase in the formation of the church is the "making of followers." This process is one in which people learn and incorporate the truths of the gospel, the theology of Christ, into their cultural system.

As Andrew Walls (1982) has pointed out, the danger in this process is that people may lose touch with the universal principles of the Word of God as they incorporate the gospel into their own worldview. Without continuous instruction in the Word, the new information may be submerged into the traditional cultural system to the point where syncretism overpowers the gospel message and the church becomes merely a local cultural system. The process of making followers is one in which believers must commit themselves to a lifelong engagement with the Word of God and the gospel. It is the living Word, "the words of life" (John 6:63–68), which free new believers from the bondage of their old worldview and bring them into a living, vital relationship with Christ.

Becoming a disciple is a personal process. Individuals receive the gospel, respond by the work of the Holy Spirit, and are nurtured in the Word of Christ so that they become his companions and followers. The church must be based upon people who are committed to becoming Christ's disciples, and who recognize that such a commitment requires rethinking basic assumptions about life, and reinterpreting them to form a biblically based, Christ-centered worldview.

Living the gospel in the social world is what the Scriptures call "bearing witness." Jesus challenged his disciples before his ascension: "you will be my witnesses in Jerusalem, and in all Judea and Samaria, and to the ends of the earth" (Acts 1:8). These disciples came together to form a social group. They gathered together in a room in the city of Jerusalem and "joined together constantly in prayer" (Acts 1:14). As they committed themselves to a ministry of prayer and service, they formed a new social system—the church, incarnate in the local society, made up of Jewish people, who understood Jewish culture and who related to one another on the basis of their history and prior social relationships. They formed a social group that was not unlike other social groups in Jewish society. Yet they were united on the basis of their commitment to Jesus Christ and to a new theological understanding gained by witnessing to the resurrection.

The *ecclēsia*, whose history is recounted in the Book of Acts, had a profound impact on the surrounding society. Their agenda was their witness to the living Christ, and they did this through individual and group relationships that were reframed on the basis of their common commitments to Christ and to one another. The social environment of the church changed. Yet throughout this process the church was the incarnate body, the witness of Christ, within the larger society.

The Greek church and the Jewish church reflected the sociocultural environments of their preconversion society. They were not anomalous inventions, but rather a new D-Collectivist assembly in which people learned the theological truths needed to complete their understanding of the gospel. At the same time, they also committed themselves to learn and live under the authority of the apostles, to surrender control of their resources to the Holy Spirit, and to embrace new kingdom principles that governed their priorities and their relationships with one another and with outsiders. Their agenda was not only to live and to serve their traditional social ends, but, more important, to bear witness to the Christ who was living within them.

The final aspect of the transformation of culture is in those who are his ambassadors, witnesses to other peoples in other cultures and contexts. These cross-cultural workers must undergo two transformations. They must live transformed lives within their own cultures, and they must be able to see through their own cultural blindness to live transformed lives in the sociocultural environment of the people whom they serve.

To fulfill its mission the church must send ambassadors who are witnesses to the good news across national and cultural boundaries. Not all of its members are capable of the dual transformations required for such ministry. The call to serve cross-culturally places great demands upon the servant for learning and humility, and requires patient and faithful prayer and support from the sending congregation. The challenge of living the Christ-centered life among people with different worldviews and social environments stretches Christian workers beyond all their normal abilities and insights.

The key to the power of the gospel for transforming culture is an unwavering commitment to the Word of God. Missionary and national alike are frequently blinded by the relationships and values of their own social environment. While they are committed to a common Christ and a common gospel, they have integrated that gospel into a cultural system that reflects in large part a transformation of their preconversion knowledge and worldview. The pressures of the old cultural system and the old social order continually work against the liberating power of the gospel and the call to discipleship in Christ. By searching the Scriptures for those kingdom principles that call believers to antistructural relationships, such as freedom from property, giving and receiving at risk, loving family relationships, and servant leadership, missionary and national discover the "trigger mechanisms" that set them free from the bondage of their cultural systems and their sociocultural environments. By the grace of God, they have been freed in the Spirit to "walk in newness of life."

> Therefore, there is now no condemnation for those who are in Christ Jesus, because through Christ Jesus the law of the Spirit of life set me free from the law of sin and death. (Rom. 8:1–2)

> Therefore, I urge you, brothers, in view of God's mercy, to offer your bodies as living sacrifices, holy and pleasing to God—this is your spiritual act of worship. Do not conform any longer to the pattern of this world, but be transformed by the renewing of your mind. Then you will be able to test and approve what God's will is—his good, pleasing, and perfect will. (Rom. 12:1–2)

References

Adams, Richard N. *Energy and Structure*. Austin: University of Texas Press, 1975.

———. *The Eighth Day*. Austin: University of Texas Press, 1988.

Archer, Margaret S. *Culture and Agency: The Place of Culture in Social Theory*. Cambridge: Cambridge University Press, 1988.

Bennett, David W. "Patterns of Pastoral Leadership in Ten Churches of Pune, India." Ph.D. diss., Fuller Theological Seminary, Pasadena, Calif., 1990.

Conn, Harvie M. *Eternal Word and Changing Worlds*. Grand Rapids: Zondervan, 1984.

Dollar, Harold E. *A Biblical-Missiological Exploration of the Cross-Cultural Dimensions in Luke–Acts*. Ann Arbor, Mich.: University Microfilms, 1990.

Douglas, Mary. "Cultural Bias." In *In the Active Voice*. London: Routledge and Kegan Paul, 1982.

Giddens, Anthony. *Central Problems and Social Theory*. London: Macmillan, 1979.

Henry, Carl F. H. "The Cultural Relativizing of Revelation." *Trinity Journal* 1 (1980): 153–64.

Hiebert, Paul. "The Missiological Implications of an Epistemological Shift." *TSF Bulletin* (May–June 1985): 12–18.

Koop, Gordon, and Sherwood G. Lingenfelter. *The Deni of Western Brazil*. Dallas, Tex.: SIL Museum of Anthropology, 1980.

Kraft, Charles H. *Christianity in Culture*. Maryknoll, N.Y.: Orbis, 1981.

Lingenfelter, Sherwood G. *Yap: Political Leadership and Culture Change in an Island Society*. Honolulu: University of Hawaii Press, 1975.

Lingenfelter, Sherwood G., and Marvin K. Mayers. *Ministering Cross-culturally*. Grand Rapids: Baker, 1986.

Mayers, Marvin K. *Christianity Confronts Culture*. Grand Rapids: Zondervan, 1987.

Murdock, George Peter. *Social Structure*. New York: Macmillan, 1949.

Netting, Robert McC., Richard R. Wilk, and Eric J. Arnould. *Households: Comparative and Historical Studies of the Domestic Group.* Berkeley: University of California Press, 1984.

Niebuhr, H. Richard. *Christ and Culture.* New York: Harper Torchbooks, 1951.

Price, Richard. *Saramaka Social Structure: Analysis of a Maroon Society in Surinam.* Rio Piedras: Institute of Caribbean Studies of the University of Puerto Rico, 1975.

——. *The Guiana Maroons: A Historical and Bibliographical Introduction.* Baltimore: Johns Hopkins University Press, 1976.

Shanks, Louis. "Characteristics of Aukan Social Structure." Paper presented at Biola University, Dec. 18, 1987.

Tillapaugh, Frank. *The Church Unleashed.* Ventura, Calif.: Regal, 1982.

Van Velzen, Thoden. "The Origins of the Gaan Gadu Movement of the Bush Negroes of Surinam." *Nieuwe West-Indische Gids* 52 (1978): 81–130.

Walls, Andrew. "The Gospel as the Prisoner and Liberator of Culture." *Missionalia* 10/3 (Nov. 1982): 93–105.

Scripture Index

216

Subject Index

Afro-Americans (see Aukan)

Adjudication (see Disputes)

Aukan in Suriname, 39–41, 133–134: community authority, 146–147, 150–151; disputes, 167–168, 174–177; exchange, 94–96, 99–100, 101; families, 121–122; regarding labor, 70–72, 79; mission employment, 73–75; regarding property, 52–53

Authority (see Family, Community)

Christian College Faculty, 34–36: community authority, 143–144; disputes, 162–164; exchange, 92–93, 101–102; families, 117–119; regarding labor, 68–69; regarding property, 50–51

Church growth, 197: New Testament church, 197–200; New Testament phases, 200–201

Church planting, 191, 200–201: making disciples, 193–194; social context of, 191–193

Community: authority and power, 140–142; biblical perspectives on authority, 151–155; conflicts about authority, 148–151; leadership types, 143–148

Conflicts (see Culture, Disputes)

Confrontation (see Disputes): biblical perspectives, 168–171; case studies, 171–177

Contextualization, 14–17

Culture, 20–21, 203, 204: cultural blindness, 23; cultural conflicts, 53–57; cultural systems, 205–212; duality of culture, 204–207; myth of cultural integration, 205; as prison of disobedience, 17, 23, 133; transforming, 19–20, 22–23, 203–212; transferring, 14

Decision making (see Disputes, Community)

Deni, Western Brazil, 33–34, 59–60, 139–140: borrowing and exchange, 85–88, 90–92, 101; community authority, 139–141, 147–148, 149–150; disputes and conflicts 159–162, 165–167, 171–172; families, 116–117; regarding labor, 59–60, 67–68, 80–81; regarding property, 49–50

Disciples: social context of New Testament disciples, 191–193

Disputes: biblical perspectives, 168–171; case studies, 157–160; chain of command, 162–164; confrontation and confrontation avoidance, 160–162; face-to-face negotiation, 165–167; net of consensus, 164–165; ritual confrontation, 167–168

Eating, 179–189: in Hong Kong, 180–181; mission candidate schools, 196–197; among Saramaccans, 94–95; social structure in the Gospels, 182–187; table fellowship in the early church, 194, 195–196, 198–199;

Exchange: asking and exchange, 87–90; biblical principles, 100–104; case studies, 83–87

Family: biblical principles, 131–133; domestic authority, 112–116; family sins, 128–131; ideal family in Yap, 107–109; marriage and domestic authority, 131–133; parental authority, 113–114,

217